C000199204

TSR2

Precision Attack to Tornado

TSR2
Precision Attack to Tornado

JOHN FORBAT

TEMPUS

To my five children, Anthony, Lance, Yolande, Wendy and Sandra,
who have never failed to support me.

KEY TO USING ENDNOTE REFERENCES

Works cited in this publication are listed on pages 185–186.
Each entry in the list is numbered and references within the text correspond to this list.

First published 2006

Tempus Publishing Limited
The Mill, Brimscombe Port,
Stroud, Gloucestershire, GL5 2QG
www.tempus-publishing.com

© John Forbat, 2006

The right of John Forbat to be identified as the Author
of this work has been asserted in accordance with the
Copyrights, Designs and Patents Act 1988.

All rights reserved. No part of this book may be reprinted
or reproduced or utilised in any form or by any electronic,
mechanical or other means, now known or hereafter invented,
including photocopying and recording, or in any information
storage or retrieval system, without the permission in writing
from the Publishers.

British Library Cataloguing in Publication Data.
A catalogue record for this book is available from the British Library.

ISBN 0 7524 3919 7

Typesetting and origination by Tempus Publishing Limited
Printed in Great Britain

CONTENTS

ACKNOWLEDGEMENTS

In the process of researching this book and filling out my own recollections, many ex-colleagues and others have made helpful comments and supplied photographs which have served well to enhance the authenticity and completeness of the Vickers Guided Weapons Dept work to create the TSR2 Navigation and Attack System. Without being certain of mentioning everybody (and apologising for any I may omit), I would like to thank the following helpful friends and colleagues.

Perhaps firstly I should thank Julian Temple, curator of Aviation at the Brooklands Museum, for suggesting I write this history in the first place. Also Museum Director Allan Winn, for his support. I would also like to thank various people from the aviation industry, as well as author Steve Skinner, who supplied a highly informative CD produced by the British Aircraft Corporation, depicting flight-testing and manufacture of TSR2 prior to its cancellation.

Finally, among other colleagues from my time at Vickers, I wish to thank Brigadier John Clemow, who (well into his nineties) has given encouragement and help. I also wish to thank those who moved from Vickers to EASAMS to develop aircraft systems for Jaguar, Nimrod and the Tornado – largely based on the systems techniques developed for TSR2 – for their helpful reminiscences and comments, particularly Jim Cole, John Goodwin, John Lattey, Richard Williams and any others I may have omitted.

PRELUDE

This fascinating personal account of the behind-the-scenes action at Vickers during the heyday of British aviation and weaponry invention in the 1950s and 1960s is both authoritative and very, very readable. A researcher's goldmine, this detailed book is crammed with facts, personal anecdotes, previously classified material and comprehensive explanations which, in a very real way, chart the evolution of today's generation of breathtakingly advanced front line aircraft and their associated weapon systems. All of the hallmarks of modern aviation: accuracy, reliability and technical sophistication, which we take so much for granted nowadays, were then largely unheard of, and today's successful front line jets are now the product of what were at the time seemingly improbable specifications, long hours of detailed analysis, complex trials and sheer inventive genius.

There is, however, a much more human side to the story and this book openly acknowledges the human failings, errors and financial battles – as well as the strong characters, leaders, and men of vision – which together combined to dictate the course of events. It is this honest mix of success and failure, trial and error, genius and prevarication, boffins and budgets, which makes this book so appealing. As recently the officer commanding 617 'Dambusters' Squadron and, having so far flown 3,500 hours in fast jets from Tornado GR4s with the RAF to F-117A Stealth Fighters with the USAF, this story of the dynamic linkages between industry and military rings very true to me. The pedigree and genetic make-up of today's famous aircraft are well described herein and most front line aircraft now contain some element of the developments orchestrated at Vickers over this period. Precision is one of today's modern Air Force mantras – this book describes how advances in technology turned any warrior's dream into an aviation reality and a real military capability.

January 2006
Gp Capt Al Monkman DFC MA BA RAF
Permanent Joint Headquarters (UK), Northwood, Middlesex

FOREWORD

Dictionaries of quotations record Confucius, Thucidides, Sir Walter Raleigh, Samuel Taylor Coleridge, and George Santanaya (an American philosopher in the nineteenth century) all as saying that, if you do not study the past, you are condemned to repeat it.

A notable example recently was that of the politician who had not read about the happenings in AD 1381, when the imposition of a poll tax resulted in the Peasants' Revolt.

I have heard many say that they value their own experiences way above those of others. However, those that rely only on their own experiences are likely to die young. To live longer (and happier) you need to have learnt the experiences of others also.

We are all descended from ancestors who survived at least until puberty. They survived by listening to bad news; and then by NOT eating poisonous berries, by NOT drinking stagnant water, nor by putting their hands in the fire, falling over cliffs, swimming too rapid rivers, fighting wild animals with no weapon, etc. Thus we are, almost certainly, descendants who are genetically programmed to want to listen to bad news and to take note of it. That is why we buy newspapers full of disasters; and why we listen to radio or watch television programmes of the same nature. The desire to survive may be even stronger than the desire to reproduce.

To get that bad news, or, indeed, any news of the past, one reads histories, biographies and especially autobiographies. Those autobiographies are the most compelling. Their authors tell what happened to themselves. Whether they tell of successes, failures or a mixture of both, their tales can be of great value to us all, but especially to those concerned with similar lines of personal life or of business.

TSR2 Precision Attack to Tornado by John E. Forbat tells of his work and experience in an area of high technology. It describes in detail the design and development of a variety of aircraft and missile systems during the 1950s and 1960s, with which the author was directly concerned. The systems include airframes, aerodynamics, structures, propulsion, navigation, guidance, control, gyroscopes, computers, warheads and their fuzes, power supplies, communications and launchers, as well as the ministries, armed services, companies and personnel involved. Of particular interest may be the early development of Head Up Displays, and the techniques for weapon delivery from fast low-level attacks.

For those less inclined towards the technical aspects, yet interested in the historical ones, some of the interactions between the private and public sectors may be eye-openers.

I met John at RAF Hastings in late 1955. I, too, had been on a year's Guided Weapons course at the RMC, Shrivenham, in 1952/53. I was, from 1953 to 1957, working at the Royal Aircraft Establishment as the Ministry's project engineer on the 'Red Shoes' (later to be renamed Thunderbird) surface-to-air weapon system, being developed by English Electric and Napiers at Luton and then at Stevenage. He was working for Vickers on the 'Red Dean' air-to-air weapon. We were both flying out on a visit to Woomera, South Australia, to deal with tests of our weapons there, as he describes in his previous book *The 'Secret' World of Vickers Guided Weapons*. The flight took eight days each way, so we did see quite a lot of each other.

Whilst at Woomera, I was shown round the test range by an Australian Artillery Major, who had been on the same guided weapons course with me three years earlier. After taking me all round, he said, 'You can try out anything you like on this range, as long as the risks for the range staff and for the farmers up-country are no greater than those for pedestrians in Sydney.' That was a quantifiable risk, which was eminently acceptable to those concerned. I have used that same principle on many occasions since then.

Later, from 1958 to 1960, I was the Liaison Officer with the USAF's Ballistic Missile Division in Los Angeles, after which (1960/62) I was the Commanding Officer at the Central Servicing Development Establishment, RAF Swanton Morley, where I had teams looking at the reliability and maintainability problems of the TSR2 as well as of Bloodhound, the other surface-to-air missile system. However, I was in Singapore from 1964 to 1966, where there was a minor war ('confrontation') with Indonesia, when I heard about the cancellation of the TSR2. From 1967 to 1969, I was the Ministry's project director for the Harrier aircraft, immediately before its introduction into RAF service on time and within budget. Not all projects are over time and budget! I do, though, remember John Fozard, the Harrier designer, telling me 'you don't design these things unless you are an optimist', when I was chiding him for being late with one of the prototype aircraft.

I met John Forbat again in 1978, after I had left the RAF and moved to Shepperton. He had patented devices for detecting potential intruders to properties, and we needed to safeguard our home. We used them again on our present home. So far we have not been burgled successfully!

This book should help all those who get involved in any way with high technology projects, especially ones with government funding. It is no simple matter to get maximum support from a mixture of government officials, service personnel and private industry colleagues, each of whom are likely to use their own objectives and past experience to guide them. This book offers considerable insight into the problems for industry, when politics get in the way of projects, whose successful completion depends both on consistent policies, and on overcoming the problems of developing new technologies.

Air Marshal Sir Reginald E.W. Harland
KBE, CB, AE, MA, CEng, CCMI, FIMechE, FIET,
FRAeS, Hon. FAPM, FSEE, RAF(Retired)
49 Crown Street, Bury St Edmunds, Suffolk IP33 1QX

PROLOGUE

Concurrently with *The 'Secret' World of Vickers Guided Weapons*, also published by Tempus Publishing, this book is intended to provide as accurately as possible, after an interval of fifty years, a historical account of the TSR2 aircraft's groundbreaking avionics developments by Vickers Armstrongs (Aircraft) Ltd in Weybridge, Surrey, including some of the political aspects of Government contracting. TSR2's trials and tribulations before it was cancelled by the Government are chronicled in some detail, relying on original Government records in the Public Records Office of the National Archive. A list of references is provided, detailing the sources of my information.

The Navigation and Attack System is described in considerable detail, but it is not intended to be a technical treatise. It is written largely from the perspective of my time as a young trials engineer, who then graduated to senior designer level, working on all of Vickers' missile projects over a ten-year period, as well as on various aspects of the TSR2 avionics. Thus, although there was a considerable depth of technical information and discussion needed to paint a representative picture, I have attempted to err on the side of making the story readable and interesting to a technically untrained lay audience. Starting at the bottom of the organisation and maturing to senior designer level – short of management status – I tried to keep myself abreast of the 'big picture' and, in this account, factual, though sometimes rather technical, data is admixed with my own personal anecdotal experiences. I hope that these may help add life to a tale of technical development at the forefront of engineering of the day, in a large and developing organisation.

The Tactical Strike and Reconnaissance aircraft, TSR2, was built to meet Operational Requirement GOR339, upgraded to OR339. The Air Staff first promulgated this in 1957, at the height of the Cold War build-up. Few aircraft have been more contentious or more written about; the TSR2 attracted attention before and after its successful flights, was a focus of interest at the time of the highly political cancellation by a Labour Government in 1965, and still invites debate today. In its time, it represented the most advanced aircraft and weapon system so far created anywhere and, even in 1978, thirteen years after its demise, no other aircraft purchased for the Royal Air Force matched its performance and overall Weapon Systems capability[9]. The Tornado GR4, still at the RAF's front line in 2006, and for some years to come, accomplishes similar operations – with the advantage of more recent technology.

The Navigation and Attack System design and development was commenced within the Guided Weapons Department of Vickers Armstrongs (Aircraft) Ltd, under the overall guidance of Brigadier John Clemow, its chief engineer. Sir George Edwards had recruited Clemow in April 1957, from his post as director of Guided Weapon Projects in the Ministry of Supply. In that capacity, he had 'sorted out' several aircraft contractors' ineffective missile development efforts and was already familiar with the situation at Vickers. Following pre-war and wartime service as a 'gunner', he became an acknowledged expert in matters of rocketry, guidance and control and, using the expertise of his Guided Weapons team, it was natural that he would lead the TSR2 avionics work. However, before agreeing to proceed with any contract for development of TSR2, the Government dictated a 'shotgun marriage' between Vickers, English Electric and Bristol Aircraft to form the British Aircraft Corporation (BAC), which finally received the contract, naming Vickers as the prime.

By late 1961, much of the TSR2 avionics design was well established and development was proceeding. However, the Guided Weapons work was now to be moved to the English Electric's GW division at Stevenage. Following my own abortive attempts together with colleagues John Lattey and Arthur Carter to dissuade Sir George Edwards from closing down the GW work at Weybridge, most of the team declined the move. Many left the company altogether but, since the TSR2 work could continue in Weybridge, others remained with what became the Aircraft Systems/E organisation. John Clemow quite openly declared that had he been, say sixty years old, he might have thought of his continuity in employment – but he was only fifty and would therefore look to newer pastures. It was 9 October before we received a memorandum from top management, setting out the responsibilities relating to the TSR2 Navigation and Attack System. This quoted a press report of the Guided Weapons work at Weybridge having now been transferred to the English Electric Guided Weapons division, and that 'further to this, Mr J. Clemow has left the Company'.

To ensure continuity for TSR2, the aircraft division's chief of electrical design, Harry Zeffert, was appointed chief systems engineer/E at Weybridge, responsible 'for the co-ordination and progress of the TSR2 Navigation/Attack System and its associated equipment'. A veteran from the starting of Guided Weapons at Weybridge, Mike Still, was appointed deputy chief systems engineer/E – effectively running the day-to-day TSR2 'Nav/Attack' work. John Lambie would continue his existing responsibilities as chief project officer on TSR2 weapon systems. The following chapter covers the many system issues, design principles and operational charac-teristics developed to meet the Royal Air Force's exacting operational requirements, up to the time of the infamous cancellation in 1965.

Another chapter describes project designs for a number of 'Missiles and Systems for the Future', including my own design project for the Navigation and Attack System of a single-seat aircraft, to navigate as effectively as TSR2 (which could only navigate accurately with a two-man crew). The lower cost implications of using a single-seat, as opposed to a two-seat, solution for TSR2 could well have changed the political landscape and prevented the eventual cancellation. But, what made me get into this business in the first place?

The magic of airplanes and flying first inspired me as a small boy before the Second World War when, occasionally, a plane would drop advertising leaflets over Kensington Gardens. There we used to fish for 'tiddlers' and watch the old men (some aged at least thirty-five), sail their big model yachts. Sometimes the planes came so low that we could see the pilot's head in the cockpit – and we wondered what it was like to fly. Being lifted up to look through the door of a corrugated-skinned Handley Page air liner at Croydon Airport was the next best thing. Then came the war and evacuation.

Newsreels of the Blitz on London and shots of diving Stukas over Poland, then Heinkels and Messerschmitts being shot down by RAF fighters, imprinted themselves on our minds and imaginations. Finding an old wingless biplane in a farm shed outside Melksham, Wiltshire, where we were billeted away from London and family, was a major coup. Safe from prying eyes, a friend and I would climb into the tandem cockpits and waggle the joystick, making engine and machine gun noises, till we were hoarse. By mid-war in late 1942, at fourteen, I was living back in London and soon got my fire guard's armband and steel helmet, for fire-watching duty – whenever we could arrange it, this was on the roof of our West Kensington block of flats. The sirens wailed, bombers roared, searchlights stabbed around in the night sky and ack-ack guns sent flak among the bombers evading the barrage balloons – then there was hot shrapnel tinkling down on to the pavement, for us kids to collect as trophies. Air-raid shelters were for grown-ups who knew the dangers. For us, they were for ping-pong during the day time when they were otherwise empty. We were trained to crawl through smoke-filled rooms, to extinguish incendiary bombs by squirting water from a hose, fed by another fire guard using a stirrup pump in a bucket of water. When bombs fell really close, it was 'you young lad' who was sent on his bike to ride the half mile over streets covered with broken glass to fetch the fire brigade – which turned out to be on fire itself.

If only we could be old enough for the RAF and fly those beautiful, magnificent Spitfires and shoot Jerries down. I was green with envy, knowing that my older brother's friends were Spitfire pilots and Mosquito train-busters. The nearest thing for me was to join the Air Training Corps – where we wore a poor imitation of RAF uniform, with high collars instead of shirt and tie, but also where we practiced rapid aircraft recognition, learned about the theory of flight and navigation by dead reckoning, practised Morse code signalling and, of course, lots of 'square bashing'. The major annual event was the two-week 'camp' at an RAF station, where we lived in Nissen huts, slept on 'biscuit' mattresses and lined up with our tin plates for our victuals in the airmen's mess, then washed them up in the trough outside, in steam boiling water, whence it was impossible to retrieve a dropped knife. Then after inspection, we would get runs in the bombing simulator, rifle and machine gun experience – and above all – the flying. Never mind that the Short Stirling bomber finished its operational training bombing runs and target shooting over the sea on my first flight with a mock attack by an American Thunderbolt fighter and took corkscrew evasive action – until I threw up. The four-hour flight entitled us to a 'flying meal' of fried eggs and bacon – my favourite, and almost totally unavailable due to food rationing in 'Civvy Street' – and I was so sick, I could not eat any of it.

But we flew as often as we could and the RAF let us feel we were part of the crew, with a trip to the flight deck, wearing our parachute harnesses and helmets with earphones. There were also days out to an airfield, where we could fly in a Tiger Moth trainer and experience the wind and the bumps and even a loop-the-loop, or an Auster side-by-side-seater, where we could actually hold the 'stick' and do a little 'dual'. The

Fig.P1. The 'Dagling' glider on Hounslow Heath, first 'ground slides' for entirely solo flying lessons.

epitome of this was for the luckier ones, who were able to go on a gliding course. On Hounslow Heath (now Heathrow Airport), where barrage balloon winches would pull us across several hundred yards of bumpy grass, in a single-seat Dagling glider – there were no two-seat gliders at the school, so we learned by flying solo from the first flight. At sixteen, this is not a bit frightening – just the excitement we craved. When we had become used to handling this almost Wright Flyer-level craft up to only about 10ft over the heath, we transferred to the much higher performance Kirby Cadet. Now instead of sitting in the open on a 'keel' with wings and tail attached, we were in an open cockpit without instruments, just a stick and rudder bar and the plug (to release the cable). The instruction was somewhat primitive – 'Just hold the stick about there, off you go' was the gist of it, perhaps adding a few shouted instructions from mid-field, while I flew over the instructor's head. In the Cadet, we could climb to ten storeys high – 100ft – and, after pulling the plug to release the cable, glide down to a good landing. This was real flying and we were really in Seventh Heaven.

And soon, we were also under the virtually twenty-four-hour rain of 'Doodlebug' flying bombs pitching down as their fuel ran out, to crash and explode on London's houses, causing much destruction and many casualties. I may have seen the first ones while cycling into Kent for camping one weekend. With its throaty pulse-jet roar, it flew quite low right overhead, with AA bursting all around it. The usual rain of hot shrapnel had us dodge into a doorway, before picking up more souvenirs. Far from being guided, these V-1 flying bombs landed indiscriminately, and we had all too real opportunities to practise the drill: when you hear one approaching, get off your bike, lie in the gutter with hands over the back of your head – and wait. If you hear an explosion, some other poor bastard got his chips. The later V-2 missiles that shot up into space before coming down at supersonic speed were equally uncontrolled in where they hit. Unlike with the V-1s, no air-raid sirens announced their impending silent arrival. Once you heard the explosion – always followed by the scream of its falling trajectory – you knew that you were all right this time.

The depth of aviation's penetration into my psyche naturally led to taking an Aeronautical Engineering degree but, after passing 'Inter BSc' at school, it was virtually impossible for me to get on to a course in London. Eventually, in the face of floods of ex-servicemen returning from the war, I was offered a course for only two days a week – as a temporary measure until a full-time course became available. At our commencing lecture, the Aerodynamics lecturer was emphatic that if we had any hopes of passing an Aeronautical degree at the first attempt, along with full-time students, 'forget it'. When the year had passed, there was still no full-time place for me, so now, having lost any opportunities for aircraft apprenticeships, I had to continue at two days per week and do private study at home on the other days. Out of a dozen or so in the aeronautical class at Northampton Polytechnic, just two of us made it and now, in 1950, I was able to look to trying for that aircraft design career, to which I had nailed my flag. It took a few months before I was naturalised from my wartime 'stateless' designation as a pre-war Hungarian immigrant, and it was March 1951 before my 'Secret' clearance came through. That is when Vickers Armstrongs (Aircraft) Ltd accepted me as a graduate apprentice.

Arriving for an 8 a.m. start on my first day in my Dad's Morris 8, borrowed for the day, the big car park outside the design office was quite empty. It was only when I backed into the first parking space near the main entrance that, through the rear window, I saw the nameplate coming into view. The name was G.R. Edwards – fortunately, I had done enough homework to realise that this was our already famous chief designer's parking spot. Quickly, I found another parking space. The first year at Weybridge was spent riveting, fitting, hammering, and gaining other factory experience with Valettas, Varsities and Viscounts in the factory, at the grand starting salary of £6 9s 8¼d for a forty-eight-hour week, while I also got a first-hand view of the Valiant V-bomber prototype being tested. To my great surprise, the wing spars I was assembling closely resembled the design I had calculated and drawn for my recent college coursework – our lecturer must have known more about practical aircraft than we had credited. I also witnessed the immediate aftermath of a test pilot's arrival that would herald an important part of my future work. 'Spud' Murphy arrived for his job interview with Chief Test Pilot Jock Bryce in his RAF Meteor fighter, which he flew like the aerobatic champion he was. Unfortunately, instead of landing at Wisley, he landed at Brooklands, where we could all see it - and suffered a brake failure that led to his Meteor being wrapped round a tree at the bottom of somebody's garden. Unhurt, afterwards he pleaded: 'Jock, you have to hire me – I'll be cashiered.' He got the job nevertheless, and later, as The 'Secret' World of Vickers Guided Weapons documents, we shared many flights. On most of these flights our navigator was Don Bowen, who flew in the navigator/systems officer back seat on most TSR2 test flights.

On commencing my second apprenticeship year I was interviewed by Assistant Chief Designer H.H. Gardner. A large man with a hawk-like countenance, he looked over his desk and said: 'I am picking people for our Special Projects Section. It is working on Guided Weapons. Would you like me to put you there?' This was not exactly the aircraft design which I had so long craved. Yet it was clearly something new, with supersonics and all that, and still very much within the scope of my degree studies. 'I want to put you into our Trials Section, with Barry MacGowan – Mac.' This sounded interesting enough – and I quickly accepted. Very soon, I entered the design office as a very junior trials engineer. I was into Guided Weapons – and later into TSR2.

Half a century later, I am back at the site of those early developments – as a volunteer at the Brooklands Museum. On the site of the famous Brooklands motor racing track, which opened in 1907 and which is also the cradle of British aviation, exhibiting the many historic aircraft, engines, racing cars and associated equipment and memorabilia, I am gathering the missiles and TSR2 material for a third 'GW and TSR2 Avionics' arm of Brooklands Museum.

CHAPTER 1

THE RAF'S MISSION REQUIREMENTS AND BASIC SYSTEM ELEMENTS

The Tactical Strike and Reconnaissance aircraft, TSR2, was built to meet Operational Requirement GOR339, upgraded to OR339. The Air Staff first promulgated this in 1957, at the height of the Cold War build-up. Few aircraft have been more contentious or more written about; the TSR2 attracted attention before and after its successful flights, was a focus of interest at the time of the highly political cancellation by a Labour Government in 1965, and still invites debate today. In its time, it represented the most advanced aircraft and weapon system so far created anywhere and, even in 1978, thirteen years after its demise, no other aircraft purchased for the Royal Air Force matched its performance and overall Weapon Systems capability.[10] The Tornado GR4, still at the RAF's front line in 2006, and for some years to come, accomplishes similar operations – with the advantage of more recent technology.

Several major aircraft companies of the time including Hawker, English Electric and Vickers-Supermarine bid for the project and, after the Government chose the Vickers-Supermarine design, it used TSR2 as the club with which to beat Vickers and English Electric into merging – eventually also with Bristol Aircraft Ltd – into the British Aircraft Corporation. The BAC was formally incorporated in July 1961 but, in the intervening period, the Vickers design team, led by Supermarine's well-informed, highly energetic and articulate assistant chief designer, George Henson, under the chief designer, Alan Clifton, proceeded with the design at South Marston near Bournemouth. They both moved to Weybridge in the summer of 1958, where the design work was thereafter mostly concentrated, in cooperation with the English Electric part of BAC, located at Warton. The team at Warton was not overly happy with design being controlled from the Vickers, Weybridge, location as the Ministry wanted, but in the end cooperated well, with much of the design and later also the manufacture being done there. Later, George Henson moved up to Warton – until he later fell out with its top management and transferred his considerable energies to Vickers shipbuilding.

A complete account of this enormous project, with all its technical requirements, could easily fill a whole book, so I will only try to give a sufficiently comprehensive – if necessarily truncated – account, to do reasonable justice to the efforts made by Vickers GW engineers. TSR2 was required to strike targets with great accuracy, after flying at Mach 0.9 or even transonically at 200ft altitude over the last 200nm

Fig.1. TSR2 taking off from Boscombe Down, piloted by W/C 'Roly' Beaumont.[53]

of a 600–1,000nm sortie. After climbing to nearly 50,000ft for a supersonic Mach 1.7 'dash', it would descend to remain below the Radar Horizon for minimum vulnerability to all anticipated defences. The aircraft and its systems also had to be capable of over Mach 2, for high-level attacks at ranges up to 550nm. Strikes against ground targets were to be made with nuclear and conventional bombs, as well as with rockets, while day and night reconnaissance was another major role. All this had to be accomplished in blind-flying or night-time conditions, without relying on any external aids from Radar or other techniques that could be vulnerable to enemy jamming. In order to minimise its vulnerability, TSR2 had to follow ground contours at down to 200ft altitude while flying at speeds close to Mach 1, and this Terrain Following capability required automatic as well as pilot-controlled flight using its Forward Looking Radar (FLR) and the Automatic Flight Control System (AFCS), supported by a Manoeuvre Computer employing information supplied by the Inertial Reference System (IRS) and other sensors. It was also required to give the aircrew a tolerable quality of 'ride', which allowed the pilot and navigator to concentrate on their intensive tasks.

In the twenty-first century, with the advent of Satellite Ground Positioning Systems (GPS), which can pinpoint a military aircraft's position within a few yards regardless of cloud cover, navigation would be relatively easier. Considered in 'broad brush' terms, in 1957 and into the 1960s, navigation independent of ground-based assistance had to rely on the relatively new technology of Inertial Navigation for 'dead reckoning' employing high-quality gyroscopes and accelerometers to sense aircraft movements and travel. In order to minimise the effects of natural drift errors accumulated by gyroscopes and accelerometers, the aircraft's velocity, also measured by the IRS, needed constant updating. This was achieved by comparison with independently measured ground speed from a Doppler Radar looking down on the ground beneath. Even this combination could not totally eliminate navigation errors, so they had to be further reduced by over-flying accurately known 'fix' points, to update the aircraft's position. To identify these fix points in blind conditions, TSR2 employed a Sideways Looking Radar (SLR) system, with which fix points could be identified. The Radar picture was built up from ground returns illuminated by the narrow beam emitted on each side of the aircraft as it moved forward. This picture appeared as a sufficiently high-resolution map, on a continually developing roll of photographic paper. Photographs from reconnaissance would provide the navigator with the means to identify the fix points (typically 100nm apart), providing a fix of where the aircraft had been a few seconds before (allowing for the Radar map developing time). With the aid of crosshairs moved over the moving picture display it was possible to compare the computed fix point with the 'actual' and so provide an accurate update at each fix point.

Approaching the target with considerable accuracy, TSR2 had to release its weapons to fall as close as possible to the target, employing inputs from the navigation system, flight instruments and Radar (FLR) equipments, controlled by a Central Computing System (CCS) that sat in the middle of the 'spider's web' of systems and subsystems comprising the Navigation/Attack System. Particularly when delivering a nuclear weapon, the bombing manoeuvre also had to incorporate a safe means of escaping from the large nuclear blast area before detonation. Thus, the bombing run had to be completed with one of a number of possible aerobatic manoeuvres, to get away from a nuclear burst in time – preferably without spending too much time at a height, where the aircraft would become vulnerable to ground-based guided weapon defences.

The foregoing broad description of the Navigation/Attack problem is already complicated enough – and not only were there a lot more equipments than I have already mentioned, as always, 'the Devil is in the details'. Following initial studies by George Henson and his team up to August 1958 (when it moved to Weybridge), taking advantage of the skills of weapons systems development honed over eight years of GW projects and of its top flight technical and managerial leadership, the Guided Weapons Department at Vickers in Weybridge was tasked with the overall design and coordination of the system's development. Although the formal ministry contract was not received until 1 January 1959, the Weybridge team had become increasingly involved, starting while George Henson was leading the effort at Supermarine. Earlier, Henson had commuted between South Marston and Weybridge, dealing with his paperwork entirely during his journeys in the back of a van!

The Ministry of Aviation (MOA) generally retained overall approving authority, policy authority and R&D authority, while design authority would mostly be delegated to contractors such as Vickers and its subcontractors. However this could lead to excessive centralisation and bureaucracy – something well known to Brig. John Clemow, a past director of Guided Weapons Projects at the Ministry of Supply (since changed to MOA) – who was now CE/W, the Vickers GW Department's chief engineer. Clemow's 11 December 1958 'Notes on Equipment for OR339' to the Controller of Aircraft at MOA[1] summarised the system's operational functions and the equipments and following receipt of the formal contract on 1 January 1959, his further 'CE/W's Plan for System Engineering' of 11 February 1959[1] dealt with management aspects. For such a major and advanced project, the plan would be commensurately thorough. Such 'revolutionary' principles had already been discussed at a meeting chaired by A/Cdre A.G.P. Brightmore, when Vickers Chief Engineer (Military Aircraft) Henry Gardner lent his support. The ministry tried to cling on to as much as possible, but agreed that Vickers control a number of equipment items, leaving decisions on others to be fought another day.[4]

John Clemow's plan[1] specified that: 'a Systems Design Group responsible for the correct integration of the various sub-systems into the overall system… must have the necessary ability to command the respect in technical and administrative matters… To ensure the attention and willing cooperation of contractors… The Group must therefore comprise engineers of broad outlook and experience…' He continued, expounding an interesting principle: 'It is sometimes said by theorists that nobody can know better than the specialist expert and that it is ridiculous, if not downright insulting, to have a group of "generalists" who monitor and check his work. This is simply not true, and anyone who has tried to engineer a system must know this.' In an appendix, Clemow listed half a dozen examples in the electronics field, among which perhaps the most stark example of 'experts' getting it wrong was during the development of the Fairey Aviation Fireflash missile (which Clemow had sorted out on behalf of the Ministry of Supply, after many problems and delays). The 'problem' related to Radar specialists' fears of flame attenuation from rocket motor exhausts affecting guidance signals. In trials, there was an initial loss of signal for one second and this was blamed by 'experts' on flame attenuation. 'A lot of unnecessary work at Westcott (Rocket Propulsion Establishment) was stopped, when a non-electronics engineer pointed out that… it took the missile approximately one second to leave the aircraft wing and get into the guidance beam at all.'[1]

He continued:

> My intention is therefore that the Guided Weapons Department of Vickers-Armstrongs (Aircraft) Limited should provide a Systems Group for the TSR2 equipment. We wish to have systems responsibilities for the aircraft control system, the autopilot, the sideways-looking navigation radar and terrain clearance, the navigational computing and bombing computing, as well as the same responsibility for any weapons for TSR2.

He then listed the members of management for this task as: himself (CE/W), Mr H. Surtees, BSc(Eng) MSc (Chief Designer (Weapons)), Mr B.A. Hunn, BSc (Deputy Chief Designer (Weapon Systems)), and Mr J.B. Lambie, MEng (Chief Project Officer (Weapons)). In anticipation of the contract, John Lambie was already actively coordinating work and progress meetings, while under Bernard Hunn, Arthur Carter and John Lattey had started working, respectively, on Radar and microwave and on AFCS and Terrain Following system studies.

Clemow listed the main tasks of the Systems Design Group:

(a)   to formulate the problems to be solved by each of the sub-systems;
(b)   To build up a mathematical model… of the sub-systems and integrate these into the overall system;
(c)   …to find out all that is known… both from Establishments and firms;
(d)   To carry out mathematical simulator studies of the difficult areas…
(e)   To draw up functional specifications in conjunction with the Ministry of Supply for each sub-system…
(f)   In conjunction with the Ministry of Supply to choose suitable sub-contractors…
(g)   In conjunction with the team managing the aircraft development to draw up… detailed programme for each of the equipments;
(h)   The equipment manufacturers then produce very detailed programmes… equipments to the specification… and time scale required. These programmes will be approved by the Systems Design Group;
(i)   The sub-contractors… submit technical reports supporting each stage of their development work… their main design parameters… block diagrams… to the Systems Design Group… will be regularly progressed.

In certain areas like antennae and Radio Frequency (RF) heads for all the radio and radar equipment, the pilot's control system including stability augmentation and the aircraft autopilot, the Vickers team would carry out the detailed design and development of parts of the systems themselves. Conceding that Ministry of Supply Establishments, RAE and RRE had a vital role as expert advisers and consultants, Clemow envisaged needing their inputs when specifications were formulated, firms were selected and the main lines of solutions were decided. However he made his principles clear:

> To sum up, what we wish to do is to set up a system that will work smoothly and quickly without too much indecision at any point as to what the right course of action is or who should do it. We wish to avoid any system where actions depend upon the meeting of numbers of committees, or even of one committee… The Ministry of Supply will then have the right to countermand this action if it thought it to be the wrong one. Little would be lost by this procedure and much would be gained… To sum up, we are proposing a procedure where, in mathematical language, Vickers-Armstrongs (Aircraft) Limited together with the Ministry of Supply settle the boundary conditions to the problem (in the form specifications and the firms to be used etc.) and then Vickers-Armstrongs Limited get on with the job of solving the problem…[1]

John Clemow instituted a format of monthly system progress meetings to be attended by key members of Vickers' Systems Group and by each of the equipment contractors. It is interesting to note that forty years later, in a seminar looking back at 'TSR2 with Hindsight',[44] Peter Hearne (at the time in question Elliott Bros manager for the CCS and AFCS contracts and later to rise to top positions in the aircraft industry) rejected a suggestion by W/C George Wilson that TSR2 had not been a complete weapon system. He cited:

…work of Brigadier John Clemow who had been appointed Chief Systems Engineer at Weybridge, charged with the systems integration of TSR2. He had run a systems integration panel which met monthly at Weybridge attended by all the relevant contractors (including Elliotts). Vickers engineers working for Clemow had provided systems integration. It had been one of the first examples of a good main contractor-sub contractor integration method with very little contractual squabbling.

He also referred to 'harmonious relationships', while Tony (ATF) Simmonds of English Electric added that: 'John Clemow managed to build a very effective team which nevertheless heard and acted on advice and ideas from outside. I remember particularly John Lambie, John Lattey and Dennis Harris – respectively for diplomacy, for well-placed enthusiasm and J-band Radar and for solid results.'

From June 1958, there had already been a plethora of studies and meetings at Supermarine and at Weybridge concerning most aspects of the Nav/Attack System, coming to a crescendo in August. Looking at each major system component in turn, Clemow's December 1958 notes[1] had listed the main technical issues.

Sideways Looking Radar for navigation and reconnaissance – the main problem anticipated being with navigation for the required fixes. A choice had to be made between Radars at X-band and J-band, with some preference for the shorter wavelength and narrower beam widths obtainable with J-band.

Forward Looking Radar with its terrain clearance, bombing, ranging and blind-landing roles. In order to 'display and replace the pilot's vision' range and angle of depression would be required and a decision had to be made, between looking at a line or an area ahead.

Doppler Radar required a choice between frequency modulated Continuous Wave (CW) and pulse operation. Existing equipments were not considered good enough for accuracy and larger antennas were needed. These needed to be stable in track (giving the wind-caused drift angle between the aircraft's heading and the track being followed) and the desirability of stability in pitch. Based on USA experience and reports from a Geneva conference, J-band appeared to be preferable.

IRS Stable Platform was already the subject of considerable activity in the UK, with Elliott Automation offering a large and heavy platform that was under development for the Blue Steel stand-off missile and English Electric offering a smaller platform based on a Honeywell design. Ferranti was omitted from this brief summary, but Clemow did not anticipate great difficulties, from work Vickers had already done.

Autopilot would ideally be specified to achieve a stable and flyable aircraft, besides augmenting stability and to provide the crew with comfortable flying conditions, especially at low altitude and a good gun platform. A second objective was to provide some boost to the aircraft's response, so that more rapid manoeuvre could be developed.

Nuclear bombing would involve loft bombing from very low altitude and medium altitude level bombing, to an achieve accuracy of about 400 yards in blind conditions. Since loft bombing might result in excessive aircraft vulnerability during loop/turn and similar manoeuvres, a powered guided bomb should be considered. Bombing with

Right: Fig.2.
Sideways
Looking
Radar Beam
Configuration
for ground
mapping.[2]

Below: Fig.3.
TSR2 elevation
drawing
showing the
SLR antenna(e)
at the position
marked 13.[3]

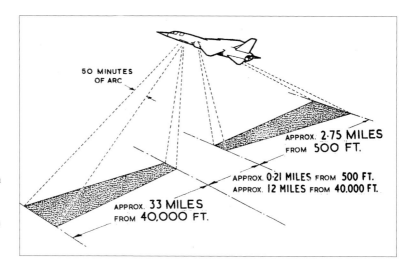

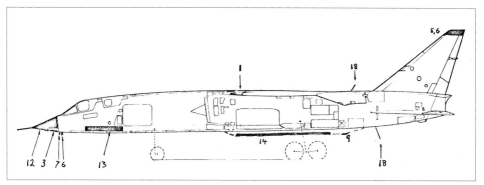

conventional high explosive bombs was expected to enable 30 yards accuracy in visual conditions, but low level blind bombing would not be accurate enough. Consequently a high definition Forward Looking Radar (FLR) would need to give the pilot a clear view of the target. At medium level, visual bombing was only expected to achieve 200 yards accuracy, except with guided bombs, offering 50 to 100 yards. In blind conditions even guided bombs were only expected to be accurate to 200–300 yards. The possible use of incendiary bombs would be considered to alleviate this problem.

High explosive rocket ground attacks would require a large guided rocket to be designed to be used in visual conditions or in blind conditions with a high-resolution FLR. TSR2's secondary fighter role would require a weapon with a large 'jump up' capability. The current Red Top Infrared seeking air-to-air missile might be suitable, he thought, or a controlled nuclear weapon. In either case, TSR2 would need to be fitted with a suitable Airborne Interception (AI) Radar.

Communications and Radio-altimeter requirements were not seen to involve unusual problems.

Computation needs were seen to be met in one of three ways. Firstly, decentralised analogue computation with existing equipments, with the advantage of the equipments being independent, and therefore development being more

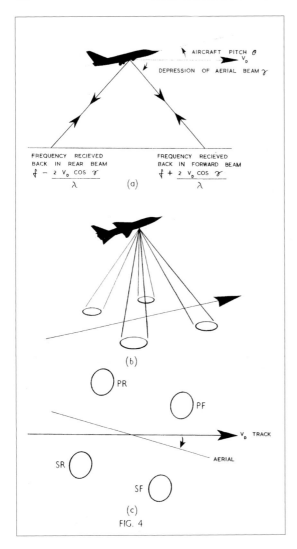

Left: Fig.4. Doppler Radar beam pattern and transmissions forward and to the rear, to port and starboard.[5]

Below: Fig.5. Relates aircraft heading to the north and east components of its velocity along the track flown over the ground.[5]

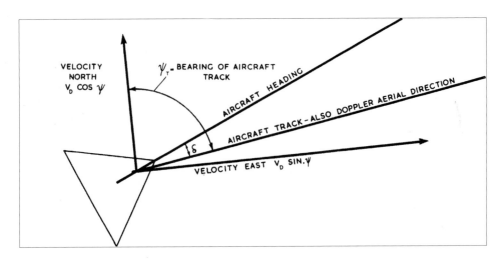

certain. However, Clemow realised that analogue computation was near the limit of its accuracy and could be wasteful of weight and power supplies. Next considered would be a central digital computer, which was reliably considered to be a possibility. A third way to consider was to use a central digital computer, which might include digital differential analysers (DDA). Digital systems would be highly accurate and could have high storage capacity (by 1950s standards!). The final solution might turn out to be partly digital and partly analogue.

Clemow's observations followed John Lambie's (12 September 1958) more detailed summaries[1] of the problems to be addressed in the main equipments within TSR2's Navigation/Attack System. Thus the conceptual scene was set, with specific equipment specification processes to be addressed. There would be many changes and much development, before the many equipment designs and the overall system would become ready for flight trials, let alone be proven and 'set in stone'.[1]

In those early days of study and specification, Lambie firstly highlighted the SLR for navigation. Prime parameters needing definition included antenna performance and the effects of installation aspects, range, power, resolution, pulse repetition frequency (PRF) and the antenna aperture (length) itself. Also, the scale of the Radar display and matching this to a conventional roller map display for general navigation; the degree of antenna stabilisation against aircraft angular movements and the number of tilt angle positions, to accommodate low altitude and high altitude operations; the effects of any nearby aircraft structure and structural deflections on the radiation pattern (Polar Diagram); the choice of accurate polar diagrams, and/or the use of swept gain; kinetic heating effects; a method for testing on the ground.

The basis of SLR ground mapping and its geometry in diagrammatic form (Fig.2) will allow the reader to visualise how the map was created.

To achieve the narrow beam of less than 1° width, studies at the 10,000MHz frequency of X-band envisaged 8ft long slotted wave-guide antennae mounted on the port and starboard sides of the fuselage, below the navigator's cockpit (Fig.3). Item 12 is the FLR's radome; Item 14 shows the bomb bay cavity mounted Reconnaissance Pack's own SLR antennae. Problems to be addressed with the Reconnaissance ('Recce') SLR were similar to the Navigation SLR, with the added question of possible interference between the two SLRs possibly leading to the need for a (time) sharing arrangement between them.

Next, Lambie looked at the Doppler Radar, where issues needing to be addressed included: the amount of stabilisation in each axis of aircraft manoeuvre, how this would be affected by wind drift angles, manoeuvre attitudes and their durations and any turbulence effects on aircraft stability, the effects of structural loading and kinetic heating on the radome's performance, the long and short-term velocity measurement errors of the systems, methods of ground-testing, and the potential for interference with other radar equipment.

The diagram shows how the Doppler frequency shifts add and subtract from the aircraft's speed as resolved along the Doppler beam paths and enable computation of aircraft speed and the determination of wind drift angle.

Many other factors remained to be determined, besides the fundamental parameters shown.

CHAPTER 2

ALL-WEATHER BLIND NAVIGATION WITH DOPPLER/INERTIAL MIXING AND RADAR FIXES

The Inertial Reference Unit, with its Stable Platform, is the heart of the Navigation and Attack System and Lambie next posed relevant questions in his outline list. The basic concept of maintaining a stable vertical and azimuth reference regardless of aircraft manoeuvre may appear simple, but in practical terms it requires solution of the most difficult engineering problems associated with making sufficiently sensitive and stable gyroscopes and accelerometers, that operate under the severe manoeuvre, vibration and temperature conditions of an advanced attack aircraft. It also requires highly mathematical considerations and analysis, just to determine the axes of reference in space and in relation to the rotating, inaccurately 'spherical' earth. George Henson had already undertaken some of these studies at South Marston and, on taking over the project at Vickers Guided Weapons Department, the mathematics of the problem, including the errors that could be expected with available gyroscopes and accelerometers, were further studied in ever increasing depth.

Fortunately, besides Chief Designer Howard Surtees' capabilities, his assistant chief designer, Bernard Hunn, was a mathematician of distinction, who relished such a problem. Bernard thought and actually 'felt' mathematics and told me at the time that he would take books about mathematics to the beach on his holidays, for enjoyable reading. He once wrote an advanced paper for a mathematical journal, which was rejected as being too 'applied' and then, on sending it to a journal of Applied Mathematics, it was rejected on the grounds of being 'too pure'! However suave, tall and elegant, in his down-to-earth manner, Bernard got down to establishing the main parameters that the TSR2 platform and its components needed to meet, from which overall navigation accuracy – and eventually bombing accuracy – could be made to meet the requirement. Along with this came considerations such as the choice between two-axis 'fully floated' gyros and single-axis 'rate integrating' gyros.

Four and a half months after John Lambie's summary at the high-level 27 January 1959 management meeting, attended by John Clemow and Henry Gardner, the Ministry of Supply (MOS) was debating whether to specify a Honeywell/English Electric platform using three Miniature Integrating Gyros (MIG) or a Kearfott

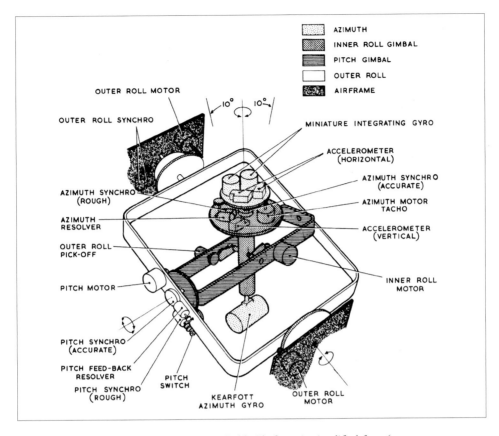

Fig.6. Representation of Inertial Navigation Stable Platform, in simplified form.[6]

platform, which they currently favoured. Ferranti at Bracknell (who eventually won the subcontract) was also described as having promising developments – in a contract the MOS wanted to control directly.

The Lambie practical points summary went on to highlight: gyro and accelerometer performance and its effects on size, shape, and weight of the platform; integration of ancillary electronic equipment with the platform; the effects of aircraft vibrations due to air turbulence; where to position the platform within the aircraft in relation to vibrations nodes; the effects of very high rates of turn during taxiing and in flight; the choice of anti-vibration mountings in the main equipment rack or to mount directly on to aircraft structure; the method of aligning to the north and the vertical before take-off; the length of warm-up period and its effect on operational readiness; the effect of starting in tropical temperatures up to 45°C and the quality of power supplies that would be needed.

The Forward Looking Radar (FLR) was his next point for assessment. Development work had started at the Royal Radar Establishment (RRE) and at Ferranti in Edinburgh, but he regarded this equipment, with its vital Terrain Following (TF) function, as being the least defined of all the equipments. The basic problems were the quality of the Radar returns from varying types of terrain, at or near grazing incidence, and the accurate measurement of angles of depression to points on the ground.

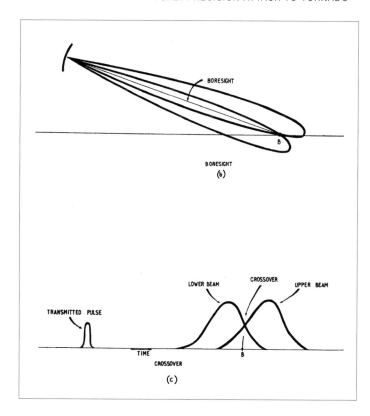

Fig. 7. The Static Split pattern of Radar beams anticipated and the nature of ground returns that would be manipulated, to create forward looking information.[5]

The theoretical boresight position to which the Radar is pointing is found where the lower and upper beams cross and where the areas on each side of the 'crossover' are equal.

Although the aircraft design was already advanced, he saw compromises being needed between the aircraft's frontal area and Radar dish size, besides the problems of rain erosion and kinetic heating of the radome. The display method also remained to be determined. Later, I shall give more detailed descriptions, particularly as affecting Terrain Following and Weapon Aiming.

As the Inertial Reference Stable Platform was the heart of the Navigation/Attack System, computation represented its 'brain'. Studies, papers and ministry documents were actively considering the advantages of the main options, which Lambie listed as: electromechanical analogue, electrical analogue – either of which could be centralised or dispersed – or, alternatively, a centralised digital computer. The full extent of the computation requirements for the whole system needed to be known, for a sensible choice to be possible.

Displays for the pilot and navigator, of information from all the detection equipment, would be required to be engineered for functional performance and for ergonomics of use, with minimised crew workload. This would lead to the relative importance of different items of information affecting the locations and sizes of the displays. Two British – possibly world – 'firsts' established for TSR2 were the pilot's Head Up Display and the navigator's Moving Map display.

The design of the Automatic Flight Control System (AFCS) would depend on the aircraft's aerodynamic 'derivatives', including the influence of motions about one axis affecting other axes, the aircraft's mass and inertia leading to its overall dynamics, the methods for navigation and bombing, as well as the basics of take-off and landing.

Other basic facilities were to be considered, such as the Radio Altimeter and its possible use in an automatic landing role, besides its supporting use during terrain following. Where would the antennae be positioned relative to other antennae and how would they be affected by various terrains at low altitude? Should there be interconnections with Forward Looking Radar and barometric height instruments? Should there be rate of climb and descent information integrated with velocity from the IRS platform and how would failure modes affect the AFCS? Also related would be the Blind-Landing System and its relationship with different kinds of ground-based systems and the achievement of automatic flare-out for landing. Basic Radio Communications by VHF, UHF, and long-range Radio Telephony (R/T) had to be considered, along with questions of power required, antenna coverage, mutual interference and emergency standby arrangements.

Finally came the highly classified Electronic Counter-Measures (ECM or RCM) that would be required. The RAE Radio Department was to be mainly responsible, but provision had to be made in the aircraft, and the effects of weight, volume, and power requirements could become critical.

This summary provided a starting point for the many choices and detailed equipment designs on which the Vickers team embarked at Weybridge, before firm specifications could be agreed for implementation by the subcontractors. Naturally, the Vickers

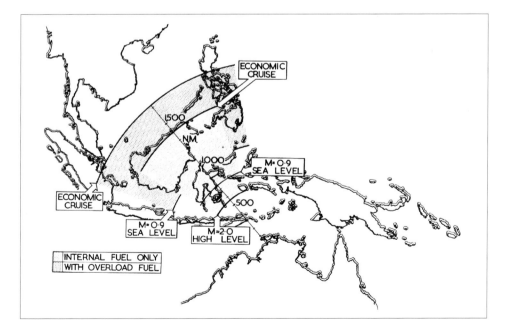

Fig.8. Radii of action from a possible basing at Darwin for the defence of Australia.[7]

Navigation/Attack systems team worked in cooperation with English Electric, whose separate studies and proposals led to their having 50 per cent of the overall TSR2 contract for the aircraft itself, headed by Vickers. Clearly a number of pointers for determining the main parameters of the IRS, the FLR and the CCS already existed from work at the RAE, the RRE, Ferranti and Elliotts, but, as of early 1959 when the TSR2 contract was formalised, and beyond, nothing was really set in stone.

The major equipments for which the MOA retained its (Category 1) authority were the Forward Looking Radar (FLR) and the Inertial Reference System (IRS) Platform, both made by Ferranti Ltd, in Edinburgh and Bracknell, respectively. However, although the MOA therefore produced the specifications for these items, Vickers remained deeply involved in the system aspects of the designs, both through mathematical analyses and by simulations of the aircraft's performance in terms of navigation and flight performance. This work in Weybridge had a correspondingly direct influence on the specifications, and a profound effect on the equipment designs.

An overall impression of the aircraft's mission requirements may be obtained from an example of its radii of action for various modes of attack and reconnaissance.

The more lightly shaded areas with internal fuel only indicate a range of 600nm at sea level and Mach 0.9, extending to 1,500nm for flight under economic cruise conditions. The more heavily shaded areas allowing for overload fuel extends the sea level range to 1,000nm and the economic cruise range to about 1,850 miles. A high level supersonic mission with internal fuel only at Mach 2 is shown to permit a range of a little over 500nm. The navigation system therefore had to achieve the required accuracy over such a range of missions.

CHAPTER 3

THEORY AND HARDWARE FOR INERTIAL NAVIGATION

As earlier indicated, the heart of the navigation system was the IRS platform and this had to operate in suitable axes related to the Earth. Mathematical studies by Bernard Hunn, John Lattey and others in the context of earlier RAE studies indicated north and east spatial axes in a true horizontal plane emanating from the aircraft's position anywhere over the earth. They also established the overall technical parameters related to navigation and bombing accuracy, which defined the detailed accuracy requirements for the platform instruments and other elements. Thus although the IRS was a MOA specified (Category 1) item, the Vickers systems team had a profound effect on the specification.

These axes were set up at the base position, usually before take-off, if sufficient time was available to run up the gyroscopes. Alternatively, they could be set up in flight, as I shall describe later. As the aircraft flies over the surface, due to the convergence of the Earth's meridians at increasing latitudes, the axes become displaced from the original true north by the angle β shown. However, to take account of the Earth's rotation, the axes nevertheless require to be precessed, at a rate depending on the local latitude, to maintain the true level in relation to the vertical (itself established by means of the 'Schuler Pendulum' that points to the centre of the Earth, as described in Chapter 16.3). Fig.10 shows the platform's rotation about the x, y and the vertical (z) axes, together with the accelerations measured along the vectors indicated by the corresponding mathematical symbols. The Earth's rotation rate and the required precession rates in accordance with the complex geometry and mathematical relationships are automatically computed in the Central Computing System (CCS).

Due to the Earth being an imperfect sphere, a further correction has to be applied before accelerometers on the platform can provide accurate information for navigation purposes.

Simplified detailing of the platform (see Fig.6) and the correcting mechanisms for azimuth and in the vertical lead to the basic instrument requirements – for gyroscopes and accelerometers.

Stability and the precession of the platform are achieved with the aid of gyroscopes whose inherent property should maintain their spin axes fixed in space. The TSR2 system employed the Integrating Rate Gyro variety, with a single degree of freedom.

Depending on bearing friction and other mechanical characteristics, a gyro spin axis is subject to wander from its initial spatial direction and errors due to this factor can be somewhat ameliorated by measurements being of airframe (platform) angular rate, which can be integrated over time to an angular displacement.

A single gimbal carries the rotor, which spins around Axis 1. The Input Axis 3 relates to airframe motions, and the gyro's inherent response to input motions is to precess the gimbal around the orthogonal Output Axis 2. The case fixed to the platform and, through that, to the airframe is shown to contain viscous damping fluid that restrains precession about the output axis.

Thus, rotation of the aircraft and platform in azimuth firstly tends to move the gyro off its axis. This causes the gimbal in which the rotor spins to rotate relative to its casing, resisted by the viscous fluid. The amount of gimbal movement (indicated by an electrical pick-off) is a measure of the angular rate, serving as an error signal, which is used to correct the platform's azimuth orientation.

The platform is continuously slaved back to the gyro's initial direction by a servomotor, driven by electronic correction signals. Thus, the platform maintains a correct indication of heading in azimuth.

Maintaining the platform level in relation to the true vertical also requires integrating rate gyros together with sensitive accelerometers (in each horizontal axis).

Whenever aircraft movement tilts the platform away from the horizontal, the 'downhill' gravity vector is sensed by the accelerometer, which signals an error. This is fed to the system incorporating the geometry of axes and appropriately scaled accelerations, which responds by simulating the movement of a synthetic 'eighty-four minute' Schuler Pendulum, whose length equals the Earth's radius and therefore always remains vertical. In practice, a torque motor in the gyro is signalled to apply an electro-magnetic precession torque to maintain its axis horizontal and, by servo action, the platform follows to maintain it in the horizontal plane, until the accelerometer error signal becomes zero. This has to be achieved in a stable and damped manner, avoiding oscillations about the desired horizontal attitude. The accelerometer therefore actually remains level to a sufficient accuracy for its readings to be electronically integrated into a measure of velocity for navigation in the appropriate axial direction. Such a system acting in the three axes of the platform enables it to be stabilised against all aircraft movements over the necessary range of climbing, diving and direction changes.

The accelerometers were of a 'forced balance' design, in which a pendulum mass moves in response to acceleration by a small amount that is sensed electrically. The sensed signal is amplified and creates an electromagnetic restoring force applied by a coil, in which the current is an accurate measure of the restoring force – and of the acceleration.

Made by Kearfott in the USA, the ±10g range accelerometers' threshold of measurement corresponded with a departure from the horizontal of 2 milliradians (approximately one-thirtieth of a degree). Subject to small linearity and other small errors, the platform employing this system would remain level and define the true vertical to this accuracy over short periods.

In the absence of gyroscope wander errors, the stable platform would continually provide the necessary spatial references for navigation and weapon aiming, as well as for pilots' displays.

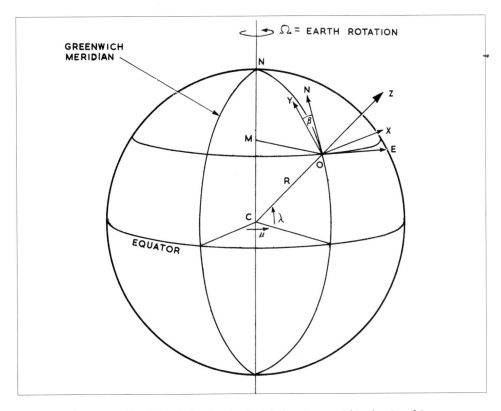

Fig.9. Axes for an aircraft at Point O, heading by the Platform's axes within the aircraft.[6]

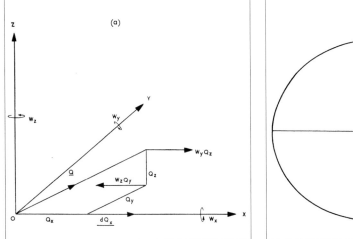

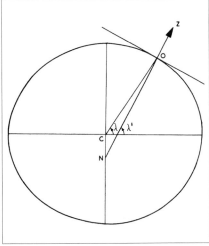

Above left: Fig.10. Rotations about and movements of an angle β to the left of the north axis and the local vertical points to Earth centre, C.[6]

Above right: Fig.11. The 'oblate spheroid' shape of Earth shown in simplified elliptic form, indicating the correction angles in the compensating precession instructions.[6]

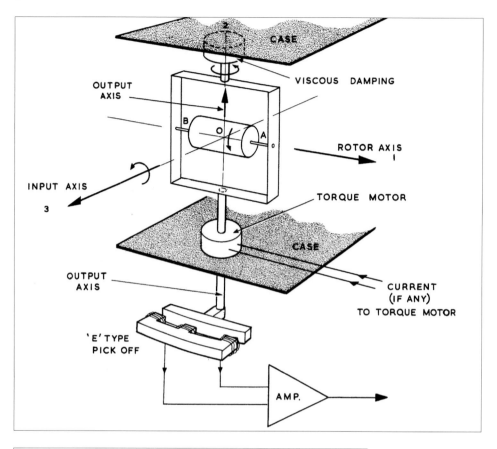

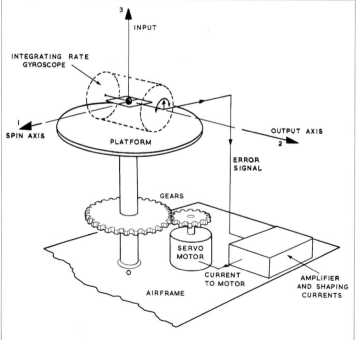

Above: Fig.12. Integrating Rate Gyro schematic.[6]

Left: Fig.13. Simple schematic platform carrying a integrating rate gyro and servomechanism.[6]

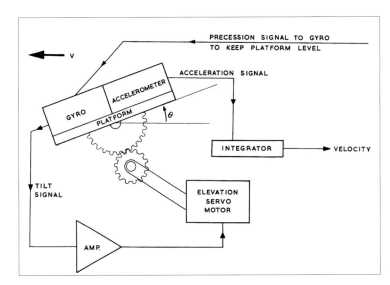

Left: Fig.14. Simple platform schematic of levelling using the Schuler Pendulum (in each of the north and the east axes).[6]

Below: Fig.15. Force balance accelerometer schematic showing the pendulum and restoring action.[6]

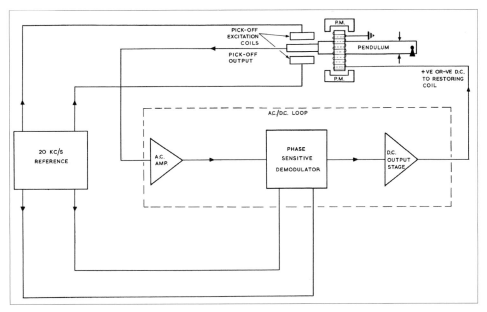

However, gyros are also imperfect – the Kearfott-supplied instruments were no exception – and long-term platform level and azimuth accuracies depend on their wander (or drift) rate. These are shown with other main characteristics of this gyro in Fig.16.

The azimuth gyro had sixty times the rotor momentum compared with the vertical gyros, all running at 24,000rpm. The random wander rates were 0.05°/hour to which the effects of fixed restraints, acceleration (g)-dependent mass unbalance and g²-dependent 'anisoelastic' wander added sufficient to result in an overall average wander rate indicated at ½°/hour in the north–south and the east–west gyros and ¼°/hour in azimuth. Such drift rates would inevitably lead to substantial navigation errors over the flight time of a mission and consequently further system elements were added – particularly the correction of velocity as measured by the IRS platform, with independently measured velocity using a Doppler Radar. Under the technical expertise of Arthur Carter and after rejecting a Marconi Frequency Modulated Carrier Wave (FMCW) Doppler Radar, Vickers specified a pulsed Doppler Radar made by Decca, enabling the velocity thus measured along the aircraft's track to be mixed with the velocity indicated by the IRS, creating a continuously corrected ground speed.

Like Janus, the Greek god who simultaneously looked both ahead and behind, the Doppler Radar, frequently called a 'Janus System' looks both forward and rearward, employing four beams (remember Fig.4). Ground reflections from the beam pattern, radiated at 8,800MHz frequency in approximately 4 microsecond-long pulses, come back at frequencies that are shifted by the speed at which the ground passes. Analogous to the rising and falling note of a train whistle as it approaches and recedes from the observer, this Doppler-shift frequency is actually measured along the beam, which intersects the ground at different speeds depending on the distance of the intersection point from the aircraft. Dependent, that is, on the angle of depression to the ground at each distance ahead and behind.

In order to measure speed along the aircraft's track rather than its heading, the forward-looking antenna assembly is turned through an angle to a position which equates the Doppler shifts measured on the port and starboard directed beams (un-shaded areas). This brings the antenna in line with the aircraft's track. The angle, between this antenna position and the aircraft centre-line is also the angle between the track and the aircraft's heading – the drift angle.

The forward and rearward-facing beams are fired together, and with some overlap due to their returns spectra being affected by differences in the terrain, then they are compared and made equal by stabilising the antenna pitch. There is no roll stabilisation, but the 9° broadside angle of fire (81° depression) and 15° beam width permit sufficient aircraft rolling during normal navigating flight. For accuracy, the forward beams, depressed by 67° to minimise over-water returns, have a width of only 2.75°.

Errors due to pitch angle errors were minimised by the combination of forward and rearward transmission returns straddling the average value, and the effects of differing returns from water were compensated by the navigator's land/sea switch, which altered the tracker scaling factor. In the event of excessive aircraft manoeuvre causing loss of Doppler functioning, a memory facility maintained the velocity output, and this was indicated on the navigator's panel. This system thus worked over a speed range between 180 to 1,800 knots, with the antenna stabilised over a drift angle range of ±20° and pitch range of ±10°. Cut-off would occur at roll angles greater than 10°. With the appropriate reference oscillator stability and mixing for intermediate frequency detection of the Doppler-shifted frequencies, the accuracy of speed measurement (averaged over a time constant of about 10s) accumulated to an equivalent distance-gone error of 0.1 per cent RMS, typically 1ft/s at Mach 0.9.

The antenna to provide the required radiations and performance was a composite of slotted wave-guides engineered into a rectangular assembly, with actuation about its pitch and lateral axes for stabilisation.

Data	Azimuth Gyro	Vertical Gyro
Type	T.2502-2-0	GG49
Rotor Momentum gm. cm²/sec	6.05 x 10⁶	10⁵
Rotor Speed r.p.m	24,000	24,000
Pick-off:– Resolution Null	<1 sec. arc 0.04° R.M.S	<2 sec. arc 0.04° R.M.S
Torque Motor:– Range Linearity	300° /hr. max Within 0.05°/hr Up to 15°/hr	± 200°/hr ± 0.5% with zero deflection ± 2½% with deflection up to 20 milliradians but constant excitation
Wander Rate:– Mass unbalance Fixed restraints Random wander Aniesolastic wander	¾° /hr/g 0.3°/hr 0.05°/hr 0.08°/hr/g²	2°/hr/g 2°/hr 0.05°/hr 0.05°/hr/g²
Characteristic Time	0.0035 sec.	0.006 sec.
Temperature Control	120° F ± 1° F	180° F ± 0.5° F
Size:– Diameter Length Weight	4 ⅛ in. 6 ⅛ in. 6 ½ lb.	1.83 in 2.82 in. 0.55 lb

Fig.16. Kearfott rate integrating gyro characteristics.[6]

Doppler/Inertia mixing entailed using the difference between the Doppler velocity V_D and the computed velocity output from the IRS platform V_C as an error signal V_D-V_C within the Doppler/Inertia mixing system. This error signal was applied to provide the required gyro precession demands for correcting any tilt angle due to N–S and E–W gyro drifts and in a system of three interacting control loops, enabling the integration of velocity from a corrected accelerometer output. A simplified block diagram (Fig.19) indicates the flow of information resulting in a finally computed velocity V_C. Because the Doppler velocity measurement is more long-term accurate than the Inertia Platform velocity, the mixing process gives more weight to the Doppler-measured velocity, as indicated by the 'K factor', being doubled for the gyro precession input. This resulting V_C was then fed to the Central Computing System for further integration with time, to arrive at distance travelled in the N–S and E–W directions.

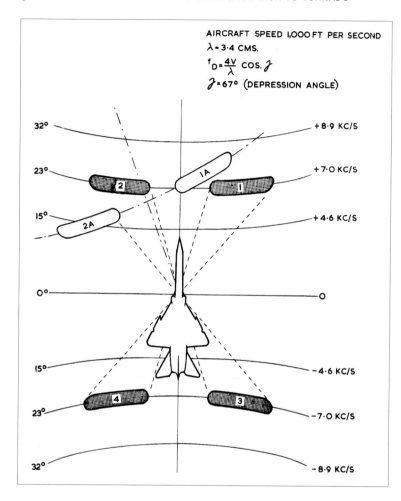

AIRCRAFT SPEED 1,000 FT PER SECOND

λ = 3·4 CMS.

$$f_D = \frac{4V}{\lambda} \cos \gamma$$

γ = 67° (DEPRESSION ANGLE)

Fig.17. Beam intersection elements on the ground shown shaded at 1, 2, 3 and 4 producing Doppler shifts that increase with distance ahead and behind the aircraft as seen.[6]

The distance travelled from initial platform and system alignment at the commencement of a mission represented the best accuracy obtainable, until any further corrections could be applied by taking fixes against known landmarks en route.

The MOA made the choice of the Kearfott-instrumented Inertia Platform to be built by Ferranti. As a Category 1 item, Vickers was able to make the system inputs already described, but was otherwise unable to influence the choice. The preference rejected by the MOA was a Honeywell platform employing Miniature Integrating Gyros (MIGs), already licensed to English Electric.

The Ferranti platform when used with Doppler mixing and the Verdan Central Computing System was expected to achieve a navigation accuracy resulting in a 50 per cent probability error of about 4–5nm per hour of flight. In the same timeframe, another inertial navigation system, manufactured by Litton Industries in the USA (the Type LN3), was in active service on 1,000 F104 NATO fighters, and achieving, at worst, 3nm per hour of flight *without the benefit of Doppler/Inertia mixing* – with tests showing nearer 1.67nm per hour. When combined with a Doppler Radar, the LN3s could attain this accuracy over a much longer period of time. The author had first-hand knowledge

Fig.18. Decca's Doppler antenna assembly showing the slotted wave-guides on the lower surface.[7]

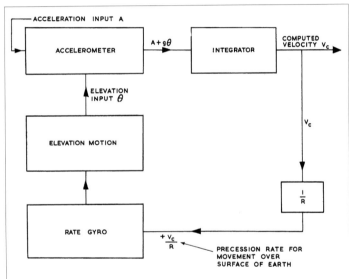

Fig.19. Doppler/Inertia mixing system block diagram.[6]

Fig.20. The Inertia Platform, made by Ferranti Ltd, employing Kearfott gyros and accelerometers.[7]

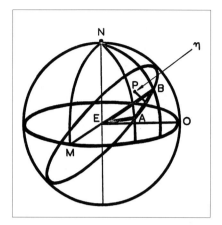

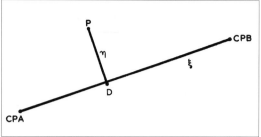

Fig.21. Great Circle navigation axes for the shortest distance between two points, indicating current position 'P' of the aircraft, offset from the intended track between A and B.[10]

about this, having discovered the existence of the Litton equipment in the latter half of 1961, following which he proposed use of an even more advanced Litton platform in another Vickers project for a NATO fighter with V/STOL capability.

When the GW Department at Weybridge was about to be closed down at the end of 1961, I had decided to take up offers either with Elliotts or Decca, but just before the year end I made a visit to the US together with Dab and Les Vine, to assist Honeywell with an anti-tank missile proposal. While in the US, I visited Litton in California and was extremely impressed by the quality of their engineering, their comprehensive laboratory test and flight results, as well as with their manufacturing and quality assurance facilities. This LN3 system employed fully floated 2°-of-freedom gyros with random wander rates of 0.01°/hour (one-fifth of the Kearfott gyros' rate), with other commensurately lower errors from the accelerometers. This well performing system included a digital computer weighing less than 80lb – well below the weight of the Ferranti platform alone. It was also capable of readiness (gyro run-up time) of three minutes, as opposed to nearer ten minutes. The more advanced system still in flight-test that I had proposed for the Vickers NATO V/STOL aircraft had still greater accuracy.

On finding out that I was about to leave Vickers, Litton offered me the job of representing them in London and, during this process, I was in regular negotiation with the Air Ministry's Operational Requirements staff and with the MOA in the context of other aircraft projects. Throughout that period, until the end of 1964 – not long before TSR2 was cancelled – the MOA resisted all offers of Litton Inertial Systems, concerning which the author received much support from the OR staff at all levels. Beyond that, when the RAF later received US Phantom F–4 aircraft – of which 400 were also in service with Litton equipment – the MOA again specified a Ferranti platform which had not yet flown. This was despite the fact that Litton had offered to establish a joint venture with a British company (discussions were advanced with GEC), or to license the manufacture of their equipment by a British manufacturer, ensuring that the technology became available in Britain. However, while recognising that there had been considerable investment in Ferranti's development work, Litton could never fathom why the MOA refused to take advantage of the opportunity to leapfrog the technology and simultaneously give the RAF a better capability.

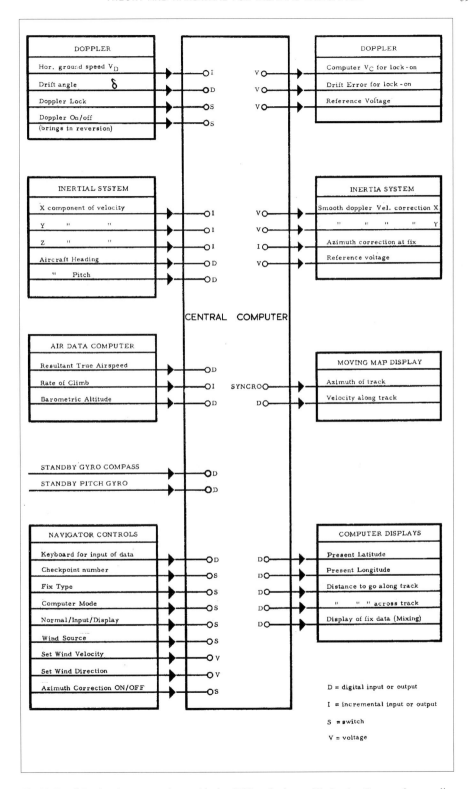

Fig.22. Dead Reckoning connections with the CCS and relevant Navigation System elements.[11]

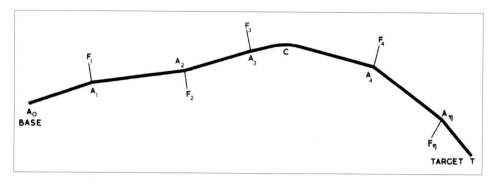

Fig.23. Legs to way points and fixing points en route to the target.[5]

Prior to take-off, allowing thirty minutes for warm-up and system alignment, once the gyros had been run up to speed, the Inertial Platform could be aligned in respect to the true vertical/horizontal and azimuth with respect to north. These parameters could be most accurately determined at fixed, well-defined sites using surveyed points against which to calibrate the north and also the height above sea level. The accelerometers on the platform would indicate any out-of-vertical (tilt) error and, as already described, their outputs would cause the platform to level until the accelerometers in the stationary aircraft showed no tilt. Considering the less prepared sites from which TSR2 had to operate, where latitude and longitude would nevertheless be accurately known, alignment would be less accurate. Azimuth could be obtained using the true north from the Fluxgate Gyro Compass, to a lesser accuracy of ten minutes of arc – or $\frac{1}{6}°$. With known starting latitude and longitude, present position could also be fed into the CCS, following which the latter would be constantly updated in each axis with velocity information from the Doppler/Inertia mixing system. The CCS would then integrate the velocities in the three axes to keep track aircraft position, heading, track, and height.

Where rapid take-off was required without time for gyros to run up to speed, the system was capable of in-flight alignment. Once the aircraft was at 150ft above the ground, enabling the use of Doppler Radar, the Doppler/Inertia mixing facility was gradually able to bring the coarsely aligned azimuth to an acceptable accuracy. Dead reckoning navigation was now possible in relation to Great Circle tracks between points on the map.[8]

Referring to Fig.21, the across-track error of point P is the value η measured from the intended track AB, pre-entered into the Central Computing System (CCS). The remaining distance to go before arriving at B is the value ξ. These values are continuously computed in the CCS, in accordance with the programmed axes and the inputs, the velocities and accelerations obtained from the Doppler/Inertia mixing system in all axes.

Central Computing System (CCS), to which I have briefly alluded earlier as the 'brain' of the Navigation/Attack System, was provided by Elliott Automation Ltd, under license from North American Aviation Inc. It comprised two Verdan computers coupled together, each containing a General Purpose Digital Computer section with a drum memory and a Digital Differential Analyser (DDA) section, each DDA performing more accurately, the kind of integration previously executed by analogue integrators. Coding and decoding equipments and a buffer store connected the computers to the various system items. Vickers specified the requirements for the CCS and placed the contract with Elliotts, following much systems analysis over many months, by the team under Bernard Hunn. As the principal engineer, Dennis Harris (initially under Arthur Carter, and later under John Lattey) issued comprehensive operation and programming notes in April 1960 for the General Purpose section of the Verdan,[29] and, thereafter, Elliotts were mainly responsible for programming the GP section. His team produced a further comprehensive note in October 1960 specifying the scaling of the DDA section[30] and thereafter did a large part of the programming for the DDAs in house. Being at the very centre of the Navigation/Attack System, the CCS interfaced with every other subsystem, essentially via incremental outputs in the form of digital pulses representing small changes in the relevant parameter values.

Inputs from the Doppler were incremental pulses (ground speed), from a digital encoder for drift angle (δ) and switched voltages from the various controls. CCS outputs were mainly digital, or voltages. The Inertial Platform provided incremental outputs of velocity in the three axes and digital heading and pitch outputs from synchros. The CCS outputs to the platform were voltages except for the incremental azimuth correction at a fix point (see below). The Air Data computer, supplied by Kelvin Hughes Ltd, has not been mentioned so far (see later). Digital and switched inputs and outputs were used mostly for the standby signals and the navigator and computer displays.

One Verdan computer was assigned mainly for navigation and the other identical computer was used mainly for bombing and reconnaissance. The store was the memory for facts such as the latitudes and longitudes of fix points and also for instructions on how to carry out calculations. An important feature was that no internal information would be lost in the event of a power failure, so that when power was reapplied, the computer would resume computation without error, except those due to any missing input information. Control was by means of an internally stored programme, which was fed into the machine by a punched tape. The GP section worked accurately but relatively slowly on the whole numbers, while the many DDAs worked on an incremental basis, being signalled by incremental changes in quantities such as velocity, angle, etc., continually bringing values up to date. In this sense, the CCS was working in real-time, operating on increments at every one-hundredth of a second. Thus for example, Doppler velocity was capable of going up to 3,000ft/s limiting the value of one pulse to 30ft/s. This system was particularly suitable for integration, such as the integration of velocities into distance travelled along the axis concerned. While errors can accumulate in a DDA, large errors were prevented by the more accurate GP section. Each value on which the Verdans operated had to be appropriately scaled, to suit the nature and the purpose of the quantity. Using the example of Doppler ground speed (V_D), the scale is 30ft/pulse for the resolution and mixing with the inertial component in Doppler/Inertial mixing.

By this method of dead reckoning, the aircraft would navigate towards the target along legs marked by pre-planned way (turning) points and navigational fixes to update position and platform azimuth at intervals of generally 100nm – that is around ten minutes of flight time apart.

CHAPTER 4

DEAD RECKONING AND SIDEWAYS RADAR FIXES

Navigation had to be of sufficient accuracy to reach the fix points closely enough for identification either visually – or more importantly by Sideways Looking Radar (SLR). When blind or at night, TSR2 had to pass over, or close enough to, the point in question for the fix point to be seen on the SLR 'map' as developed by the Rapid Processing Unit (RPU). This Vickers-specified item was developed and made by Kelvin Hughes Ltd. In addition, a computer-driven 'Moving Map Display' (MMD), made by Ferranti, projected colour topographical maps from a pre-prepared film strip on to displays for both pilot and navigator. This simplified the normal process for map-reading over a rapidly changing territory, assisted by a computer-generated marker indicating the aircraft's computed position. The position marker sat on a line indicating the aircraft's track and the whole display was thus track-stabilised, with the map moving to keep the position marker in the lower segment of the display, with the future positions showing along the track line.

The navigator would first enter latitude and longitude manually at points where fixes had been taken. Receiving velocity and drift inputs from the Doppler Radar (and drift information also from the gyro compass in reversionary mode), the MMD continued to update latitude and longitude on the navigator-selected map frames. The scale of the map could be selected at 1:500,000, representing a 50nm-diameter area on the 6in diameter screen; it could be enlarged (mainly for use at high altitude) up to 1:4,000,000, to display an area of 400nm diameter. A graticule generated in the plane of the transparency and calibrated with a diameter scaled in nautical miles was also projected, and this could be rotated through 360° so that the navigator could determine the relative bearing of any ground feature. This rotation was duplicated by a servomechanism on the pilot's display. In the event of a CCS failure, the navigator could select velocity and track information direct from the Doppler and compass heading (with auto variation correction), to which Doppler drift angle was added.

Fixing to correct dead reckoning errors was aided by the MMD, but essentially utilised the EMI-manufactured SLR beam coverage, earlier shown in Fig.2. The Radar map produced by the Rapid Processing Unit (RPU) is somewhat distorted by the drift angle and also by yawing and pitching of the aircraft carrying the SLR antennae, as shown in Fig.27. However it was sufficiently representative for

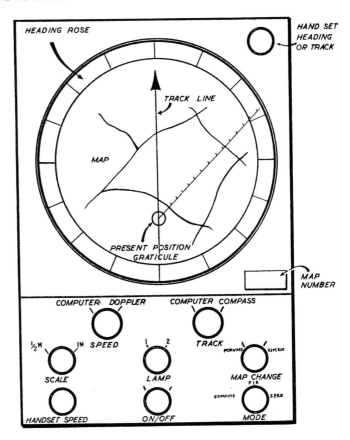

Fig.24. Moving Map Display and controls.[13]

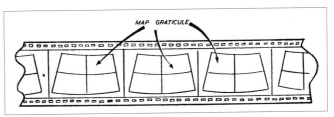

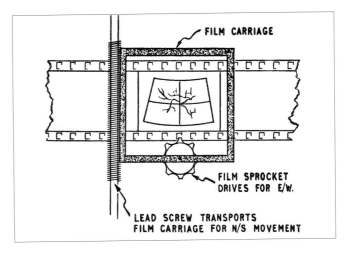

Fig.25. Moving Map film strip and film drive.[13]

recognition of fix points alongside a reconnaissance photograph of the same area and was further correlated by the fix position indicated on the Moving Map Display.

The procedure for a planned fix commenced with the navigator setting up the SLR scaling to give the optimum display on the RPU. He then compared this with the MM Display, giving an idea of track-keeping accuracy. The area displayed by the RPU could be controlled either manually or, normally, under computer control (it was offset by the planned distance at which the fix point was to be passed, so that the fix point would appear within the area viewed). At 10 miles from the fix point, a warning lamp was lit, and at 5 miles the computer started painting a range marker on the Radar map and the aircraft would 'freeze' in roll, to hold the wings horizontal for minimum picture variation. Repeated at intervals until the fix had been made, this range marker was printed on the Radar map at a point corresponding to the computed across-track distance of the fix. Thus, the line leading to the fix point was shown by the heralds and eventually the fix point itself, as shown in Fig.31. Maintaining a constant heading, the navigator looked out for the Radar paint that identified the fixed point. Thus the actual fix point as identified from the reconnaissance folio picture appeared on the Radar map – and also the computed fix point.

The navigator could then control a pair of cursors in the up/down and left/right positions using handwheels. Intersecting first on the computed fix point and then on the actual fix point, with appropriate controls and buttons he could input the coordinates of each point into the CCS, defining the error between computed and actual fix positions (usually less than ½in on the Radar map). The CCS enabled the cursor position to move with the paper at the 'aircraft speed', enabling easier fine-tuning of the cursor settings (to an accuracy of 0.03in). This constituted the fix correction and enabled the CCS to update the navigation data, velocity, and azimuth error on the inertial platform. If the along-track distance between computed and actual fix points exceeded 2.5in, the navigator could temporarily select a slower paper speed than the normal 18in/min that corresponds to a ground speed of 700 knots. Variations of the fixing procedure permitted unplanned (random) fixes. Using his control panels, the navigator could change the sequence of fixes or miss out fixes if the sortie plan changed. The MMD also required updating after a fix and this process also updated the pilot's MMD.

The navigator's display and control panels were designed for clear readout and simple execution of these operations, enabling speedy input of navigation requirements, with flexibility.

Employing 'Nixie' tube number displays on the left, (see Fig. 32) the Fix No. (of up to forty stored check points) was displayed, together with the planned miss distance across track in nm, and the track direction in compass degrees. Fix point altitude, in 100ft units, and latitude and longitude, defined down to one second of arc as stored, were also shown. Below this, the present position, in degrees north and west, was shown to the nearest minute of arc (about 1nm). These and the values on the right of the display were dynamic displays continually updated by the CCS, in the form of mechanical counters. Similarly, distance to go to the fix point across and along track were recorded to the nearest 1nm. These values were an indication of deviation from the desired path and were complemented above, with computed wind speed and direction.

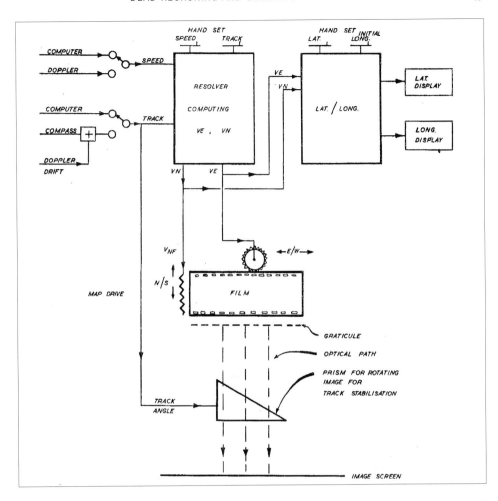

Above: Fig.26. The Moving Map Computer, showing inputs from the CCS, Compass and the Doppler.[13]

Right: Fig.27. Effect of yaw or drift on the SLR beam positions.[2]

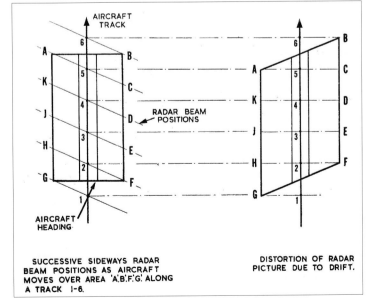

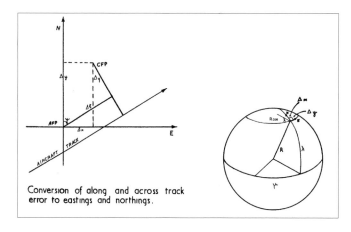

Conversion of along and across track error to eastings and northings.

Fig.28. Eastings and northings in Earth axes after allowing for along/across track conversions.[2]

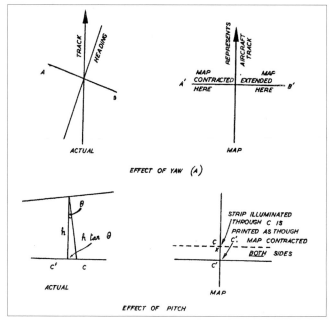

EFFECT OF YAW (A)

EFFECT OF PITCH

Fig.29. The above diagrams represent the geometrical calculations required in the CCS, to operate on the SLR fixing information, to update aircraft position, allowing for drift, height, aircraft attitude in flight and picture distortion.[2]

Initial conditions including manual inputs of wind conditions could be entered by the navigator (Fig. 33), who selected the checkpoint to be displayed by the Nixie tubes. The upper sets of square buttons were interlocked, such that when, in any group, a button was pressed down to select a condition, any other that had been depressed popped up.

The right-hand set of three buttons was for use before take-off, to freeze the computation while entering information ('off'), to check correct storage of programmes, and ('comp') to start the computation from the initial conditions before the aircraft moves from the position in which the IRS was aligned.

The four interlocking buttons controlled which values were to be displayed by the Nixie tubes. The normal in-flight condition ('auto') selected information for the next fix, which automatically changed as fixes were taken. A 'fix after next' button enabled the navigator to look ahead at upcoming data.

The SLR map displayed by the RPU is seen in Fig. 34 with the cursor alignment and controls near the centre. The Forward Looking Radar display is just visible at the top right. The FLR provides an additional fixing facility, by using the Radar map as produced on the cathode ray display tube.

It may seem like the Rapid Processing Unit (RPU) 'tail' was wagging the Navigation/Attack system 'dog', but this small part of TSR2 was an absolute key to the aircraft's capability. With this went the question: would the navigator be capable of doing his job to the accuracy and at the speed required, under the turbulent terrain following conditions of near-sonic speed flight at 200ft? I will cover the Terrain Following System in Chapter 7. However, at this point, the reader will be interested in its potential effect on navigator performance and how this was overcome. I have already indicated that, in order to navigate and make fix corrections to the required accuracy, (besides the operating criteria of other equipments), the placing of the RPU cursors needed to be within 0.03in – corresponding to an error of 125ft. This had to be possible through significant portions of a sortie lasting more than an hour under the difficult conditions at low level, where gusts could create a very bumpy ride for the aircrew.

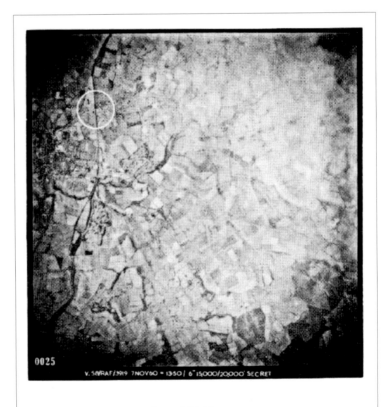

0025

V. 5&RAF/3919 7NOV60 = 13501 6" 15000/20000 SECRET

Fig.30. Photograph of fix point in the navigator's folio for the sortie.[14]

FIX FOLIO

PHOTOGRAPH PRODUCED AT 1:50.000 SCALE.
FIX POINT RINGED IN TOP LEFT CORNER OF PICTURE

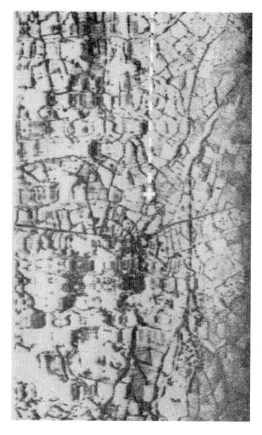

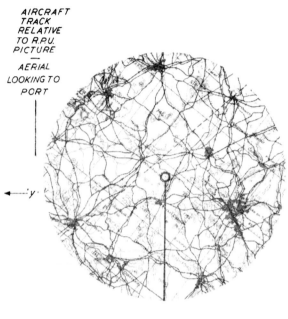

AIRCRAFT
TRACK
RELATIVE
TO R.P.U.
PICTURE
—
AERIAL
LOOKING TO
PORT

← 'y'

NOTE: *This Display is normally in Colour*

R.P.U.
SCALE 1 : 50,000

ACTUAL FIX POINT INDICATED
BY ARROWS 'x' AND 'y'.
COMPUTED FIX POINT SHOWN
BY WHITE HERALDS TERMINATING
IN CROSS.

MOVING MAP
SERIES G.S.G.S. 4715.   SCALE 1:50,000.

AIRCRAFT PRESENT POSITION, INDICATED
BY CIRCLE, HAS ADVANCED APPROXIMATELY
5 N.M. BEYOND FIX POINT SHOWN ON R.P.U.

Above: Fig.31. Relative views of aircraft position as seen on processed SLR map and on the Moving Map Display.[14]

Opposite above: Fig.32. Navigator's Display Panel, located at eye level.[15]

Opposite below: Fig.33. Navigator's Control Panel.[15]

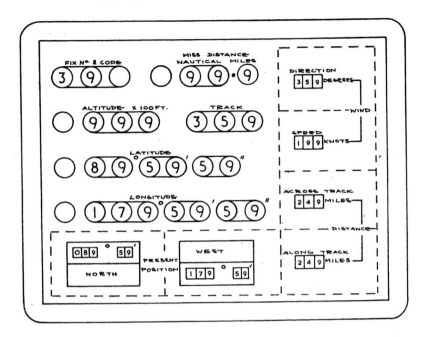

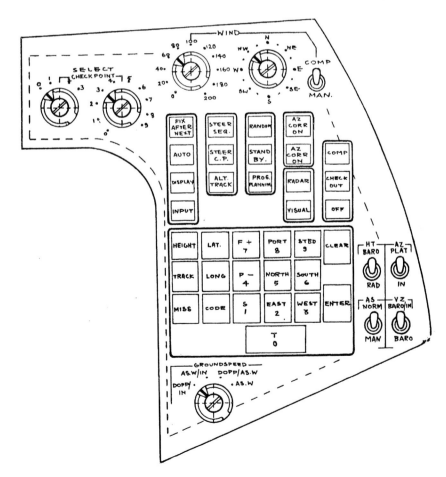

Fig.34. Photograph of prototype navigator's displays.[7]

For this very reason, TSR2 was designed for minimised response to gusts, by adopting a high wing loading and low aerodynamic lift/incidence curve slope. The resulting gust spectrum was described by mean RMS velocity producing random vertical accelerations ('g's) applied to the aircraft and its crew. From trials of the nearest comparable aircraft (Scimitar, Hunter, Lightning, Canberra) and computer simulations, the critical figure for the mean RMS velocity was given as 4ft/s, incurred in the region of 0.5 to 25Hz. To study all the aspects of this problem in the most realistic manner possible, Vickers built a simulator of fully equipped pilot's and navigator's cockpits, which could be shaken in accordance with the anticipated (and much greater) rough ride conditions. This was used in a comprehensive test programme completed in January 1961 and conducted under contract by Vickers Research Ltd (VRL), under the supervision and guidance of Harry Hitch (department Head) and B.W. Payne of Mathematical Services at Weybridge.

The equipment included the RPU made by Kelvin Hughes Ltd, initially as a Category 2 item, but later changed to Category 1 where the design authority was with the MOA's Royal Radar Establishment (RRE), from where the specification was issued. At all stages, Vickers GW Department was concerned with this specification and its integration with the SLR's display – the source of the Radar picture produced on photographic paper by the RPU.

CHAPTER 5

ACCURATE FIXES UNDER VIBRATION IN TURBULENT FLIGHT

In conducting the test programme, consideration was given to the navigator's task, the Moving Map Display and the SLR display, the fix folio of reconnaissance photographs, the nature of the sortie, vibration patterns and the physiological effects of vibration on the navigator under different seating and restraint conditions. Considering the navigator's performance in great detail, the study and tests covered: the ergonomics associated with optimising the display control loop; recognition of fix points; illumination of the cockpit and the displays and instruments in day and night time conditions; the cursor setting task, the associated system, and the navigator's physical controls with regard to 'feel', pressure, hand movements and the use of mechanical inertia (as for handwheels); positions of displays and controls. Scaling of 1:50,000 at low level corresponded to showing a strip of ground 3.4 miles wide, moving at a speed of 1in every four seconds. No detail appears to have been overlooked in considering all the influences that could affect the accuracy of obtaining fixes with consistency and reliability. It was clearly essential to verify that accurate-fix-corrected dead reckoning navigation would be truly possible under operational conditions.

To apply the specified vibrations to the navigator and his instruments, the ejection gun at the base of his ejection seat was replaced by an electro-hydraulic position system, driven up and down its near-vertical guide rails in a manner proportional to an electrical signal representing the inputs due to turbulence. Tests were carried out at the specified 4ft/s mean RMS velocity level and, at higher levels, up to 10ft/s. Besides engineers from the Vickers GW Dept., a number of professional navigators from the Vickers Flight Test Department endured many hours of tests in the turbulent seat of the simulator. A number of vital design requirements emerged, resulting in conclusive test results confirming the ability to achieve the required fixing accuracy under realistic conditions.

The report,[16] of thirty-four pages, four appendices, and twenty-seven illustrations, gives full details, from which the following results emerged. Firstly, taking account of worldwide variations of turbulence effects, as well as the aircraft's own structural vibration patterns, it was found that, far from isolating the navigator's seat from anti-vibration mounted instruments and operating controls, it was most effective to fix the ejector seat firmly to the structure holding the RPU controls, so that they moved together. Secondly, for his comfort and operating efficiency, the navigator should be firmly strapped to his seat. A belt at abdomen level should then be inflatable by mouth – until he finds it difficult to take a deep breath! This was to prevent excessive movements of his abdominal organs for improved comfort – a feature not used in twenty-first-century combat aircraft.

Most importantly, viewing of the RPU display should be through a collimating lens that focuses the image at infinity. The absolute need for this was discovered by my colleague John Garrett, who rode the seat during many of its tests, when he found difficulty in keeping a clearly focused view of the Radar map picture and the cursor with which fix locations were input to the CCS. After yet another difficult ride and attempts to make accurate cursor movements on to the fix point, he threw back the canopy and looked out through a window in the simulator building. Noticing a row of birds perched on a telephone wire a hundred feet or so distant, he had an idea. Before the test engineers could shut down the hydraulic turbulence equipment, he called them back to turn it on. With the seat vibrating to its full extent, he found that, despite the vibrations, he could easily count the relatively distant birds sitting on the wire. This led him to realise the importance of collimating the view to the RPU display, and an experimental collimating lens was soon added to the cursor carriage over the Radar picture. Sure enough, he found that the vibrations no longer made it difficult to see the fix point detail and to adjust the cursor position.

The addition of a collimating lens to cover the top 5in of the SLR viewing area was added to the specification, though after some difficulties encountered by Kelvin Hughes in modifying the cursor carriage design, this remained the subject of meetings and correspondence through most of 1961. However, with this modification – and taking account of recommendations for the exact nature of the cursor lines, their illumination and the resulting little square placed over the fix point, the nature of cursor movement in the left/right and up/down directions (as opposed to joystick controls), and the use of vernier control handwheels with inertia, for rapid yet delicate and accurate control – a most satisfactory means of fixing was verified (Fig. 36).

Relative ease of identifying a fix point from the SLR map produced by the RPU was confirmed, so long as the fix point features were well defined and the aircraft did not exhibit excessive yaw motions at a critical time. Under these conditions, few navigator subjects identified points incorrectly. With the collimating lens, fixing to the required 0.03in (125ft) accuracy was achieved on 90 per cent of occasions, and some scores were 100 per cent. Even with the turbulence level increased from the specified 4ft/s RMS to 10 or 12ft/s, 75 per cent scores were common and 100 per cent scores were still gained by several people. The time required between recording the computed fix point and the actual fix point was usually thirty to forty seconds, and the shortest time was less than ten seconds. This confirmed that, in the actual aircraft flying at 1,000ft/s with 1:50,000 display scaling and the paper and the cursor selected to run together at the slow speed, the distance moved by the SLR beam represented ½in on the paper map – well within the available display area. The effect of fatigue over runs between twenty minutes and fifty minutes indicated no change in navigators' ability to make accurate fixes. Thus the system was shown to allow accurate fixing under anticipated, and even more severe, flying conditions, without difficulty in achieving the fixing task within the available time.

Fig.35. Navigator's cockpit mock-up with full complement of displays, instruments and controls used in the VRL tests.[16]

Thus, before the closing down of the Weybridge Guided Weapons Department in early 1962 and the work moving to the Weybridge aircraft team offices, employing mostly the original engineering team, the basic navigation system was well proven, and its manufacture for the first in-flight testing on the third TSR2 aircraft could begin.

Flying the aircraft to the target in response to the navigation system under terrain following conditions required similar, if not even more stringent, human engineering criteria. A similar test programme was therefore completed at VRL, to verify pilots' ability to carry out their tasks under severe terrain following conditions, reporting in March 1962.

The Head Up Display (HUD) was key to the pilot's task for a number of operating modes in TSR2, particularly terrain following and weapon aiming, but also for normal instrument flying, including use as the director for roll and pitch control, as well as for take-off, approach to landing, and homing onto tanker aircraft. Weapon aiming modes included Radar ranging and sighting for direct attack with rockets or when dive-bombing, and as the director for nuclear weapon delivery. Along with the automatic Moving Map Display, the concept of HUD was new to flying instrumentation and TSR2 broke new ground, becoming the British first aircraft in which this was specified.

Adapting the principle of the pilots' reflector gun sight for air combat to a windshield display system for low-altitude bombing was flight-tested in a simple form by the AMES Research Laboratory in the USA, reported in a 1958 NACA document.[17] Aimed at improving bombing accuracy in similar manoeuvres to those that TSR2 was to utilise, it showed that, while pilots could follow director signals accurately, greater bombing errors were experienced due to other factors related to the release point. However, the biggest single factor militating towards using

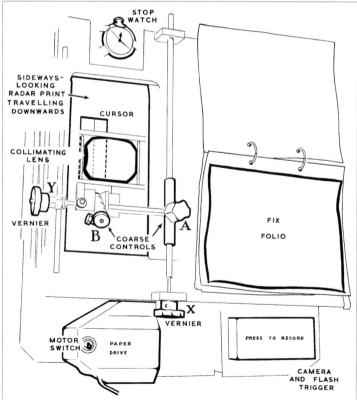

Fig.36. Experimental SLR display and cursor controls with collimating lens, photo and schematic.[16]

Head Up Displays was the need for the pilot to avoid the time-consuming change from viewing conventional (head down) instruments in the cockpit to visual flight information through the windscreen. This changeover could take up to two seconds, resulting in a 'there and back' changeover taking up to four seconds.

In the same timescale, the RAE at Farnborough made a study of Head Up Displays *viewable simultaneously with the outside world* and, in a December 1959 report,[18] presented arguments for the geometrical configuration of display information applicable in the various mission flight modes. These led to the 'Highway in the Sky' format, eventually adopted for TSR2 and many later aircraft. Rank Cintel was contracted to make the experimental HUDs, employing a cathode ray tube which displayed markers produced by an electronic waveform generator. These were projected onto the windscreen and collimated to appear at infinity. As with the navigator's SLR display, this collimation avoided the blurring or confusion of the pilot's display which was caused by vibration.

George Henson originated much of the exploratory work, in conjunction with the English Electric aircraft design group, which was then implemented by the Vickers Aircraft Design Office team's Jock Graham and R.W. Penney under Assistant Chief Designer Mike Salisbury, who coordinated the design and testing programmes. In early tests looking up the Brooklands track's Test Hill, after months of engineering, test pilot Roly Beaumont took one look before walking away with a 'that's no good'. This verified that it was essential to collimate the display at infinity. At each stage of designing the HUD, the nature and layout of orientation markings and director markings for piloting operations were tested on the simulator at Weybridge with pilots, whose opinions as to suitability and suggestions for optimisation were key to the choices made. Besides the VRL vibrating rig programme work, John Lattey and John Garrett in the Vickers GW team ran these simulations and other work for determining many of the display parameters. Typical of these choices were given in John Lattey's

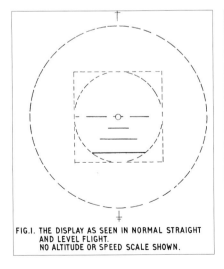

FIG.1. THE DISPLAY AS SEEN IN NORMAL STRAIGHT
AND LEVEL FLIGHT.
NO ALTITUDE OR SPEED SCALE SHOWN.

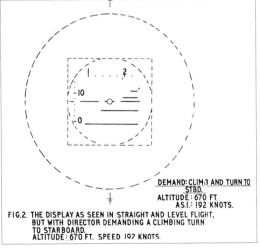

DEMAND: CLIMB AND TURN TO STBD.
ALTITUDE: 670 FT.
A.S.I.: 192 KNOTS.

FIG.2. THE DISPLAY AS SEEN IN STRAIGHT AND LEVEL FLIGHT,
BUT WITH DIRECTOR DEMANDING A CLIMBING TURN
TO STARBOARD.
ALTITUDE: 670 FT. SPEED 192 KNOTS.

Fig.37. Pilot's view of HUD 'Highway in the Sky' presentations in straight and level flight (left) and with demand for turn to starboard (right).[19]

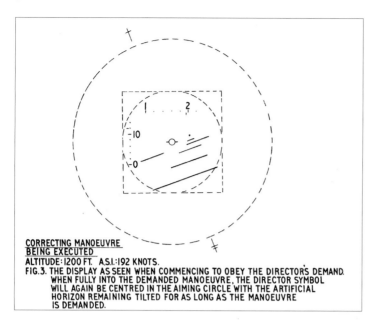

CORRECTING MANOEUVRE
BEING EXECUTED
ALTITUDE: 1200 FT. A.S.I.: 192 KNOTS.
FIG. 3. THE DISPLAY AS SEEN WHEN COMMENCING TO OBEY THE DIRECTOR'S DEMAND.
WHEN FULLY INTO THE DEMANDED MANOEUVRE, THE DIRECTOR SYMBOL
WILL AGAIN BE CENTRED IN THE AIMING CIRCLE WITH THE ARTIFICIAL
HORIZON REMAINING TILTED FOR AS LONG AS THE MANOEUVRE
IS DEMANDED.

Left: Fig.38. Display of a demand for climbing turn to the right, the aiming mark (circle with short horizontal 'winglets') needing to move above the horizon and towards the director symbol (dot at the top of the inclined 'highway').[19]

Below: Fig.39. Complete set of information available on the HUD display with weapon aiming mode.[19]

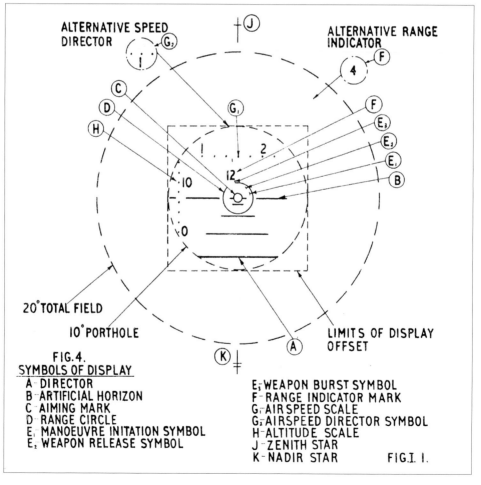

ALTERNATIVE SPEED
DIRECTOR

ALTERNATIVE RANGE
INDICATOR

20° TOTAL FIELD

10° PORTHOLE

LIMITS OF DISPLAY
OFFSET

FIG. 4.
SYMBOLS OF DISPLAY
A - DIRECTOR
B - ARTIFICIAL HORIZON
C - AIMING MARK
D - RANGE CIRCLE
E₁ MANOEUVRE INITATION SYMBOL
E₂ WEAPON RELEASE SYMBOL

E₃ WEAPON BURST SYMBOL
F - RANGE INDICATOR MARK
G₁ AIR SPEED SCALE
G₂ AIRSPEED DIRECTOR SYMBOL
H - ALTITUDE SCALE
J - ZENITH STAR
K - NADIR STAR   FIG. I. I.

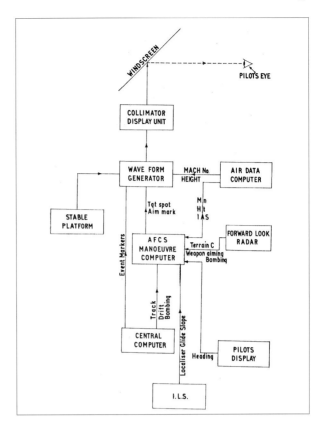

Fig.40. Block diagram of interactions between the pilot, the HUD, and the Nav/Attack system.[19]

3 May 1961 memorandum to R. Penney relating to the HUD's approach director role, discussing the use of an aerodynamic incidence probe at low speed, the need for an airfield altitude input, air speed accuracy requirements relating to the Air Data computer, FLR inputs for the approach and how such items may need to be specified in order to create the required utility of the HUD in that role.

Many such basic parameters had to be optimised, including the relationship of 'wing' and horizon markers to the real view of the outside world to be seen simultaneously through the windscreen. Also, the brightness and scaling of the markers against varying intensities of sky background, the flight director marker size and the rate at which it should move for accurate tracking by pilots, and the amount of additional information to be presented, such as current speed and height. These needed to be as comprehensive as possible to give the pilot the best information about the flight condition and the manoeuvre demands relayed by the CCS, without overburdening the pilot's view to the point of confusion. After completing the specification, Vickers put this out to tender. Rank Cintel was the only respondent to propose a collimated display and was selected as the contractor for engineering and manufacturing the unit. Shortly before the first 'A' model was due, the digital means of creating the alphanumeric characters was found to result in broken-up figures. Vickers and Elliotts worked day and night to create a new analogue design, without excessively delaying delivery.

Low-altitude test flights under turbulent conditions in a Javelin and other aircraft provided practical experience, on the basis of which Roly Beaumont and other test pilots checked out display suitability and their own ability to control flight in terrain clearance and other modes.

The displayed 'horizon' would be parallel to the visible true horizon seen through the windscreen. Current speed and height are indicated with simple scales and figures.

In TSR2, the pilot could thus use the HUD and follow directions manually, 'flying' the aiming mark smoothly and constantly over the director symbol, which was placed in the appropriate location on the display by the CCS, as if following normal external visual clues demanding the required manoeuvre. As described later, through the Automatic Flight Control System and the Manoeuvre Computer, the aircraft could be flown on autopilot to follow the required manoeuvre automatically – including terrain following and weapon delivery. In this case, the pilot would use the HUD to monitor, rather than control, the aircraft's flight path, with the ability to switch to manual control at any time.

Thus, the HUD was integrated into the wider Navigation/Attack system with interconnections to the Central Computing System and the various instruments feeding information around the overall system. These system connections and interactions required detailed analysis, integration and verification by the GW engineering team, with inputs from virtually all sectors of the systems team at Weybridge. The overall system block diagram showing the operation of the HUD within the system is shown in Fig.40.

CHAPTER 6

'HANDS OFF' AUTOMATIC FLIGHT CONTROL

The Automatic Flight Control System (AFCS) enabled the aircraft to be controlled without immediate pilot input in any of its flight modes. Using his HUD the pilot could nevertheless monitor the aircraft's correct response, assisted by normal visual inputs through the canopy (when not flying blind). All depended on the design of the autopilot and the control systems operating the pitch, yaw, and roll controls via the 'tailerons' for pitch and roll, and the all-moving fin, acting as rudder. The aircraft was aerodynamically stable in pitch and roll, but at high Mach numbers (over 1.7) it was unstable in yaw. Consequently the AFCS had to provide auto-stabilisation in yaw, as well as enhancement of performance in pitch and roll. Much depended on the use and performance of gyroscopes and accelerometers strategically placed at appropriate locations in the aircraft.

Based on the aircraft's aerodynamic characteristics, its mass and inertia in the three axes, and its structural vibration characteristics, lengthy and comprehensive mathematical analysis was combined with simulation exercises by John Lattey and his systems team in the GW Department, in consultation with the aircraft design teams at Weybridge, English Electric at Warton, and Elliott Automation, the chosen equipment contractor. These activities commenced within the Guided Weapons Department in 1958, which issued the first (draft) Specification No. VES 1006 to Elliott Automation in September 1960. Working closely with Elliotts and exchanging study and simulation results, the work continued with much the same Weybridge team after the GW Department there closed down in 1962, becoming the BAC Systems Division.

These analyses progressively led to defining the type of stabilisation employing rate gyroscopes and accelerometers and to the specification of particular instruments, their scalings and locations for optimum performance and minimised effects of structural vibrations. Locations had to be on the centre-line and appropriately placed, relative to the aircraft's centre of gravity (CG). Thus the normal (vertical) accelerometer and the pitch rate gyro were near the CG to avoid increased or decreased readings otherwise measured ahead of or behind the CG. The lateral accelerometer and rate gyro were placed ahead of the CG, to provide an element of phase advance to provide damping of oscillations in the yaw loop. Abetted by Harry Hitch from Mathematics Services, John Lattey's consequent choice of locating the lateral accelerometers in the middle of the fuselage fuel tank caused a significant flutter in Henry Gardner's office. However,

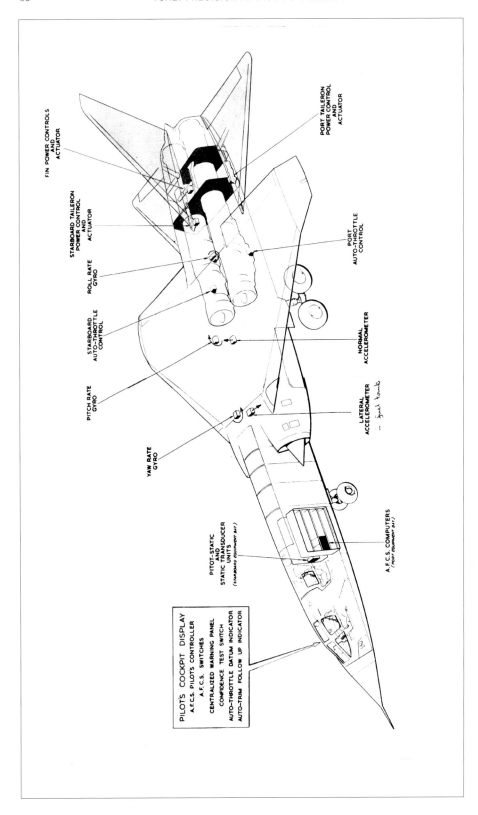

Fig.41.Locations of Gyroscopes, Accelerometers and other main control items for AFCS.[20]

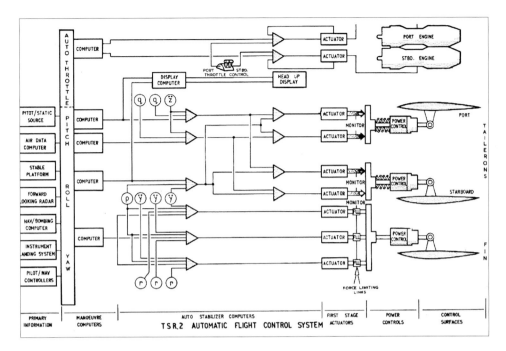

Fig.42. AFCS block schematic showing the channels of control and the actuation system.[20]

it remained there and proved to be within 3in of the optimum and well within likely minor positioning errors, when the total systems were tested in the third TSR2 aircraft – which was ready and due to fly on the day the project was cancelled.

With the basic automatic control system defined, the major factor was the nature of the actuation system for the flight controls and the degrees of redundancy required for flight safety under failure conditions. Duplicated flight controls were already common in aircraft employing power controls, automatic pilots and artificial feel, and with TSR2's complicated AFCS requirements over the very wide speed and height range of its operations, the choices were to use single-channel controls for roll, duplex for pitch and triplex for yaw (where the AFCS was absolutely essential due to aerodynamic instability).

Amusingly enough, the Ministry of Aviation demanded a learned paper to support these choices and, despite John Lattey's many highly mathematical treatises related to the AFCS, terrain following and such, he found it more effective to take the technical common sense solution and work back to the necessary assumptions to arrive at them mathematically. The MOA accepted the paper with alacrity!

Inputs of information can be seen on the left (Fig.42), from the Air Data computer and independently from the pitot-static air pressure sensor, the IRS Stable Platform, Forward-Looking Radar (FLR), Navigation/Bombing Computer and from the pilot and navigator controllers and the ILS landing system. These are handled by the Manoeuvre Computer and the Autostabiliser Computer in the three axes, and the Auto Throttle Computer handles the engines. After the amplifiers in the simplified control system depicted at the centre of this diagram, two hydraulic actuators are seen applied to each of the left and right tailerons, each signalled from both pitch and roll control loops for their differential operation as elevators and ailerons, also acting as a redundant pair in case of one failing. A monitor between the two actuators detected any difference in demand in the event of a failure, leaving the good loop control demand and actuator force to be applied to the control surface. The three independent channels of yaw control are seen to apply demands for fin movement, again monitored for any disagreement. In the event of failure, a voting system applied the required demand for fin movement. Force limiting sensors prevented excessive demands being transmitted by three channels that would normally each demand the same movement.

Such redundancy in aircraft flight control systems was perpetuated in military as well as in civil aircraft, where it is common to duplicate controls and even to triplicate Inertial Navigation platforms. The American Lockheed F-117 'Stealth' fighter, which first saw service in the 1990s, would be totally aerodynamically unstable were it not controlled by computer. However, since this formidable attack aircraft can have no safe means of manual reversion for multiple redundancy, it carries no less than four computers in its automatic flight control system.

The artificial 'feel' units and pilot's control column and rudder pedals on the left of Fig. 43 in the simplified schematic also show the navigator's controls and the separate manoeuvre and (yaw) autostabiliser computers, with inputs from the various sensing systems in the aircraft. The taileron and fin control surfaces, driven from the mixed outputs of the AFCS, are shown on the right.

Under manual control (pilot), the AFCS provided facilities to improve aircraft handling and to compensate for natural deficiencies in stability. In the pitching axis, auto-stabilisation increased the damping, as well as increasing the speed of response to tailplane (tailerons together) movements. It thus provided augmentation in the form of a 'g' manoeuvre boost, increasing the rate at which maximum normal acceleration was reached in response to stick movements at subsonic speeds. In the lateral 'weathercock' yaw axis, auto-stabilisation provided damping of a common aerodynamic oscillation known as 'Dutch roll', where yaw and roll oscillations combine. In this mode, aileron movement was applied proportional to roll rate and to lateral accelerations. In addition, at speeds from Mach 1.7 the instability was countered by artificial directional stiffness by sensing sideslip and applying proportional opposite rudder. In the automatic flight regime, the latter auto-stabilisation was applied in the 'weathercock' direction, but no manoeuvre boost, nor aileron-to-lateral acceleration, was applied. However, the AFCS controlled all the modes already listed, in automatic flight.

In the auto-control modes, barometric altitude and/or height locks demanded a pitch rate proportional to height and/or Indicated Air Speed (IAS), or Mach No. error signals from the Air Data computer, while the combined lock also demanded operation of the auto throttle. The latter had a limited authority of +800rpm and -400rpm, the pilot applying the main throttle settings. These controls all operated in their own stabilising loops, applying damping as required. Semi-automatic controlled climb and descent was controlled by speed or rate of climb via the tailplane (tailerons together), the pilot controlling the throttles. Fully automatic climb and descent were possible at around Mach 0.9 and at 8,000ft/min climb or descent rates, employing automatic throttle control in addition to tailplane control. Track and heading lock

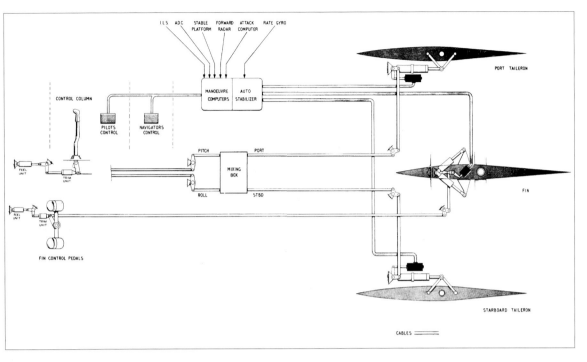

Fig.43. Control diagram of the system, including the pilot's controls and artificial 'feel' system.[20]

with rate of turn commands for azimuth control was based on a system of bank angle demands. Here, the error signal of roll angle caused a roll rate demand, with roll angle limited to 45° and roll rate limited to 15°/s.

Automatic approach using ILS controlled height, speed, and azimuth, down to the 'break-off' height of about 200ft. The aircraft was maintained in the descent (track and glide) mode until intercepting the glide path beam, when the aircraft would be pitched down to hold the usual 3° glide slope, with automatic speed control. I will discuss AFCS control for the terrain following and for bombing manoeuvres later in the relevant sections.

Gyroscopes and Accelerometers, made by Elliotts, were at the heart of the AFCS, and were located as indicated in Fig.41. The two types of sub-miniature gyros 3in long and 1in diameter cylindrical construction were of identical construction except for their operating range. They were not capable of field servicing, being oil-filled and sealed and of very high reliability. The Type GR-H4-17G was the sensing element in the triplex yaw rate gyro unit and the Type GR-H4-35G was used in the duplex pitch rate and roll rate gyro units. Their sealed gimbal assemblies were filled with nitrogen to provide an inert atmosphere for the 24,000rpm spin motors and for heat transfer reasons. Spring restraint, required for rate measurement, was provided by a torsion bar, the assembly being capable of withstanding shock loads of up to 500g. For low damping characteristics, the whole gyro was filled with low-density silicone oil. The duplex and triplex units were appropriately mounted with their related torque motors, amplifiers, locking solenoids, electronic interfaces, and power inputs within a sturdy assembly.

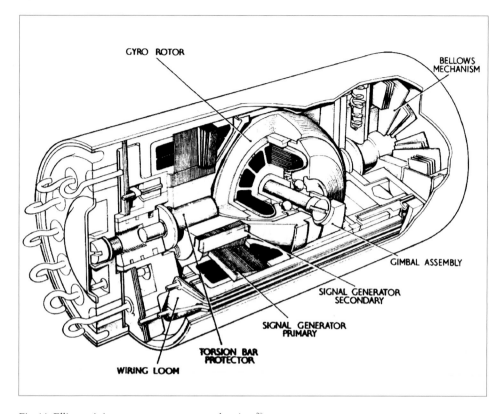

Fig.44. Elliott miniature rate gyro cutaway drawing.[20]

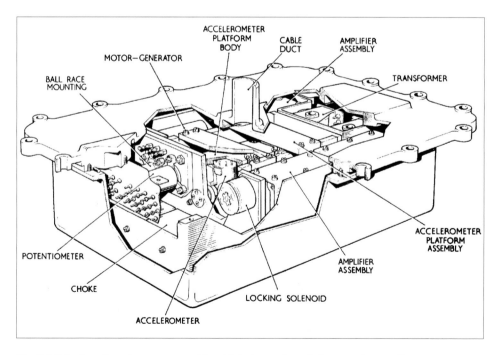

Fig.45. Triplex lateral accelerometer assembly, with locking solenoid, for ground testing.[20]

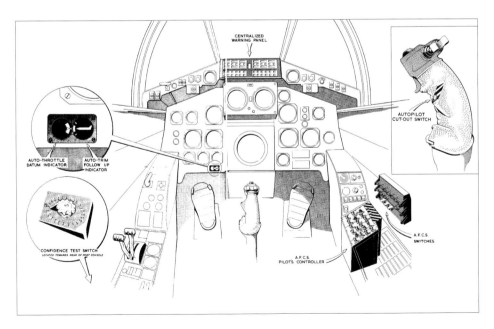

Fig.46. Photograph of AFCS controls and indicators in No.3 aircraft pilot's cockpit, with explanatory diagram below.[20]

Constructed identically to the gyros but with the rotor replaced by a pendulous weight, Accelerometers were similarly mounted in triplex units for yaw auto-stabilisation and in duplex units for pitch stabilisation controls. Under acceleration, the pendulous weight exerted a rotational force on the gimbal assembly which turned a signal generator rotor, and this produced a signal proportional to the acceleration.

Similar to the duplex pitch Accelerometer assembly, the Accelerometers were caged to the airframe in order to measure airframe accelerations. For ground testing purposes, the Accelerometers could be uncaged and rotated by a known angle, for the gravitational force to simulate given accelerations that could be fed into the AFCS.

Each of the independent control loops and the instruments feeding into them were created in common electronic units of standard 'brick' size, employing silicon transistors and diodes for high reliability. These electronic units were suitably connected into the complicated system, represented in simplified form by Figs 42 and 43. The total system flow diagram and the many engineering diagrams relating to the control facilities I have described would occupy many pages. Pilot's and navigator's controls and displays completed the AFCS, enabling the aircrew to function in the required modes.

The resulting AFCS was required to ensure the aircraft's safety in the event of any single failure and the crew had to be warned of the failure condition. The system performance had to meet the control needs of the Terrain Following system and the Weapon Aiming system and the pilot had to be able to revert to manual control by cutting out the AFCS at any time. The AFCS gave him the choice of the aircraft being flown automatically 'hands off' or, as described earlier, he could fly manually in response to flight director commands via the HUD in any of the various modes. These included:

(a) maintenance of track and altitude using guidance signals from the (CCS) navigation computer and FLR – down to 150ft above ground level, between Mach 0.7 and Mach 0.9;

(b) loft bombing and dive toss manoeuvres using guidance signals from the (CCS) attack computer;

(c) three-axis auto-stabilisation under manual control including synthetic stiffening and manoeuvre boost in the longitudinal channel at low indicated speeds;

(d) locks for altitude, barometric height, speed and heading existing at the time of their engagement, together with the ability to 'inch' the datum manually after the lock is engaged;

(e) pre-selection of height or heading datum and the means to home to these without overshoot (subject to override of the barometric altitude control by the Terrain Following system);

(f) automatic airfield approach using ILS Type guidance signals with primary selection and initiation made by the pilot. Primarily to meet the in-flight refuelling and airfield approach requirements, automatic throttle control was also incorporated, with separate control for each engine.

CHAPTER 7

TERRAIN FOLLOWING
AND VULNERABILITY

Having described the systems capabilities for navigating to the target under pilot or automatic control, I can now move on to elaborate on the already mentioned Terrain Following System (TFS), essential for delivering weapons with minimised vulnerability to attack by ground-based guided weapons. Criteria for vulnerability were extensively studied during 1960 by the RAE and by Arnold Roberts with R. W. Penney under Mike Salisbury in the Vickers Aircraft Aerodynamics Department, with parallel and intertwining studies by John Lattey in the GW Department. The issues of vulnerability were addressed in the context of terrain avoidance/clearance or terrain following – 'clearance' implying flying over hilly terrain from crest to crest, while 'following' required hugging contours as closely as might be safely possible. The former method clearly exposed an aircraft to ground Radars for longer periods at the heights between crests than would occur if the aircraft followed contours down into valleys. Experimental terrain following was also being tested by Cornell Aeronautical Laboratories near Buffalo, NY, USA, with B-57 (Canberra) aircraft, where many ideas had originated, and where these engineers made visits to discuss the subject and test results with CAL staff.

The vulnerability study by Arnold Roberts issued in September 1960 was particularly enlightening.[21] He concluded that terrain following at 200ft and Mach 0.95 was less vulnerable than terrain avoidance at 500ft and the higher speed of Mach 1.2. The effect of height was more important than speed and reducing from 500ft to 200ft was roughly equivalent to increasing speed from Mach 0.95 to Mach 2.4. Also, peak-to-peak flying was found to be roughly equivalent to an increase from Mach 0.95 to Mach 1.4.

Vulnerability was assessed by considering three main threats. Firstly, the Long-Range Missile, such as Hawk, was considered. The Long-Range Missile is designed to attack medium and high altitude aircraft flying at high speed. Such missiles are complex and result in a relatively long time period between detection of its target and missile launch. To achieve a satisfactory coverage, such a missile would require a long flight time and successful interception would require the target to be visible for some forty to fifty seconds. Ideally, such missile sites would be expensively mounted on towers surrounded by flat country – which a well informed strike aircraft plan would try to avoid. Secondly, the Light Anti-Aircraft Missile, such as the Vickers Light AA (later to become the BAC Rapier Missile), designed specifically to close the gap left by the Long-Range Missile, was considered. Such mobile and flexible missiles would require the target to be visible for twenty seconds at most, and such a comparatively cheap missile system could be widely dispersed to cover sectors 8 miles wide. Reduction of vulnerability against such missiles required both reduction in the nominal minimum clearance height and a more active form of terrain following. The third threat was from the Ultra Light Missile (such as Red Eye) which could provide an effective defence at very short range under visual conditions. Most likely using infrared homing, they would be most effective protecting tactical targets against air-to-ground rocket attacks. These had a rapid (eight second) warm-up and lock-on time, making them distinctly marginal against aircraft flying at Mach 0.95, with only four and a half seconds before the target passed overhead. Where such missiles were known to be deployed, for reduced vulnerability TSR2 would have to make its attack at Mach 1.2 at 200ft.

Employing contour maps of areas with varying roughness of terrain and differing proximities to valleys and more open country, Roberts used the above considerations to evaluate the degree of vulnerability for specific attack profiles.

The upper diagram in Fig.47 shows how terrain clearance at a nominal 200ft over peaks leaves the aircraft vulnerably high over the valleys. The lower graph shows how the 'g' felt by the aircrew varied under the less vulnerable terrain following conditions. The maximum considered tolerable (and tested in the VRL simulator rigs earlier described) was positive 1g and negative -½g. The above curve fell well within these tolerable limits.

The desirable terrain following system was therefore conceived to be essential, much as described in the introductory paragraphs of this chapter – namely a static split Radar with a 3kHz pulse repetition frequency, scanning the terrain ahead at the rate of two scans per second. The up and the down scan planes would be separated and both used to provide terrain following signals. This separation was intended to provide wider coverage required for turning flight. As described in greater detail later, a function of range was to be mixed with the associated depression angle of the Radar boresight and the steady aircraft incidence for the current flight condition, to provide the manoeuvre demand for clearing the element of terrain seen along the boresight.

Valley following typified by Tracks 1 and 2 of Fig.48 were clearly vulnerable to long-range missiles. The shaded areas delineate where an aircraft flying at 200ft would be shielded by higher terrain, while an aircraft flying from peak to peak would be seen. A light missile might have coverage against an aircraft over a 40 miles valley width, indicating the importance of varying flight paths from mission to mission. Peak-to-peak flying would place an aircraft within the visibility range of the indicated missile sight for twenty seconds, while Track 7 would be in range for the long-range missile, but for too short a time for that missile. The long-range missile would be able to intercept along Tracks 1, 2 and 6 flown peak to peak, but not Tracks 3, 4 and 5. An aircraft attacking with terrain following and avoiding the line of a valley, the time in sight of the missile site would be reduced in all cases. With shadowing by hills, only Track 3 would leave the aircraft in sight long enough to risk interception. These conclusions are summarised in the table Fig.49.

After considering various alternative Radar scanning modes and radio altimeter combinations up to early 1959, the USA work at Cornell with the Autoflite system aroused interest in the UK and resulted in the visits from Weybridge and elsewhere

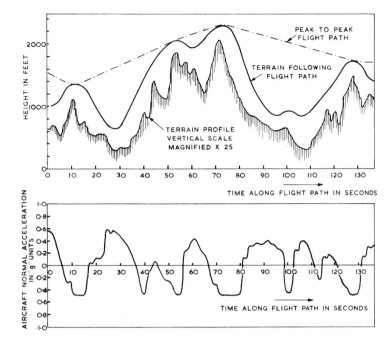

Fig.47. Terrain clearance and terrain following paths over ground profile and aircraft 'g's.[21]

to which I have alluded. CAL had demonstrated Radar shaping techniques with consistent returns, to an accuracy of 4 milliradians (0.23°), producing voltages proportional to ridge line depressions as seen by the Radar. This was to form part of the CAL automatic terrain following system and was linked with the UK development work employing a vertically scanning Radar. The terrain avoidance locus of the system was combined with the autopilot and a radio altimeter could then also be used as an override for flight over water, where Radar returns would not be available.

Effectively, a 'ski-toe' locus of the shaped Radar returns was rotated until it touched the terrain and the locus was fed into the AFCS as a proportional signal. This rotation of the locus was also combined with a pitch attitude signal, to provide a 'climb high' override for improved response over high peaks. Fig.7 already showed the nature of the radar returns employing the Static Split monopulse transmissions to be used. Now this could be applied to create the ski-toe locus, and its fitting to the terrain profile.

The ski-toe concept, originated and developed by Vickers aerodynamicist Arnold Roberts (who had produced the above vulnerability report) and R.W. Penney, ran parallel to work at CAL. John Lattey from Weybridge and aerodynamicist Ian Hall from Warton visited CAL, where computer simulations were carried out employing the ski-toe concept together with aircraft control criteria in the AFCS being derived in the GW Department. Back in Weybridge, the next stage of the work required John Lattey's team to simulate the aircraft's response over analogues of terrain profiles, with variations made in the AFCS and in the FLR output criteria. Roberts' development progressed through a series of studies and digital simulations on the Pegasus computer from 1960 through 1964, in order to home in towards optimised overall performance, stability and invulnerability[22-25]. Confluent with this, it was

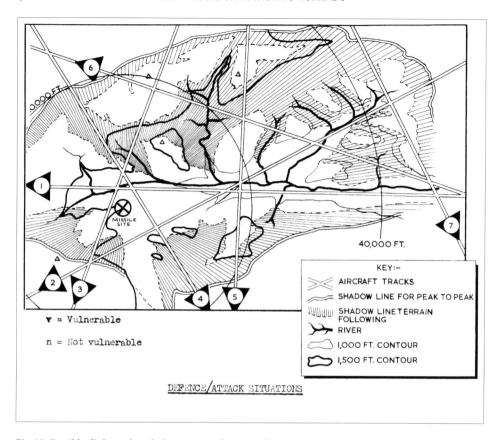

Fig.48. Possible flight paths relative to a missile site indicating their relative vulnerabilities.[21]

TRACK NO.	SHORT RANGE MISSILE			LONG RANGE MISSLE
	PEAK TO PEAK	TERRAIN FOLLOWING	VALLEY FOLLOWING	
1			v	v
2			v	v
3	v	v Just too short shadow area to drop out of sight		n
4	v	n Drops out of sight		n
5	v	v In sight just long enough		n
6	v	n Passes behind hill		v Peak to peak n Terrain following
7	n Out of range	n Out of range		N Time in sight too short

Fig.49. Analysis of each track's vulnerability against short-range and long-range missiles.[21]

necessary to confirm suitable performance in the flight director mode, when the pilot would terrain follow manually, under flight director commands on his HUD. It should be noted that the CAL concept of terrain following using a FLR was rejected by the US Air Force as 'unworkable'!

A key factor in using the FLR was the nature of the double vertical scan, to give breadth of coverage during turning flight. Initially, Ferranti proposed a horizontal scan similar to that of a navigation Radar and using the mapping facility to provide the signals for terrain following. However the Vickers team persuaded Ferranti of the deficiencies of a mapping style scanning system and opted for a vertical scan.

The scan was stabilised about the aircraft's track, which is shown here to be displaced from the aircraft's physical heading by the wind drift angle. The 20° elevation scan range is shown by way of example to be divided between 8° above and 12° below the radar roll axis.

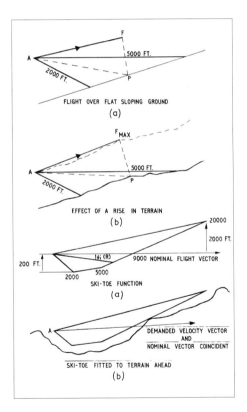

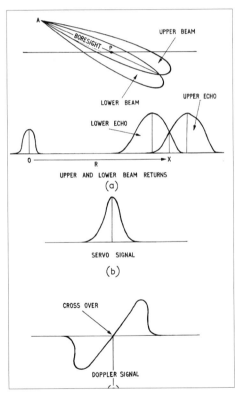

Above left: Fig.50. Derivation and fitting of the ski-toe locus to the terrain, indicating typical distances ahead of the aircraft. It minimised manoeuvre demands from terrain at the shortest ranges and smoothed out the higher demands from high terrain at longer ranges.[5]

Above right: Fig.51. reproduces Fig.7 in the two upper diagrams. The two lower diagrams show how the echoes from the split beams are summed to produce the servo signal (b), whose strength has to be above a critical point over the noise level for it to be used. The lowest diagram shows the difference between the two returns, applying one as positive and the other as negative. The crossover or zero point represents the boresight axis of the Radar beams identifying a 'point' on the ground.[5]

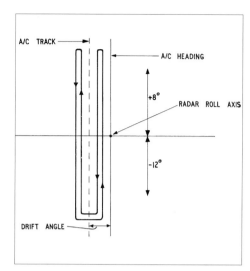

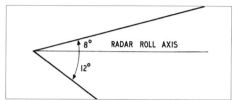

Left: Fig.52. On the right above, the vertical two-bar scan pattern, repeating at two cycles per second.[5]

Below: Fig.53. Scan axis in vertical plane.[5]

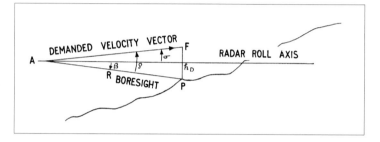

Fig.54. Boresight line to point on the ground 'P'.[5]

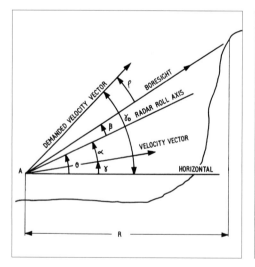

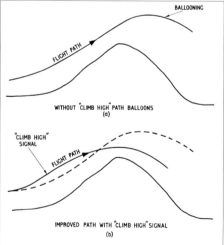

Above left: Fig.55. The demanded velocity vector and its angular relationships to the Radar roll axis, the boresight, and the horizontal, shown at the angle α above the actual velocity vector being followed. If the aircraft faithfully followed this demand, it would fly a path over the undulating terrain such as indicated below.[5]

Above right: Fig.56.[6] Flight paths in relation to a peak in the terrain showing (a) an overshoot taking the aircraft higher than desired over the peak.[5]

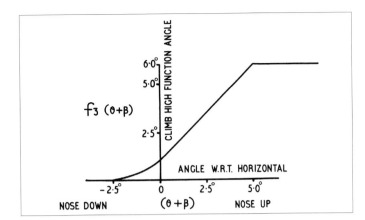

Fig.57. The 'climb high' function built into the TF system, for avoiding overshooting peaks.[5]

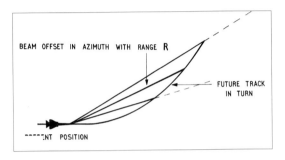

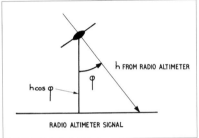

Above left: Fig.58. Radar scan axis offset from the present position towards the direction of the azimuth.[26]

Above right: Fig.59. Effect of bank angle in turning and on use of Radio Altimeter.[26]

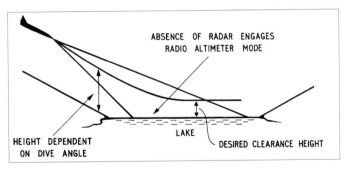

Fig.60. Approach to a body of water and the automatic engagement of the Radio Altimeter mode.[27]

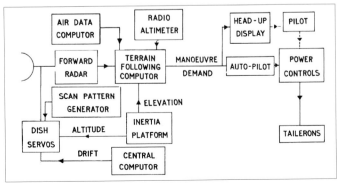

Fig.61. Principal elements of the Terrain Following System.[28]

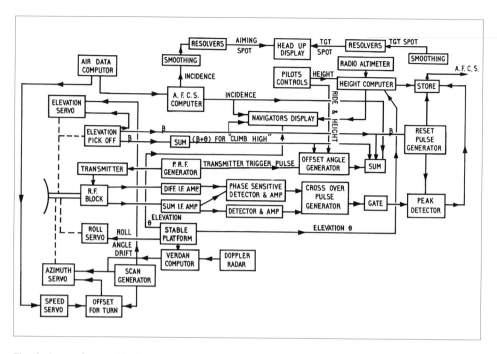

Fig.62. Comprehensive block diagram of the TFS within the overall Navigation/Attack System.[28]

In accordance with the ski-toe function relating demand to the distance ahead of the terrain features being scanned, the aircraft received a velocity vector demand into the AFCS and to the director icon on the HUD.

In order to avoid this overshoot, the system included a 'climb high' function, which altered the velocity vector demand to anticipate the peak and to fly the aircraft over the highest point on a level flight path (b). At the same time, if any conflict between demands occurred, the pitch control demands were constrained always to follow the higher pitch demand, for safety from 'ground clobber'.

Radar ranges along the boresight over rough terrain typically varied between 2,000ft at short range and 20,000ft at long range, giving an adequate five seconds and twenty seconds for reaction time at a speed of 1,000ft/s. Over the control range between 5,000ft and 20,000ft at 200ft clearance height, the values of the demanded velocity vector to boresight angle ρ typically ranged from 2.5° to 0.6°.

The effect of the ski-toe locus method was likened to the locus contour shape representing a strong spring, somewhat like a motor car suspension's leaf spring, that touches the terrain and is forced up and down as differing terrain profiles pass beneath it. The aircraft then responds in sympathy, to follow over the terrain at a selected height, typically 200ft. Corresponding with the conditions applied in the VRL cockpit simulator tests described earlier, the aircraft's manoeuvre would ideally be restricted to avoid 'g's applied to the aircrew exceeding 1g in the upward direction and 0.5g in the negative direction. This degree of aircrew 'comfort' was to be achieved over any terrain likely to be met on a sortie, also under any likely degree of turbulence due to wind conditions at low level.

The questions of terrain following during turning flight (required for navigation) and for flight over water required specific solutions.

The double scan beam pattern occupies 4.5° in each of its two 1.5°-separated vertical scans, resulting in a coverage of 7.5° (or ±3.75°) along the future path of the aircraft. By displacing the space-stabilised beam scan pattern ahead of the turn, the FLR terrain signal covered ground over which the TFS was required to control the aircraft's height as it turned on to a new track. The amount of azimuth beam displacement was determined by the angle of bank applied to generate the turn. Bank angles up to 45° were accommodated and the width of the azimuth beam coverage was sufficient to allow for wind drift angles, as well as the accuracy of predicting the turn.

Returns from a FLR over water are normally absent or effectively useless and this required alternative means of controlling height – with less onerous clearance requirements than over undulating land. However, lakes are frequently surrounded by mountains and the TFS had to cope with high ground arising on the far side of any body of water. The Radio Altimeter was the back up for providing accurate height information to the TFN when over water, for altitudes from 2,000ft down to 50ft – a credible flying height for reduced vulnerability to missile defences.

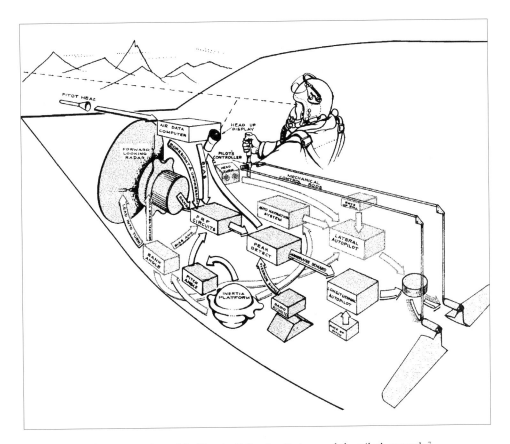

Fig.63. Pictorial representation of the Terrain Following System and the pilot's controls.[7]

The ski-toe locus remained available with the FLR, to detect the need for following any rising terrain on the far side of the body of water and automatic reversion to the normal mode occurred as FLR returns resumed.

A fuller system diagram (Fig. 62) will show how every part of the Navigation/Attack System had to be integrated in order to enable the Terrain Following System for all modes of operation with minimum vulnerability to missile defences and in the safest possible manner.

In developing and testing the stability and performance of the TFS working in conjunction with AFCS, John Lattey and his team's comprehensive analogue simulation exercises at Weybridge, were conducted in cooperation with members of the English Electric aerodynamics team from Warton and AFCS engineers from Elliott Bros at Rochester. They utilised the GW analogue simulator for realistic representations of the interacting servo loops inherent in the TFS and the AFCS working together. Within the design programmes pursued by Arnold Roberts and R.W. Penney of the Vickers Military Project Office under the guidance of Mike Salisbury, a fundamental series of simulations was conducted to establish performance against the most realistic available terrain and turbulence inputs, coupled with airframe vibration effects. These employed the Pegasus digital computer operated by the Vickers Mathematical Services Department headed by Harry Hitch.

Checking the Radio Altimeter backup for the TFS involved comparing with a (pulsed) Radar Altimeter operating on a similar frequency. Jim Cole, complete with parachute, was the lone volunteer to attempt this comparison, installed in a replica of the TSR2 fuselage in which he hung under a barrage balloon at 1,600ft. No amount of manoeuvring and nauseating bobbing about to better use the restricted amount of cable succeeded in reaching the preferred 2,000ft, but the comparison was adequately proved.

In the event of Radio Altimeter failure, the TFS had to protect the aircrew against 'clobber' (flying into the ground), by a logic system that demanded a climb.

CHAPTER 8

TESTING
AND SIMULATION

Overall Navigation/Attack systems testing including the analogue simulators and individual equipment verification testing was originally under the direction of Dennis Harris, who left the company for a while, when John Goodwin took over as group leader. This group had created the 'four part' operational specifications, also covering environmental factors, safety and interference. This involved the testing of all the 'hardware' – prototypes were used in every part of the Navigation/Attack System, enabling all of the system's interacting loops to be closed. This had to represent how the equipments would work together in the aircraft when interconnected by totally representative power supplies and cables, in the locations they would occupy in TSR2.

The major systems rig for this latter purpose was housed in the special T362 Systems Hangar under the management of Peter Mobsby, whom I have already mentioned elsewhere in relation to Red Dean (and other projects) and his famed cartoons. Another veteran GW (electronics) engineer, John Doyle, oversaw the operations and testing of the equipment and instrumentation, along with Barry Bailey.

A clearly cardinal element of TSR2's terrain following and weapon delivery systems to which I will soon refer was, of course, the Forward Looking Radar. The FLR was a Category 1 item contracted direct by MOA to Ferranti Ltd in Edinburgh, under its general manager, Mal Powley, and chief engineer, Don McCallum. A prototype of this FLR was among the equipments integrated into the systems rig before any installation in a TSR2 aircraft could be contemplated.

Tests of the FLR prototype at Vickers were not without their excitements, as when a visiting VIP was exposed to a loud 'bang' caused by short circuit during pitching movements, when the antenna support structure fouled circuitry employing the latest (exposed) wire wrapped joints.

The parabolic dish antenna, with its centrally protruding microwave feed to create the static split beams pattern, is on the left of the unit, controlled through the electronic chassis complex held in the test cradle.

The engineers in the pictures (Figs 65 and 67, around 1964) are operating test rigs for providing input signals, monitoring and recording test data during system-exercising operations representing the real aircraft installation.

Fig.64. Ferranti Forward Looking Radar prototype under test by system rig engineer Ted Hurst.[1]

Fig.65. The systems rig TSR2 mock-up complete with cockpit and equipment bay behind it.[1]

Fig.66. Stage III test rig for full Nav/Attack system, Central Warning System with cooling rack.[1]

Fig.67. System Support Group computing area (smartly turned out engineers of the 1964 era!).[1]

Above: Fig.68. Seven-axis cockpit motion simulator used in AFCS and Terrain Following simulations.[1]

Left: Fig.69. Dennis Moore (overall system rig manager) with Colin New at the Stage III system PERT chart.[1]

Besides the Project Evaluation Review Technique (PERT) work, Colin, who was a highly experienced designer of many GW electronic units, designed test units for TSR2 systems development work.

Over the period from 1960 up to completion of the first fully equipped aircraft flight installation in April 1965, confidence in the systems' operation and integrity was progressively established, with each item of equipment integrated and fully tested for overall compatibility and correct functioning.

CHAPTER 9

THE CENTRAL COMPUTING SYSTEM

CCS – the brain of TSR2's Navigation/Attack System – was involved in virtually every control loop, as one can see from Fig.22 and Fig.62. Computations for the navigation equations involving Earth axes, Earth rotation, inertial platform outputs, fixing, and all the other items I have described, required the No.1 Verdan of the CCS to operate on twenty-nine separate functions. These ranged from pre-take-off and alignment to details of the fixing process and providing the navigator with the 'next fix' position. Computations in Verdan No.2 for the bombing equations were required in all of the nuclear (lay down, loft and dive toss manoeuvre) modes and the conventional HE weapon delivery modes, again with ballistic information to be stored on the variety of weapons to be delivered. Having specified the accuracies of the Inertial, Doppler, SLR and other sensing systems, the CCS computation accuracy had to be sufficiently high to avoid the creation of greater errors. In this context, while the GP sections operated on whole quantities represented by the contents of each word and its changing value as updates occurred, it interfaced with the magnetic storage system operating at 332,800 pulses per second. The DDAs, operating incrementally to integrate values in 'real-time', had to be capable of updating quantities 100 times each second.[32]

Compared with computers in the twenty-first century, where a laptop computer may contain 60Gb of hard drive space and work at well over 1GHz rate, it is almost inconceivable that two Verdan computers, each 85lb in weight and each operating at a clock rate of 332.8kHz, had a combined memory of only 2,048 words (26 bits – or an equivalent 6,656 8-bit bytes) – and some 256 Digital Differential Analysers. Dennis Harris' and Elliotts' programming somehow squeezed sufficient computing capacity into the two Verdan computers, so that they initially appeared to permit the whole range of operations described in this chapter. However, as the project proceeded beyond the time of the 1960 Summary Brochure (see References) and the mission profiles became more complicated and diverse, some difficult choices had to be made as to which facilities to discard or reduce. By 25 September 1964, soon after the aircraft's first flights without the Nav/Attack System, Dennis Harris issued a report approved by John Lattey outlining the CCS capacity problem.[12] (Bernard Hunn was by then at Elliotts as manager of the Airborne Computing Division). Allowing 15 per cent to 20 per cent spare capacity for requirements that may arise due to increased Operational Requirements during the TSR2's operational lifetime, TSR2's six operating modes, as then envisaged, required considerably more than the capacity indicated above. These were for the combined roles of: dead reckoning navigation and fixing, nuclear strike (low level and medium level with a FLR fix), nuclear strike (dive toss), conventional weapon aiming, reconnaissance, and ferrying. However, as a result of flight trials in other aircraft before TSR2 was due to fly with the whole system, no less than sixteen features for refinement of performance, various reversionary modes, and operational flexibility, considered to be essential by the OR staff, were indicated as requiring extra computing capacity.

While the total capacity available was 256 DDAs and 2,048 GP section words, the capacity required for all six modes to be present together had risen to 838 DDAs and 7,817 words!

It was clear that, while a workable system was possible with the two Verdan computers, the Operational Requirement could not be met in full. Besides considering possible reductions in the OR, the report outlined a number of possible solutions, such as employing enhanced Autonetics computers, or using entirely different Elliott MCS920 computers and a GEC airborne computer. These time-consuming and costly alternatives all implied the need for considerable reprogramming, or new programming work, which now led to recommendations for urgent further study.[12] However, it should be noted that the proposed reductions in operating modes or sorties really related to the RAF's desire for these *all* to be available at any one time. In reality, sorties would generally only require (typically) the navigation mode and one or two bombing modes (nuclear or conventional weapon aiming). The reconnaissance and the ferry modes would not normally be required at the same time as the bombing modes. Thus, as the above report showed, the capacity required for sorties employing only the nuclear bombing modes with the necessary navigation was only 234 DDA's and 1,947 words and, individually, each of the other main modes required less than this capacity. The report explored the whole range of possibilities among the different sortie modes.

Solutions to the capacity problems considered included a reduction in the number of bombing modes and in the number of navigational fix positions to be stored (initially forty, reducing to thirty or fewer), as well as doing away with the requirement for airspeed and wind reversion and dispensing with the FLR fixing option. A constant battle ensued: OR wished to maximise its continually escalating requirements, leading to computer hardware change possibilities and, as a result, cost. It may not be surprising that the continually rising cost of the Elliott contract remained a major problem. The rise was due to developments, changes, and associated support work. While the estimated ('fixed') cost of the CCS contract with Elliotts ran to £2,250,000 in late April 1963, by October of the same year it had risen to £3,161,252, and by November 1964 it stood at £4,664,295. Not surprisingly, this led to a 'frank' discussion between BAC (headed by Harry Zeffert, i/c BAC Systems/E) and Elliotts (headed by Jack Pateman, head of Elliotts at Rochester). While the meeting was cordial enough and was followed by an Elliott letter indicating their equal embarrassment at the cost increases, coupled with thanks for the 'close and cordial relationship between the companies', the meeting was not entirely devoid of somewhat aggressive suggestions from Harry Zeffert as to how the costs might be reduced – or even be overstated.[33]

Meanwhile, by December 1963, preliminary flight trials of the CCS were planned and carried out by the RAE from Boscombe Down, in an RAF Hastings aircraft. These were complementary to the Stage III rig tests at Weybridge, but besides verifying the systems' operation in the airborne environment, only by flight trials could the full effects of aircraft manoeuvre be reproduced, with inputs from an inertial platform and Doppler Radar – which could not be simulated on the ground. Stage I of the Hastings flight trials were to verify navigation by Doppler/Inertial mixing, with fixed monitored azimuth and the creation of steering demands to the pilot and/or the AFCS, all dependent on proper information flow and calculation accuracy in the Verdan computer.[31]

Stage II flight trials exercised the various revertionary modes to be handled (in the event of failures of the Doppler, when attitude limits were exceeded, when there was a failure of the inertial platform, and reversion to a compass azimuth). Furthermore, computations were required from the CCS to achieve airborne alignment of the inertial platform, as was expected to be necessary when operating from remote field bases without full airbase facilities. Simulation of Sideways Looking Radar was accomplished by carrying a Dexan computer, whose outputs could be made to mimic the SLR as seen by the CCS Verdan. Similarly, fixes could be simulated using Decca Navigator, enabling the CCS to be tested in the computations it would normally make with a live SLR (to check the CCS computations relating to bombing manoeuvres, employing suitable weapon ballistic derivatives and computation of the release point and, in the case of loft bombing manoeuvres, computations for the 4g pull-up point). The flight-test programme was completed by early 1964.

CHAPTER 10

WEAPON DELIVERY

Weapon delivery was, of course, the final purpose of TSR2 and, besides the evident participation of the CCS in every aspect of Navigation/Attack, the Forward Looking Radar had a cardinal function in conventional HE weapons delivery, providing target identification, conventional weapon-aiming computations, and the measurement of target range until weapon release.

However, TSR2's primary nuclear role in this deadliest aspect of the Cold War dictated much of the aircraft's design and specification. The accuracy of the navigation system under blind flying conditions at low altitude was the key to determining where the target lay ahead of the aircraft and when precisely it would be in range, without any last minute external references, even from the FLR. Thus, after navigating over hostile territory via a series of fix points to update the aircraft's present position, a final fix point was designated at not more than 30 miles from the target. At this point, the azimuth reference and aircraft track and heading were also updated, enabling the inertial platform within the Inertial Reference System to become the principal medium over the three minutes until accurate arrival at the weapon release point. The tolerable accuracy of delivery with a nuclear bomb allowed much greater error than was allowable with the much smaller lethality radius of HE weapons.

The least accurate delivery error is shown as 1,200ft (edge of the dark shaded area), within which 50 per cent of high yield nuclear bombs would fall. This corresponds to blind bombing from an altitude of 25,000ft, in straight and level flight at Mach 1.7. The circles are seen against the shadow of a factory complex. The middle, paler shaded circle extending out to 825ft represents the 50 per cent CEP level of accuracy obtainable by means of a blind pull-up (Low Altitude Bombing System or 'LABS') manoeuvre, following a navigation updating fix taken 30nm from the target, and assumes that the LABS delivery manoeuvre was initiated by the CCS navigation computer. The much more accurate 50 per cent CEP figure within the 250ft radius smallest circle was achievable from a visual dive toss manoeuvre with the aid of FLR ranging, beginning at high altitude and terminating in delivery at about 15,000ft.

Enemy missile defences, expected to be intense in the areas around targets for nuclear attack, made it essential for attacks to be executed in the least vulnerable way. Having survived a long flight to the target, often by terrain following at 200ft, the principal mode of delivering a nuclear weapon had to minimise the duration at which

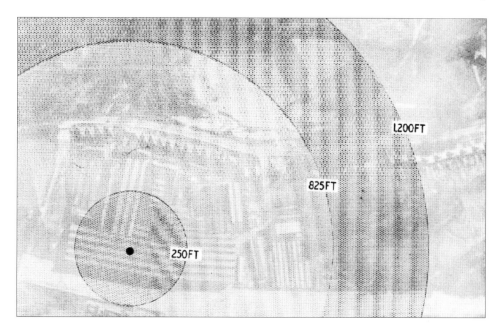

Fig.70. Circles of 50 per cent critical error probability (CEP) for three types of delivery.[7]

the aircraft may be detected at a greater height. At the same time, the yield of a nuclear weapon made it even more essential that the aircraft rapidly escape from the large area to be incinerated by a nuclear burst. The LABS manoeuvres were developed (initially in the USA), to achieve such nuclear delivery with maximum safety for the aircrew. A number of different versions of this highly aerobatic manoeuvre were to be used by TSR2 – usually to be automatically directed by the CCS through the AFCS. The first task after making the fix correction closest to the target (assumed to be at 30 miles) was to correct the track, to pass through the target's position.

The process started with the navigator setting the mode of attack and then making the fix. The navigation system then corrected the errors, by the CCS transferring the origin of coordinates to the target, setting up the pair of axes with X-T (Fig.71) leading directly to the target. The CCS continually held the error distances along Track (x) and across Track (y) and issued steering instructions for either automatic AFCS or manual steering by the pilot tracking the target 'spot' on the Head Up Display.

The bomb had to be released at an appropriate height, speed, climb angle and the correct range from the target corresponding to the bomb's ballistic trajectory. Trajectory information for specific weapons was held in the CCS and the forward throw of the bomb, and burst heights required over the target, was continuously computed while approaching the actual release conditions. With the CCS having steered the aircraft on to the correct track (datum plane) allowing for Doppler Radar-measured wind drift and for height, via the Air Data computer, bomb release would occur when the computed forward throw equalled the actual distance to the target. A considerable amount of calculation was required to determine the information required for programming the computer, the author being one of several engineers employed in these calculations.

The pull-up for a LABS toss manoeuvre delivery was typically at 4g. As the aircraft gained climb angle and height, Doppler information was soon lost and, after that, aircraft trajectory inputs to the CCS were entirely dependent on the Inertial Reference Unit stable platform, and on the Air Data computer. The bomb ballistics calculations continued as described above, until the forward throw computed by the CCS equalled the range to the target, allowing for the required burst height.

From the aircraft's vulnerability viewpoint, the height gain would bring distinct dangers, which can be appreciated when considering the trajectories in greater detail.

The straightforward 'Immelman' loop and roll-off-the-top here involved rising to 14,000ft. This would be reached just after bomb detonation a little over 3 miles away. It would take nearly one minute before TSR2 had descended back to 1,000ft – possibly long enough for interception by a surface-to-air guided weapon (SAGW). By rolling into a steep turn immediately after bomb release at four seconds from start, the height gain was reduced to a still vulnerable 4,000ft, but by just after the time of bomb detonation at twenty-three seconds from start of the manoeuvre, the aircraft would be back down to a safer level approaching its 200ft terrain following height. Either way, there was little chance of interception before the bomb was released, ensuring completion of the mission.

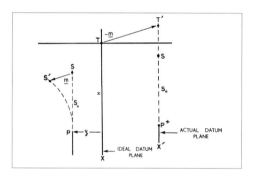

Fig.71. The uncorrected target position T' and the datum plane through the real target T. Launching from position P would land the bomb at S, except for launching errors and any errors due to wind, that could land the bomb at S'.[34]

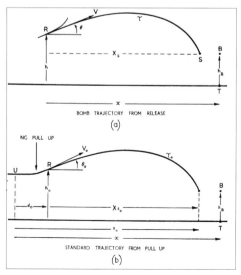

Fig.72. Standard bomb trajectory and trajectory from a pull-up manoeuvre at given number of 'g's.[34]

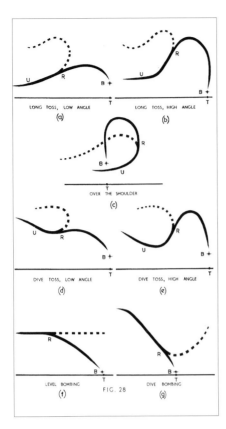

Left: Fig.73. The main forms of attack manoeuvre, in tossing the bomb by LABS and dive-toss methods. The dotted escape trajectories represent differing aerobatic manoeuvres resulting in the aircraft gaining height.[34]

Below: Fig.74. Escaping from the blast effects of a nuclear bomb.[34]

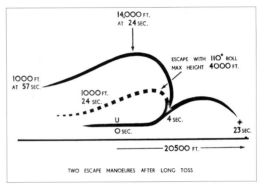

As seen from Fig.73, variations on this blind attack mode were available, including long toss with low angle release (typically less than 45°), such as a 30° release at Mach 0.9, resulting in tossing a distance of 30,000ft – nearly 6 miles. A high-angle toss could release at, say, about 60°. A more accurate form of toss was the 'button hook' method, for a long toss. Here, the aircraft passed right by the target using it as the fix point, before turning back in a much shorter time than from a fix point 30nm distant. This leaves less time for errors to build up in the IRS, resulting in automatic control through the AFCS, allowing smaller errors to be built up. An even more accurate delivery was the 'over the shoulder' method, in which the aircraft flew directly over the target visually and pulled up through the vertical, to release in a very short time with minimum time for errors to accumulate. However, height gain would be considerable, increasing vulnerability.[34]

The release conditions were not expected to be in error greater than ±100 knots in speed, ±90ft in height and ± 10° in release angle. The CEP bombing errors I have described allow for these errors, as well as those due to inertial platform drift during pull-up, wind drift measurement errors, aircraft control inaccuracies in response to demands of the CCS, and any computing inaccuracies in the CCS.

High-level dive toss attacks, as shown in Fig.73 (d) and (e), could also be made at low and high release angles, again carried out automatically by control from the CCS. For these kinds of attack, the central computer stored data in each mode, including medium-altitude-level attack and 'lay down'. The latter refers to time delay-fuzed nuclear weapons that were aerodynamically retarded after release over the target.

Visual nuclear attacks were provided for, where conditions for visual acquisition of the target had to exist at a sufficiently early stage of the attack. Initially, the Forward Looking Radar (FLR) would be employed in a ground mapping mode for identifying the target. In a high-level approach (Fig.73(g)), the aircraft was automatically steered towards the target in the usual way. In a transition manoeuvre, the HUD director display took the aircraft into a suitable dive towards the target. On seeing the real target through the head up display, the pilot would put the aiming mark over it and the FLR would now be operated in the target ranging mode. This would occur with at least thirty-five seconds to go, when it would initiate the CCS to generate bomb trajectories and wait for coincidence between the computed strike point and the target, as in the other modes. At about thirty seconds to go, the pilot would follow the computer driven aiming mark on the HUD to pull-up (see Fig.73(g)) and the aircraft would release the bomb when the conditions were satisfied. Control in the vertical plane would be less important, since the computer would keep track of the actual flight path in that plane. Prior to pull-up, for steering in azimuth the pilot needed to track the HUD aiming mark lying on the aircraft's velocity vector (fed with drift information), to keep in the correct vertical plane. Again, this delivery could be effected automatically through the AFCS manoeuvre computer, the CCS remembering the aircraft's track at the beginning of pull-up, as obtained from the Doppler/Inertia inputs up to that point.

If Radar ranging could not be selected until too close to the target, the attack would be inhibited, and a warning light lit, indicating danger of flying into the burst zone. In any case, at no later than thirty seconds to go, the pilot had to press a button to 'accept' the attack (when all the necessary conditions were satisfied). At bomb release, both the target spot and the aiming mark would disappear from the HUD and the pilot would recommence terrain following.

Conventional weapon aiming with HE required visual conditions as well as greater accuracy.[35]

The inner 50ft-radius (inner shaded) circle represents 50 per cent CEP accuracy with 2in rockets. The 100ft-radius accuracy was obtainable with 1,000lb HE bombs delivered in dive-toss attacks and the 110ft radius corresponded with straight, dive attacks. These could be initiated from low and medium altitude, with the aircraft starting at 550 knots indicated air speed (IAS), the corresponding Mach No. depending on the altitude and the air temperature.

Since visual acquisition of targets from altitude was possible earlier than from low altitude, conflicts would arise between the desire to keep low for reduced vulnerability and to dive from a greater height for greater accuracy of Radar ranging and subsequent visual acquisition for delivery. The bombing system therefore contained data for a wide range of attack conditions. Since acquisition would only occur shortly before bomb release, blind attacks were possible, albeit with lower accuracy. With the aid of the HUD, the procedure and pilot actions were similar to the earlier described long-toss attacks. However, an alternative 'depressed sightline'

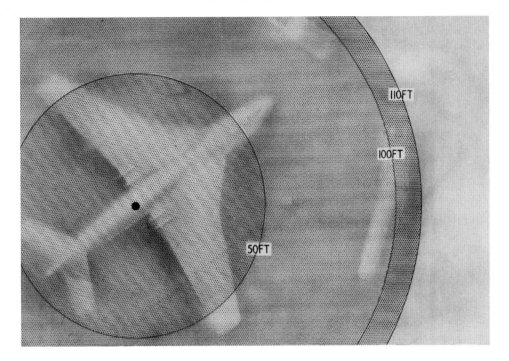

Above: Fig.75. Circles of 50 per cent CEP in visual conditions, with conventional weapons, seen against the dimensions of a Valiant bomber.[7]

Right: Fig.76. Low-altitude approach before briefly climbing to initiate the 'Depressed Sightline Attack'.[35]

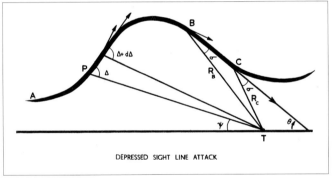

DEPRESSED SIGHT LINE ATTACK

attack method was capable of better accuracy, since the target would be in view of the pilot throughout the attack, until the point of release.

The details and the mathematics of the bombing equations were somewhat complex, and here I only attempt to describe the main aspects of controlling the aircraft to achieve release conditions resulting in a hit. The sightline depression angle to the target (shown as σ) was set into the FLR and the HUD aiming mark, at an angle related to bomb trajectory ballistics and inversely proportional to the aircraft's speed. This gave the aircraft a constant speed perpendicular to the sightline. In this mode, the bombing computations were executed entirely in the FLR's Conventional Weapon Aiming computer. A significant advantage in this mode was the greatly reduced effect of any navigation position errors, when the attack commenced. If the aiming mark and the Radar were aimed at the target giving an accurate range, allowing for computer-held bomb ballistics, the target would be hit.

As indicated in Fig.76, minimising his time above terrain following height, the pilot would initiate the attack while at low altitude at a point 'A'. At the same time, a programme was generated to position the aircraft's velocity vector at an angle above the sightline to the target, as indicated by the navigation computer. This was designed to put the then climbing aircraft initially into a ½g bunt (as seen going over the top in Fig.76). At a fixed time to go before release, the target elevation angle was changed to become a function of aircraft speed only, and the path thus transposed into the depressed sightline trajectory (a spiral). With the objective of creating the steepest dive angle (for Radar ranging accuracy) and the minimum time at increased altitude, the aim was also to provide a reasonable period of six seconds of steady tracking with the depressed sightline indicated on the HUD director spot, before reaching the release point. The bomb's time of flight would then be six to eight seconds. The target spot on the HUD would be positioned at the expected position to be seen through the windscreen – except that the target would not come into view until the dive angle became steep enough, so the target spot was made to rest at the foot of the HUD area until the target really came into view, when it would move as required for pilot tracking to the release point. The errors to be expected, beyond factors properly accounted for in the bombing equations, would be due to second-order factors, such as changes in the wind along the bomb's descent path and disturbances when the bomb was ejected from the bomb bay. Although it is inappropriate to describe them all here, there were many more detailed and subtle considerations in detailing the flow of data and the operation of the HUD director spot for tracking by the pilot.

The interactions between elements of the navigation system, including the CCS, the FLR, and its own Conventional Weapon Aiming computer, will be seen from the block diagram.

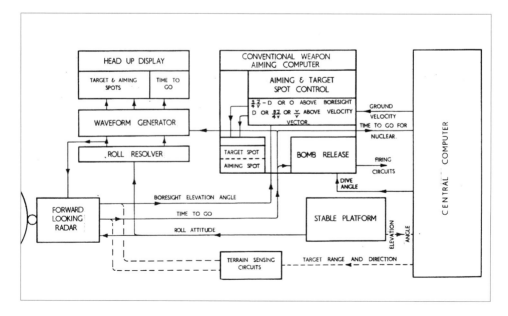

Fig.77. Conventional Weapon Aiming with Forward Looking Radar, schematic.[35]

Similar techniques were applied for level bombing from higher altitudes and for other dive attacks. The techniques applied to attacks with rockets were again similar, but with the ballistics modified due to their acceleration. This resulted in shorter flight times and distances and in the depressed sightline angle being generally smaller – at about 2° compared with up to 10° for free-falling bombs. The effect of faster and shorter flight times and the reduced sightline depression contributed to the 50 per cent CEP error circle being of only 50ft radius, shown in Fig.75.

Ferranti had made a comprehensive study of weapon aiming with its FLR, including both nuclear and conventional attacks, where Radar ranging could be required. This covered the many modes and the methods described above, including the variation of parameters such as the attack profile, the pilot's view at different angles of dive, the HUD aiming mark movements, tracking capabilities, weapon ballistics, and a vulnerability index based on the time spent at altitudes giving SAGW defences opportunities to intercept. In a series of reports commencing in November 1959, the study (under contract to the MOA) detailed all aspects of each attack mode and developed criteria related to the release points, time to go, leading to weapon delivery accuracy estimates. Error analyses at a time prior to flight trials depended very much on the accuracy of Radar ranging and the effect on this, of the sightline's angle of incidence with the ground and the nature of the terrain illuminated. For a low-altitude worst case, with an aircraft speed of 1,000ft/s and only 5° beam grazing incidence at a range of 8,000ft, assuming arbitrary ground non-uniformity, the overall ranging error was indicated as 287ft (standard deviation). Increasing the incidence angle corresponding to a dive angle of 15°, the ranging error estimate reduced to 146ft (s.d.). The range error estimated at this same dive angle, from an altitude of 25,000ft, as may be appropriate to a high-level nuclear attack, increased back to 290ft.[36]

Attacks with air-to-surface guided weapons (ASGW) such as the American Bullpup missile added another, more accurate, capability for 'pinpoint' targets. The confidently anticipated accuracy with Bullpup was a 50 per cent CEP of 30ft.

CHAPTER 11

COMMUNICATIONS, ANTENNAE AND SYSTEM LOCATIONS

The Navigation/Attack system so far described was installed either in the modular equipment bay behind the navigator's cockpit or, in the case of the FLR, the Radio Altimeter, IRS and Doppler units, in locations appropriate to their functions (see Fig.78). Whereas most of the electronic units and the Verdan computers were in the modular equipment bay, the 8ft-long SLR antennas look down from beneath the navigator near the Radio Altimeter antennae.

Summarising the overall system, the Inertial Platform is co-located and accurately aligned with the Doppler Radar and its antenna, just behind the nose wheel – close enough for navigation purposes to the aircraft's CG for its instruments to recognise the aircraft's steady state accelerations, even during manoeuvres.

The Air Data computer (ADC) made by Kelvin Hughes was also located in the equipment bay. Fed with air pressure sensing from the pitot-static head at the tip of the aircraft's nose, this relatively standard piece of equipment, employing highly sensitive pressure sensors and temperature sensors, supplied essential information – principally barometric altitude, rate of climb/descent, indicated air speed (IAS) and true air speed (TAS), which allows for effects of air density variations with altitude, and Mach No. (dependent on temperature). This information is used in the pilot's prime flying instrument displays, but it also interacted directly with the Central Computing System in its control of the overall system and with the Automatic Flight Control System (see Figs 22 and 42).

Inputs to the Air Data Computer from the pitot-static and temperature sensors are on the left, the CCS in the block above it and outputs to the AFCS in the block below it. Further system ancillaries appearing on the left include the Sperry gyro compass and the standby vertical gyro reference.

In its central position, the Air Data computer is called upon in several reversionary modes, such as in the event of failures of the Radio Altimeter, or height or speed outputs from the Inertial Reference Unit to the CCS. It is also provides height and angle of incidence information to the Terrain Following System and for the weapon aiming computation during the pull-up in loft manoeuvres.

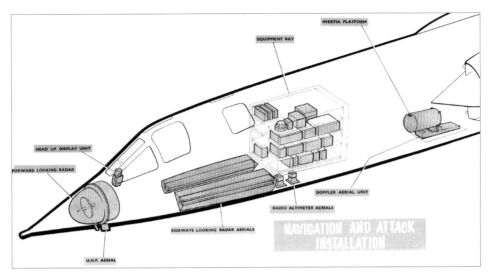

Above: Fig.78. Location of Navigation/Attack System equipments.[37]

Right: Fig.79. Schematic of the complete Navigation/Attack System, showing the flow of information between units of the system and the block for the Air Data computer near the middle.[38]

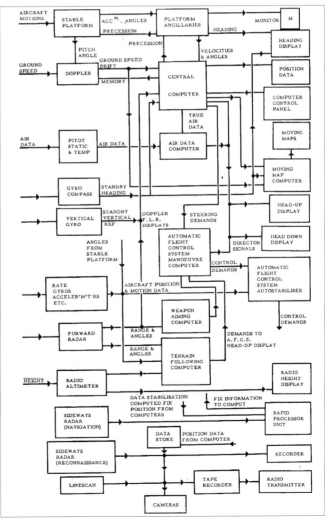

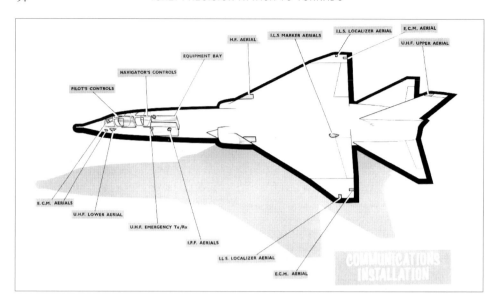

Fig.80. Locations of TSR2 communication antennae, showing multiples for all-round coverage.[37]

Fig.81. Ray Allen's design of the HF Notch Antenna tuning unit under test in the TSR2 wing root, with high current bonding to the wing skin panels to achieve the required radiation at high frequency.[42]

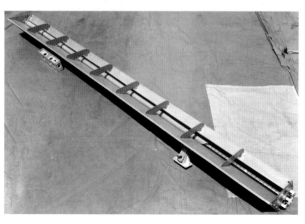

Fig.82. The 8ft-long X-Band Sideways Looking Radar antenna, to provide a beam width of less than 1° for creating a Radar picture of terrain accurate enough for a navigation fix. (Vickers Laboratory picture)[42]

Communications required reliable High Frequency (HF), Very High Frequency (VHF) and Ultra High Frequency (UHF) radio transmissions in all directions relative to the aircraft during its wide range of manoeuvres. Besides the specialist Radar systems, the basic communications package reflected relatively standard technology for modern military aircraft of the period. Under the leadership of Arthur Carter, the Aerial and Microwave Laboratory at Wisley, within the GW Dept, later BAC Systems/E, undertook the specification of antennae ('aerials') and their testing for their radiation 'polar diagrams' at multiple locations around the aircraft. These covered all requirements associated with operational missions, including antennae for Identification Friend or Foe (IFF), Electronic Counter-Measures (ECM), and for the Instrument Landing System (ILS) used for approach. The laboratory issued reports approved by Carter, covering subjects such as HF transmitters for Model Aerial Plotting,[39] Grounding Studies or Communication and Radar Aerials[40], Microwave Propagation Studies for Pulse and Pulse Doppler Radars.[41] His team also designed the SLR antennae, which had to be structurally integrated with the airframe, and was later provided by EMI under direct contract to the MOA. A most comprehensive report in the Aerial brochure for TSR2[42] covered a total of twenty-three antennae used on TSR2, covering frequencies ranging from 2MHz for the HF radio, all the way to S,C,X and J-Band for the Warning Receiver, to 35,500MHz (Q-Band) for the Reconnaissance SLR.

Besides the option of a Missile Control Antenna for SAGWs, provision was made for TACAN, Telemetry, Beacon Transponder, and Decca Dectra for trials purposes during aircraft and system development. Manufacturing studies also undertaken at Vickers included wave-guide bending techniques.

Vickers/BAC designed the Notch Antennae for HF transmissions, between 2 and 25MHz, located at the wing roots.

At HF, the Notch Antennae enabled the whole airframe to radiate signals via its metal skin covering. These large (3ft x 1½ft) notches buried in the wing roots coupled the radio frequency (RF) outputs of transmitters (Collins and later Marconi) to the aircraft skin. A current of the order of 10–60A was made to circulate around the notch surfaces, which induced in-phase skin currents, that radiated the power from the entire length and breadth of the airframe. A unit in each notch had to be frequency-tuned to match the transmitter in the airframe and a frequency pre-selector tuning system was also fitted, to enable the crew to match the transmitter to the airframe without transmitting RF energy during radio silence. While the units were omni-directional at low frequencies, at 25MHz they only radiated on their side of the aircraft, requiring the two notches and manual crew selection. Great attention had to be paid to grounding (Earth bonding) in and around the notches, to achieve good current transfer to the aircraft skins.

The Navigation and the Reconnaissance SLR antennae also went through the Aerial Laboratory.

CHAPTER 12

RECONNAISSANCE SYSTEM

TSR2's reconnaissance role was to be executed in a different configuration (see Fig.3), where the bomb bay contained a 'Reconnaissance Pack', with a powerful combination of very-high-resolution Q-band Sideways Looking Radar for mapping in all weather conditions, fixed long-range film cameras and linescan. The latter was capable of producing an even higher resolution photographic record of terrain in clear weather – by day or by night. Besides recorders for the reconnaissance data, a microwave data transmitter in the 'Recce Pack' enabled Radar and photographic linescan information to be transmitted to base, while the aircraft was still on its mission. TSR2 also had a useful degree of reconnaissance capability in the strike configuration, employing the navigation SLR, a retracting forward facing camera and oblique cameras facing port and starboard. Specification and development was centred on the Royal Radar Establishment (RRE), with Vickers coordinating, integrating and testing equipments.

The Q-Band SLR antenna for reconnaissance, with nearly twice the Navigation SLR antenna's length, and operating at four times its frequency compared with X-Band, produced a beam width of only about ⅙°, resulting in its extraordinarily high resolution.

This SLR was also capable of recognising moving objects, with Moving Target Indication (MTI). This enhanced the system's ability to show up railways and motorways, due to the traffic moving on them.

The MTI record (used at low altitude) shows faint traces where the motorway and the main roads run through Northampton. They can be recognised by looking at the map in Fig.86. When operating at low altitude, the Radar aperture was stopped down for better performance. At high altitude, the whole record would be occupied by the Radar picture.

Depending on the altitude, this high-definition Q-Band Sideways Looking Reconnaissance Radar scanned strips of terrain up to 10nm wide on either side of the aircraft's track. The recording system was capable of producing photographic film covering 1,500nm at a scale of 5nm per inch, or 3,000nm at a scale of 10nm per inch. A central portion of the strip between the Radar maps on each side contained digital navigation and flight parameters. After a sortie, this film could be rapidly processed and new film inserted for the next sortie.

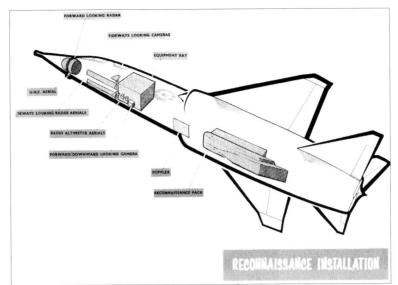

Right: Fig.83. TSR2 Reconnaissance System, with the 'Recce Pack' in the bomb bay space.[37]

Below: Fig.84. Recce Pack equipment content and layout.[37]

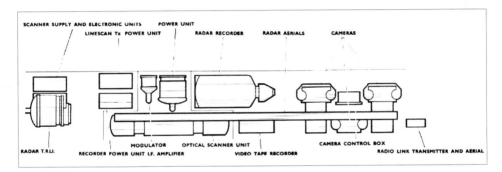

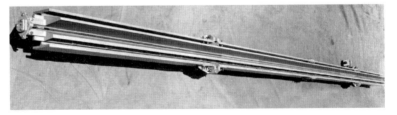

Fig.85. 15ft-long Q-Band SLR antenna for reconnaissance. (Laboratory picture)[42]

A 20nm-wide strip 400nm long could thus be reconnoitred and recorded and the data could be in the hands of a field commander within two hours of his request for reconnaissance information.

Besides long-focus lens still photography with FX 126 cameras, the highest photographic resolution obtainable employed Optical Linescan – Passive Linescan by day and active linescan by night. Its resolution was almost as good as that obtainable by conventional (FX126) cameras and the reconnaissance information could be transmitted by radio link to a ground station where the pictures could be printed, before the aircraft had returned to base. The data could also be stored in a video tape recorder for processing after the aircraft returned.

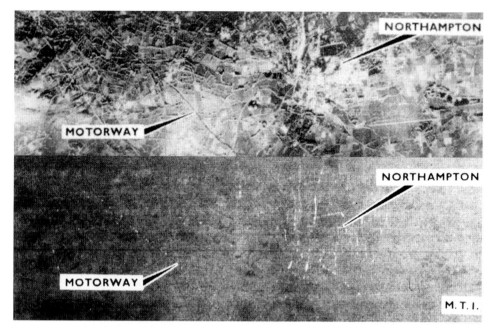

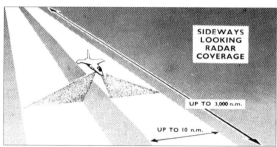

Above: Fig.86. 'Photo'/map created on a flight trial with the Q-Band Recce Radar and the MTI below.[37]

Left: Fig.87. Sideways Looking Radar reconnaissance coverage capability.[37]

Above left: Fig.88. Example of passive linescan picture taken by day.[37]

Above right: Fig.89. Example of active linescan picture, employing a rotating light beam at night.[37]

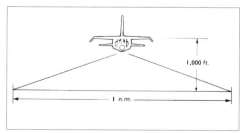

Left: Fig.90. Breadth of linescan coverage, from 1,000ft altitude.[37]

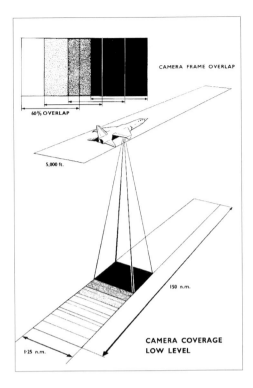
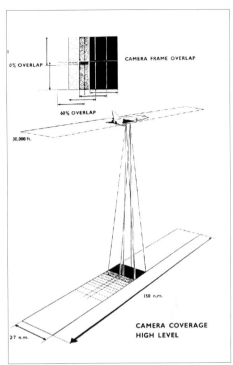

Fig.91. FX126 camera coverage at low altitude and at high altitude, showing picture overlaps.[37]

Fig.92. Reconnaissance Pack aligned with TSR2 wing mock-up for antenna polar diagram test.[1]

Fig.93. Reconnaissance Data Link antenna, with rotatable corner reflector to direct transmissions toward the receiving ground station, while TSR2 flew on an otherwise unsuitable course.[1]

Essentially for use below 1,500ft, at 1,000ft a strip of 1nm wide was covered immediately beneath the aircraft, with a recording capacity of about 100nm length in the daylight mode and about 350nm in the night mode. Passive linescan (for daylight) employed a rotating mirror, which scanned successive strips of terrain. The varying intensity of light seen was converted into an electrical signal by a photoelectric cell. This electrical output could be recorded or transmitted back to a forward ground station up to 110nm distant, controlling special printing equipment which would produce a map-like picture.

Active linescan compensates for the inadequacy of light by night by rotating a narrow and powerful light beam in synchronism with the rotating mirror, in order to illuminate the ground. The speed of the light beam's rotation and the consequent velocity of its traverse over the ground was too high for it to be seen by any observer on the ground, rendering the reconnaissance scan undetectable.

Besides the three conventional reconnaissance cameras permanently installed in TSR2 (which, together with the Navigation SLR, gave the aircraft a reconnaissance capability in its strike mode), in the Recce Pack, the FX126 cameras employed 24in and 36in lenses. These gave a photographic scale of 1:10,000 from 20,000ft, or 30,000ft respectively. Each camera contained 250ft of film. The image movement compensation, and the exposure intervals, were controlled by the navigation system.

The data link for transmitting reconnaissance information in electronic form had to use a special antenna employing a corner reflector whose direction of maximum gain could be directed in the required direction by the navigator.

CHAPTER 13

FLIGHT READINESS AND AUTOMATIC CHECKOUT

Flight readiness and pre-flight testing have already been mentioned in the context of aligning the Inertial Platform to the true north and to the local vertical. Overall readiness and checking of the Navigation/Attack System was largely to be accomplished by the 'go, no-go' self test features of individual equipments, and this had to be compatible with the requirement for local deployment of the aircraft on standby, for periods of three days without support and dispersion, followed by thirty days standby. This was intended to provide instant aircraft readiness with very little support. With roll-away disconnect couplings, the aircraft could be rolling for take-off within sixty seconds following a signal to go.

The Royal Air Force considered Automatic Checkout systems to be essential for TSR2, particularly when operating from forward airfields – and considered the need for more comprehensive equipment for base operations, to enable a quick aircraft turnaround following sorties. These were intended to permit comprehensive tests and diagnostics, enabling faults to be located to replaceable module level. The English Electric Aviation Ltd Guided Weapons Division of BAC made detailed design studies of Mobile Automatic Checkout Systems ('MACE'),[43] both for forward field operations and, with much more complex systems, for main base operations. Such testing was designed to include all of the Nav/Attack System components described in this chapter and, where applicable, the main RF transmitting equipment – the FLR, Doppler Radar, SLR and Radio Altimeter systems. RF radiation into the FLR system for testing of the static split sum and difference circuitry was also planned.

The addressable matrix and function generators, comprising the forward base version of MACE scheme, made connections into the Verdan computers via an input/output unit and produced test results on a tape reader for confirmation of functions and for analysis. The navigator's computer display unit also provided necessary indications before commencement of a sortie.

Considering the complexity of the Nav/Attack System, the Vickers/BAC systems team considered the complexity of MACE to be equally high and posed the question: 'what would check out the automatic checkout equipment?' Although MACE was designed in considerable detail, including its air transportability by AW 660 Argosy aircraft, there was little enthusiasm for proceeding with a development. Its high cost could greatly inflate, if not rival, that of the Nav/Attack System itself.

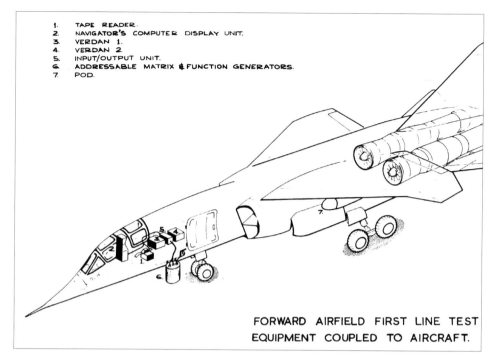

1. TAPE READER.
2. NAVIGATOR'S COMPUTER DISPLAY UNIT.
3. VERDAN 1.
4. VERDAN 2.
5. INPUT/OUTPUT UNIT.
6. ADDRESSABLE MATRIX & FUNCTION GENERATORS.
7. POD.

FORWARD AIRFIELD FIRST LINE TEST EQUIPMENT COUPLED TO AIRCRAFT.

Fig.94. Scheme for Automatic Checkout equipment to be used at 'unprepared' forward bases.[43]

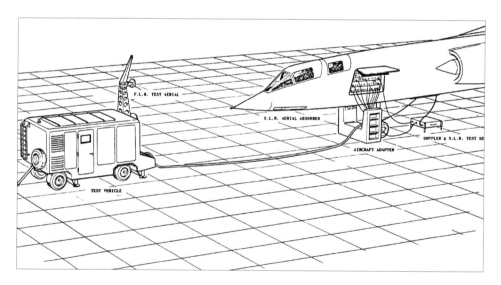

Fig.95. Comprehensive main base Automatic Checkout vehicle, complete with RF input radiations.[43]

MACE was certainly not available on 5 April 1965 when, after several days of twenty-four-hour working by the systems testing team, the first fully installed Nav/Attack System was proven and approved for flight in No.3 aircraft – the very day on which the Government cancelled the whole TSR2 project.

CHAPTER 14

POLITICS AND THE CANCELLATION OF TSR2

The tempestuous history of TSR2's birth, development, and premature death has been the subject of many articles and books. In concluding this chapter, I will summarise some (greatly abbreviated) highlights, partly in the context of the Vickers Guided Weapons team – which became the BAC Systems/E team, after Vigilant was moved to Stevenage for quantity manufacture in 1962.

BAC was itself born of a shotgun marriage between Vickers Armstrongs (Aircraft) Ltd and English Electric Aviation Ltd, forced by the Government in 1960/61, essentially to satisfy ministry insistence on the Vickers being prime contractor for TSR2 – but in partnership with the other main design bidder, English Electric. At the same time, the ministry laid down the condition that the engine to be used would be the (then Bristol) Olympus 22R, forcing another marriage between Bristol and Armstrong Siddeley (a combination soon to be purchased by Rolls-Royce). Sir George Edwards wanted to use a more advanced and lighter Rolls-Royce Medway engine, with greater potential. He remarked at the time: 'This is the first time I have ever been told what engines I must have for an aeroplane and I have taken the precaution of getting the Minister [Aubry Jones] to give me the order in writing.'[97] According to some knowledgeable observers, this one early decision could have doomed the aircraft to be much heavier, larger, and more expensive than otherwise, and so set the scene for some of the most acrimonious politics regarding the cost of the project.

From the earliest days, there was strong opposition to TSR2 in many Government quarters, not least from Lord Mountbatten at the Ministry of Defence, who lobbied for development of the Royal Navy's (subsonic) Buccaneer and from Sir Solly (later Lord) Zuckerman, chief scientific adviser. Their 'closet' opposition[44] extended to overt influence on the RAAF, the main non-UK potential buyer of TSR2. Researching relevant files in the Public Records Office of the National Archives brings out further nuggets of information, some of which could make one's hair stand on end.

As early as 15 May 1962, an Air Ministry minute (M.64) concerning a financial authority request to the Treasury commenced: 'I cannot believe that there is a possibility of our dropping the TSR2 altogether at this stage…' A week later, on 23 May, the request went forward for eleven pre-production aircraft. In parallel with this, lobbying rose and intensified for purchasing the American swing-wing F-III, originally known as the TFX. This was under development in the USA and was offered at an attractive 'fixed price' and delivery, which appeared to be much more secure and less expensive than had been anticipated, as a result of the complexities demanded under the RAF's Operational Requirement. The unparalleled technological advances required to meet the RAF's OR, in respect of uncharted territory for both the aircraft and the Navigation Attack System, led to delays and rising costs that increasingly opened the project to competition from the F-III. It is ironic in the extreme that, while the Strategic Air Command of the US Air Force was apparently receiving all the priority over the US Tactical Air Force, the TAF was pressing urgently for a replacement to the B-57 (Canberra made under licence from the UK). The TAF considered the TSR2 specification to be what it wanted – and US Defence Secretary Robert McNamara effectively specified the TSR2 – but with variable geometry (swing) wings. This became the TFX/F-III, which would compete with TSR2.

Following equivocal support by the Conservative Government up to 1963, as the 1964 General Election loomed, the Labour Party embarked on its campaign with a firm undertaking to cancel TSR2 (among its general reductions in defence expenditure). Having initially regarded the F-III as a fall-back prospect in case TSR2 failed to materialise, in October 1963 the RAAF purchased twenty-four F-IIIs at the 'fixed price' of US$90,749,040 – an apparent bargain compared with figures by then anticipated for TSR2.[45] The RAAF waited ten years before receiving their F-IIIs – at three times the original 'fixed price'. By the summer of 1963, the Labour Party campaign to vilify the TSR2 grew more widespread and strident. By the time the first aircraft flew, with great success, on 27 September 1964, the campaign had reached such a pitch that the Press hardly knew how to handle the story.[45] Former Chief of Air Staff, Sir Dermot Boyle, by then with BAC, commented: 'The less people knew about TSR2, the more they talked about it.' The F-III was being offered at the same 'fixed price' already accepted by the RAAF.[45]

When Labour won the election in 1964, no immediate cancellation announcement followed, to everyone's surprise. However, the wheels were grinding, and more (mostly uninformed) negative statements were bandied about – an example, according to Chapman Pincher,[97] being Denis Healy's remark to Harold Wilson at a Defence Committee meeting: 'By the way, Prime Minister, we think you should know that the wing of TSR2 broke under test at Farnborough yesterday.' Chapman Pincher reckoned that this sealed TSR2's fate – however, what the Cabinet did not know or understand was that this was a test to destruction as normally applied to a structure under development and that the wing had withstood many times the design load it could expect to encounter in flight!

At the Prime Minister's 5 January 1965 meeting with Sir Solly Zuckerman, Harold Wilson suggested that, in the event of a cancellation, BAC could employ the people put out of work in the development of a 500-seat transatlantic jet airliner. Such proposals took no account of realistic commercial realities nor, as Sir Solly pointed out, the duplication with development already being pursued in the USA. On 14 January, the president of the Board of Trade met with Lord Portall and Sir George Edwards, asking for their preference if they had to choose between cancellation of TSR2 or of Concorde. Both replied 'Concorde'. On the following evening, 15 January, Sir George Edwards, Sir Arnold Hall (Hawker Siddeley Aviation), Sir Denning Pearson (Rolls-Royce) and C.E. Wrangham (Short Bros & Harland) met with Harold Wilson at Chequers over dinner, and later in the Long Gallery. The whole scenario was discussed in depth, covering not only TSR2, but the (Hawker Siddeley) P1154 supersonic jump-jet and the HS 681 being built by Short Bros. The discussion encompassed the suggested 'airbus', all aspects of the endangered projects' costs (the Prime Minister gave the TSR2 costs to date as £750 million with prospects of them reaching £1,000 million – although this figure probably included all the costs incurred by the many ministry departments), and the perceived attractiveness of the RAF ordering the TFX (F-III). Uneconomic compromises, such as ordering fewer TSR2s and additional F-IIIs were suggested, bringing the per aircraft cost of TSR2 even higher, along with the effects on the balance of payments due to imports and lost exports. Everything was to be 'off the record' and the Press were to be merely told of a 'frank exchange of views'.[46]

Sir George made good on the PM's request to write to Roy Jenkins, Minister of Aviation, concerning export prospects following a cancellation of TSR2. The main thrust of this was that, in the absence of the TSR2 work and its contribution towards BAC overhead costs, the price of the BAC 1-11 civil airliner could no longer remain competitive and therefore excellent worldwide export prospects would be lost. In his concluding paragraphs, Sir George added: 'Whilst not wishing to join in the feather-bedding controversy, I think you might like to know that, in addition to the risk on the BAC 1-11, we are also at considerable risk on the VC-10 and Super VC-10 projects.' The 'chapter and verse' of many more meetings and memoranda, up to the Chancellor of the Exchequer's 5 April Budget speech, occupies many pages of Public Records Office documents, which the author has brought into the Brooklands Archives. In his September 1973 *Aeroplane Monthly* article,[45] Bill Gunston's analysis shows that: 'TSR2 was (outwardly, at least) judged by the Labour Party to be the supreme example of a giant confidence trick by a "featherbedded" industry which had "taken the public for a ride"; and was "a mentally retarded and overgrown" child in the national economy, and ought to be "cut down to size" (these are all actual quotations).' Here is some more of Bill Gunston's article: 'Beaumont, for example, prepared a lecture on TSR2 for the Royal Aeronautical Society and got it security-cleared shortly before cancellation; then he was forbidden by the Government to read it (till 1966) because impartial comment, which would inevitably make TSR2 sound like an uncommonly fine aircraft, was strictly out.' Disinformation seemed to be the order of the day. Defence Minister Denis Healey was quoted[45] as saying: 'TSR2 will only drop ordinary high explosive on tanks and bridges… new anti-aircraft weapons will be able to shoot it down by the time it is in service, so at £16 million per aircraft it is going to make all Mr Amery's [Conservative Minister of Aviation in the previous Government] other blunders look like chickenfeed.'

On that Budget day of 5 April 1965, the main worries for the Government appear to have been the effects on employment and the trade unions. George Brown, Minister for (the Department of) Economic Affairs, wrote to the Prime

Minister, advising of arrangements for meeting trade union representatives at the House of Commons. While the Minister of Aviation (Roy Jenkins) would meet representatives of BAC and Bristol Siddeley Engines, George Brown would meet representatives of the Confederation of Shipbuilding and Engineering Unions. A note for the record indicated that: 'The Prime Minister was content with the arrangements for consultations…', and that 'The Minister of Aviation … *Should indicate to Sir George Edwards that if the aircraft companies affected by the cancellation wanted sympathy and help from the Government at a later stage then they must co-operate over the decision and not, for example, indulge in histrionics with the Press* [author's emphasis].'[46]

Once the cancellation was announced in that Budget speech, following which the F-III was ordered at the same (eventually tripled) price as that for the RAAF, 'the very next morning the Weybridge workers were instructed not only to destroy every TSR2 on the production line but also the jigs used to make them.'[45] As may be expected, many of the Vickers and English Electric members of BAC lost their jobs. Sir George Edwards remarked that 'The stuffing has been knocked out of BAC' and made known his opinion: that the company may not survive.

After the cancellation, John Lattey visited the RRE looking for work to occupy his team. RRE had shown Lattey round their TSR2-funded projects only two months earlier. To his fury he was told that nobody there had become redundant because they were not working on TSR2-specific projects! How these Government establishments justified maintaining their staff and funding under these savage defence cuts remained a mystery. Fortunately for the RAF's longer term prospects, some of the original Weybridge Guided Weapons team (Howard Surtees, J.E. Daboo, Frank Bond, Dennis Harris, John Goodwin, Jim Cole, John Garrett, John Doyle, and others) turned up at Easams and at Panavia in Munich, working on the Multi Role Combat Aircraft (MRCA), later to be called Tornado. In its strike role nearly thirty years later in the first Gulf War and, later, in the twenty-first century, with the aid of still newer technology which became available in the meantime, Tornado executes the same missions as TSR2 and owes a great deal to the Navigation/Attack System work of the Vickers Guided Weapons team, and later the BAC Systems/E team, at Weybridge.

CHAPTER 15

SINGLE-SEAT 'TSR2' NAVIGATION FIXING FOR NATO V/STOL FIGHTER

In late 1961, this project had unexpected consequences for the author. It has direct relevance to the work of GW Department with the TSR2 supersonic long-range attack aircraft discussed in the earlier chapters. The similarities related to TSR2's Navigation/Attack System, in that both that, and the NATO V/STOL fighter were to be navigated using an Inertial Platform and, as with OR346, both were to utilise a Sideways Looking Radar.

TSR2 already used the 'eighty-four-minute' Schuler Pendulum for the maintenance of an accurate vertical reference, which had to remain unaffected by any gyrations of the vehicle carrying it. To be independent of external aids, such as Radar, which could be jammed, both TSR2 and the NATO V/STOL project were specified with entirely self-contained Inertial Navigation Systems (INS). For the NATO V/STOL project, my role included the choice of the most suitable INS system. I also studied the possibility of this aircraft navigating in a similar manner to TSR2, but with one important difference.

INS systems suffered a degree of inaccuracy due to gyroscope drift as well as their inability to measure very small accelerations below an error threshold. The resulting navigation error was usually measured in miles per hour of flight. Thus, if the drifts and other errors resulted in 10nm navigation error after an hour's flight, the system was said to err by 10 miles per hour. This figure (like 'miss distance' in guidance systems) was often given as the 50 per cent Critical Error Probability of 'x' miles per hour – or CEP of 10 miles per hour. Without regularly correcting errors during the journey to the target, such accuracy was still not good enough for finding the best starting point for an accurate bombing run, even assuming terminal bombing aids. One way of reducing the INS error was to apply a continuous correction of the inherent velocity measurement within the INS and thereby update the system. In TSR2, this was achieved by means of independently measured aircraft ground speed obtained with reasonably good accuracy from a Doppler Radar carried in the aircraft. The overall navigation error could be substantially reduced in this way. However, even a fraction of a mile/hour error after several hours flight would be unacceptable, so a third correction was necessary – by means of taking highly accurate 'fixes', such as a ship might take on a lighthouse. For high altitude missions, the latest technique was to take fixes on stars, which could be seen at high altitude even during daylight. This considerably raised the complexity and cost of the navigation system, but was nevertheless used on some US aircraft of the time.

In the twenty-first century, highly accurate Global Positioning Satellites (GPS) provide sufficient accuracy to obviate much of what was necessary for navigation in the 1960s.

A significant part of TSR2's long-range bombing mission would be flown below cloud as, if the target was under cloud cover, even at night, Stellar-Inertial Navigation (SINS) would not be suitable. The most suitable system for the aircraft was to take regular fixes from the ground, employing the very narrow beam of a Sideways Looking Radar (SLR) radiating from lengths of slotted wave-guides on each side of the aircraft. These beams would illuminate a narrow strip of the ground on either side as the aircraft passed over and, if evolving strips could be rapidly assembled into a map, the reconnaissance-briefed flight observer/navigator could identify fix points. He could then enter absolute corrections into the Doppler/INS and update the aircraft's position with great accuracy. One immediate prerequisite was the ability to create a 'moving map' and apply a correction quickly enough to avoid unacceptable deviations from the desired track to the target. In TSR2, this was to be achieved by means of an auto-developed, photographic-style continuous map that would be visible to the crew within six seconds of passing over any point. Even then, the crew would only know where it had been 'six seconds ago', but that would nevertheless enable an accurate enough navigation update.

However, another immediate consequence was the need for a fairly large piece of equipment in the cockpit to produce the moving map, with means of entering the coordinates of a recognised feature – and therefore cockpits for two crew members.

Sideways Looking X-Band Radar antennae of 4ft length would create a beam of about 1.75° width. This could produce a map with sufficiently high resolution for recognition of a fix point at a distance of, say, 200 yards abeam the aircraft and locate it with an accuracy of about 6 yards. My challenge was to assess the possibility of achieving this kind of fix accuracy *in a single seat aircraft*.

We needed a way to dispense with the bulky auto-developer and to present the moving map information in such a way that the pilot could recognise the terrain, and enter fixes into the INS system himself, without excessively increasing his workload. Besides flying the aircraft, he would now also be navigator and have to handle all communications and weapon systems. This would frequently be during low flying sorties requiring the highest concentration. A ray of hope lay in the development of cathode ray tubes (CRTs) such as those used with Radars and for Head Up Displays (HUDs), with ever improving resolutions. A moving map display CRT would need to be small enough to fit into the pilot's cockpit and conveniently located for ready viewing and manipulation. This might be by the movement of crosshairs, which the pilot would align with a feature on which to take his fix, and then the entering of fix coordinates with the press of a button that would automatically update the INS.

Conventional Radar displays, such as H2s, worked with relatively slowly scanning antennae, leaving a 'trail' and 'afterglow' behind individual target scans. This system would have to create a continuously unfolding map that would remain coherent with aircraft travel as it moved across the screen, keeping an icon representing the aircraft apparently stationary on the screen as the map passed by. There would still be a delay between the time of passing a point and its input to update INS, where the order of six seconds would most likely be acceptable.

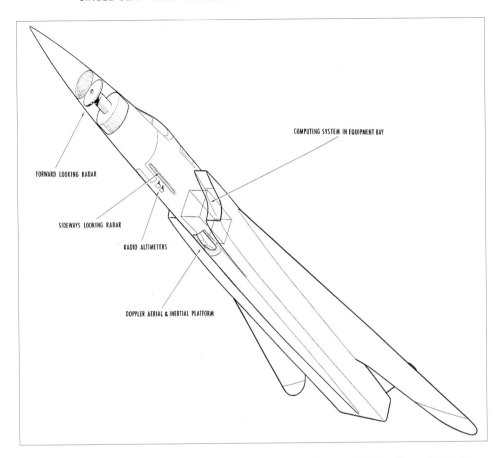

COMPUTING SYSTEM IN EQUIPMENT BAY

FORWARD LOOKING RADAR

SIDEWAYS LOOKING RADAR

RADIO ALTIMETERS

DOPPLER AERIAL & INERTIAL PLATFORM

Fig.96. Typical disposition of the main navigation elements employing INS, Doppler, and SLR.[105]

In discussing such CRT displays with manufacturers and the RAE, clearly the critical factors of refresh rate and 'spot' size would be cardinal to creating a moving map with the necessary resolution to display a Radar map showing sufficient detail for the recognition of small features. For a resolution equivalent to, say, 100 lines per inch, a 6in or 150mm-diameter display would require a spot size equal to half the line resolution – or about 0.75mm. Judging by the result of using today's computer scanner at such resolutions, this resolution might be quite sufficient.

The examples overleaf used aerial photos taken by the author from our Canberra at about 20,000ft. The amount of information retrievable from the scans of this picture is shown by the visible detail of a town and fields and illustrates that, even at 50 lines per inch, it is possible to recognise enough detail to navigate. The corresponding spot size would be 1.5mm. At 96 lines per inch, roughly corresponding to the example of 0.75mm spot size, the quality of detail appears to be more than adequate. So, in the absence of archival information dating back to the NATO V/STOL study, it is possible to confirm our 1961 finding that a display was available with the requisite resolution.

Assuming that a suitable display would be available and that the aircraft's navigation computer could be programmed to move the picture around a marker representing

Fig.97. Scan of an aerial photograph at 96 lines per inch resolution.[106]

Fig.98. Scan of an aerial photograph at 50 lines per inch resolution.[106]

the aircraft, it remained for the pilot move crosshair cursors on to his fix point as it moved across the picture and to press his 'fix' button. The feasibility of this depended on the ergonomics of the display, its positioning in the cockpit and, above all, the pilot's workload. I explored these points with our test pilots and, in particular, with Mike Lithgow of Supermarine, who was regularly flying transonic Supermarine Swifts and Scimitars in both fighter and ground attack roles. We postulated positioning the display in a convenient position clear of other controls and displays, possibly to one side of the cockpit somewhat below eye level. This would make for rapid viewing and terrain recognition, without unduly taking his attention from the terrain or HUD information seen through the windscreen. Clearly, layout design for any aircraft cockpit would need to be very carefully thought out, and would require proving by simulator trials before flight trials. Considering all these points, Mike Lithgow felt confident that, with assistance from the available autopilot control of the aircraft, pilots would cope with the short periods of extra workload and make successful fixes at suitable intervals, to update any navigation errors.

Most tragically, Mike Lithgow was killed in the 1962 crash of an early BAC 1-11 commercial jet.

At that time, Vickers had a cooperation agreement with the Minneapolis Honeywell Corporation in the USA, and the conventional wisdom was that we should specify a Honeywell INS platform. INS systems were being offered by several US firms besides Honeywell, including Sperry, Kearfott and Litton Industries. In the UK, Elliott Automation at Borehamwood and Rochester were best known to us, and I had become acquainted with their platform in connection with TSR2, meeting with their executives Jack Pateman (later Sir Jack) and Peter Hearne (later president of the Royal Aeronautical Society). The NATO V/STOL project was for some time in the future – later than TSR2, whose design was well advanced towards its eventual 1964 first flights (and Harold Wilson's Labour Government's precipitate cancellation in 1965). We needed higher performance than the Elliott INS, and looked to the USA, where Honeywell was Vickers' natural partner.

I looked wider and obtained technical specifications from most of the American INS manufacturers, in order to make comparisons. While Honeywell had an excellent reputation and their latest platform for aircraft applications was promoted with a 50 per cent CEP around 2–3 miles per hour of flight, Litton Systems in Woodland Hills, CA, claimed to have their LN-3 platforms with less than 2 miles per hour of flight CEP in service in 1,000 NATO F-104 fighters. Furthermore, they were now offering their next generation LN-9 platform with much higher specification gyroscopes and accelerometers to achieve a 50 per cent CEP of about 0.32 miles per hour of flight. What was more, this platform system weighed about 50lb, half the Honeywell platform's weight. Litton clearly appeared to have the advantage of extensive operational experience with their LN-3, and their LN-9 was claimed to be through its main development stages and in flight test.

On the strength of this solid information, I rejected the Honeywell platform for our proposed NATO V/STOL aircraft. Instead, I included the Litton LN-9 inertial navigator and added the all-electronic Moving Map Display for single-seat pilot execution of navigation fixes.

In the process of obtaining top management approval for this proposal, I had to fight off objections and arguments from Henry Gardner, who wanted to stay with Honeywell. It took considerable argument but, after standing my ground, the proposal went forward as I had intended.

The only doubt in my mind was that nobody had visited Litton to see the equipment and its test results at first-hand. Fortuitously, at this time, in November 1961, I was asked to visit Honeywell with Dab and with Les Vine, to assist its Ordnance Division with its design proposal for the TOW tube-launched anti-tank missile. During the two weeks in the USA, I took a couple of days to visit Litton in California, for a thorough inspection of their whole operation and to grill their engineers over their test results. At every turn, I was extremely impressed with their engineering skills quality and overall professionalism. Their INS systems were by no means imaginary, but very impressively real. I telexed my confirmation of the choice for NATO V/STOL back to Weybridge and felt that my choice had been thoroughly vindicated. As the Epilogue will reveal, this trip to Litton had deeper implications.

CHAPTER 16

VICKERS GUIDED WEAPONS DEPT – MISSILE PROJECTS FOR THE FUTURE

Besides TSR2 and the four major missile projects – Red Rapier, Blue Boar, Red Dean, and Vigilant – a number of forward-looking missile designs were taken to a relatively advanced stage.

16.1 THE 'LIGHT ACK ACK' PROJECT

The 'Light Ack Ack' project, which eventually became the Rapier missile system, started as a private venture design study at Weybridge in 1957. During the MOA's period of agonising as to whether Vickers should be encouraged to entertain any hope for new Government GW contracts, one of the two £10,000 designs studies it was considering placing with the company ('with the object of picking their brains')[54] was for a 'Field Army Low Altitude SAGW' (surface-to-air guided weapon). This contract was placed before August 1959, under the project designation ET316 (superseding the 'unattainable' automatic PT428) only after Vickers had already expended about two years on private venture work.

Led by Bernard Hunn, Assistant Chief Designer (Projects), the concept was to make direct hits on aircraft flying at up to supersonic speed, at a range from 0.3 miles to 4.5 miles. The aim was to rely on the simplest possible low-cost system, mounted on readily mobile transport for rapid deployment and firing in most tactical situations. With this in mind, the system was initially conceived as optically sighted, with eight missiles being carried on the mobile launch platform.

This slender 9ft 6in-long design of only 6in diameter is shown with four tail-mounted controls and without the usual mid-body wings, evidently relying on body lift for its manoeuvre at the low altitudes at which it would operate. The aerodynamics and control equations of the proposed autopilot and guidance parameters were fed into Vickers' Pegasus digital computer, where studies were already in progress for the GW Department's work on the TSR2 Terrain Following Radar System. These computer simulations enabled the principal control and guidance parameters to be determined. Unusually, being a hitting missile (as opposed to most missiles, which it is assumed will miss the target, and therefore require a proximity fuze and a large warhead), the LAA required only a small, lightweight warhead.

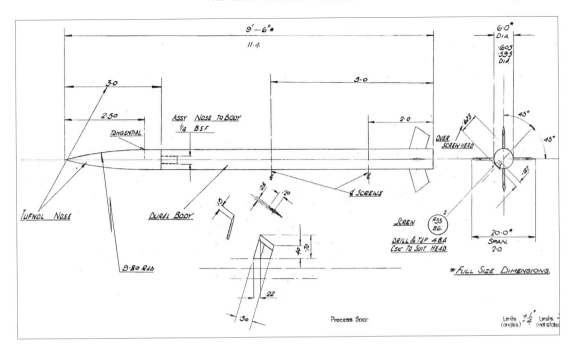

Fig.99. Early scheme for Light AA Missile 89908, Sheet 1, November 1957.[50]

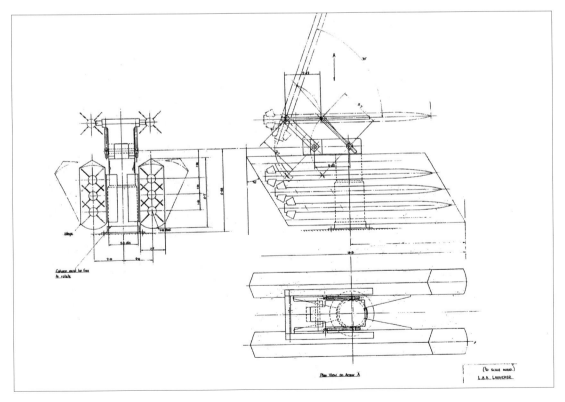

Fig.100. Scheme 89908, Sheet 3, for mobile launcher carrying eight Light AA Missiles.[50]

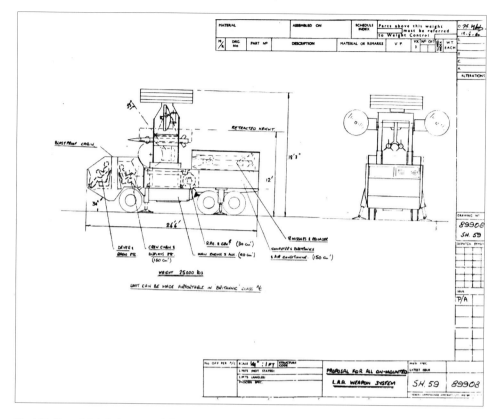

Fig.101. Peter Mobsby's proposal for All On-Mounted LAA Weapon System.[50]

In parallel, design of a launch vehicle to carry eight missiles, their sight tracking and guidance was outlined, resulting in the scheme drawing (Fig.100).

One missile on each side is seen in its ready-to-fire position and a further six below, ready for placing into their firing positions as missiles are fired from above. The missiles were to be elevated to a launch angle of up to 70°. A simple operator-tracking optical sight was to be used, with which missile deviation from the target sightline would be measured. This would transmit command guidance signals using a Radio Frequency (RF) link to the missile. Later designs would utilise Radar tracking capable of use in poor light and at night, with a similar RF link for guidance.

Simulator control and guidance studies and overall weapon system studies continued, along with details of field handling equipment to meet the Army's tactical requirements. In mid-1960, Vickers produced a further complete scheme for the All On-Mounted LAA Weapon System. This carried two command link microwave dishes and a modified method of loading, carrying and positioning of the missiles for firing, at elevations of up to 55°. The scheme provided for the carriage of missile and guidance electronics in an air-conditioned container, with onboard electrical power generation, all transported on a self-contained six-wheeled vehicle, complete with the loading and firing structures and the guidance sight. Two crew members were housed in a blast-proof cabin – a driver and a rearward facing missile operator, with displays and controls. The whole system, nearly 27ft long and over 18ft high, and weighing 25,000lb, was designed to be air-portable in a Britannia Class aircraft.

On completion of the Ministry of Aviation Study Contract in 1960, in accordance with the ministry policy of keeping Vickers from any mainstream GW development work and the putative merger of Vickers, English Electric and Bristol Aircraft into the British Aircraft Corporation, the main development was placed with the English Electric Company's Guided Weapons Division at Stevenage.

English Electric built on the basic concept as proposed by Vickers and, as may be expected after its own lengthy design and development process, there were many changes and modifications. The missile itself received more conventional mid-body wings of 15in span on a slightly reduced 5.25in-diameter body. Missile overall length was 88.2in, with a launch weight of 94lb including its IMI Troy dual-thrust solid rocket motor, which accelerated it to around Mach 2. BAC eventually announced the programme in September 1964 and Rapier went into service in 1971.[51]

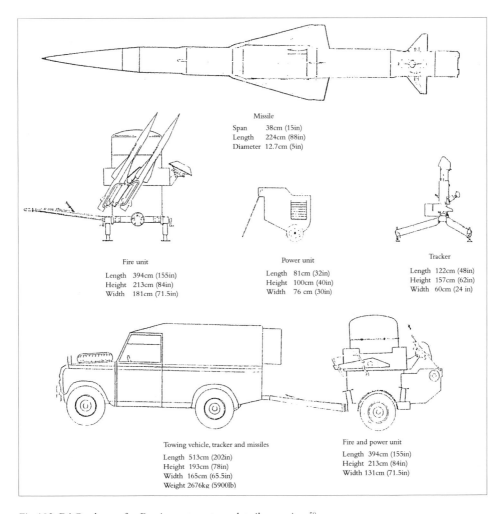

Missile
Span   38cm (15in)
Length   224cm (88in)
Diameter 12.7cm (5in)

Fire unit
Length   394cm (155in)
Height   213cm (84in)
Width   181cm (71.5in)

Power unit
Length   81cm (32in)
Height   100cm (40in)
Width   76 cm (30in)

Tracker
Length 122cm (48in)
Height 157cm (62in)
Width   60cm (24 in)

Towing vehicle, tracker and missiles
Length   513cm (202in)
Height   193cm (78in)
Width   165cm (65.5in)
Weight 2676kg (5900lb)

Fire and power unit
Length   394cm (155in)
Height   213cm (84in)
Width   131cm (71.5in)

Fig.102. BAC scheme for Rapier system, towed trailer version.[50]

Above: Fig.103. Rapier Missile Battery on show at BAC's display at the SBAC Show, Farnborough.[53]

Right: Fig.104a. Rapier being fired from M548 tracked vehicle.[51]

Fig.104b. Field-deployed Rapier Missiles with fire control.

Named Rapier, the tactical system now included the option of tracking and acquisition Blind Fire Radar, and was carried either on trailer or mounted on a tracked M548 vehicle. The system included many features for Identifying Friend or Foe (IFF) and minimising the effects of Electronic Counter-Measures. Carrying a simple 1.1lb. semi-armour-piercing warhead, Rapier confounded many sceptics by successfully hitting targets as small as 7in in diameter.[51] With its rapid deployment and simple operation, it is no surprise that some 18,000 Rapiers were sold to armies, by 1978 including the British Army, RAF Regiment, Australian Army, Zambia, Oman, Abu Dhabi, Brunei, and the Imperial Iranian Air Force. Rapier was a major player in the 1991 Gulf War and remains in service to this day.

16.2 SMALL LONG-RANGE PERIOD ANTI-TANK GUIDED WEAPON WITH BACK SCATTER GUIDANCE

Vickers' brilliant Chief Designer (Weapons), Howard Surtees, undertook a feasibility study under Contract No.KF/2F/03/CB.23(B) for the Ministry of Aviation through ARDE in November 1959,[47] reporting in November 1960. With help from Dab and other experienced designers, he appeared to perform the lion's share of the work himself. Over this period he also oversaw his Vigilant team, which was intensively engaged in the development and trials leading to eventual acceptance by the War Office, and there was much interaction with all the relevant ministries. Having been moved from leading the Test Group, where I was heavily engaged in the development testing and environmental testing of Vigilant as senior designer, I became a project engineer reporting directly to Howard. Soon, I found myself struggling to revise my somewhat rusty degree-level mathematics, aerodynamics, physics – and more. Now sitting in my own little office next to Dab's office designing weapon systems, I was fortunate enough to become somewhat involved in Howard Surtees' largely one-man study.

Vigilant was a 'Manual Command Line of Sight' – or MANCLOS weapon, requiring manual guidance. Ideally, a missile would be specified to be totally automatic, requiring no human operator for achieving a hit, something that even in 2004 was still under development as the vehicle-mounted Tri-National Anti-Tank Weapon (TRIGAT), anticipated for service use by about 2006. Short-range TRIGAT will be laser-guided, still requiring the target to be illuminated by an operator. This will only be marginally better than an improved version of Swingfire, which was developed immediately after Vigilant. To be fully automatic, the long-range 'fire and forget' version of TRIGAT homes (passive homing) onto the heat signature of a tank and therefore does not require illumination by an operator, but merely to be pointed in the right general direction. The Government tried an interim approach in the 1950s under the Orange William programme using semi-automatic line-of-sight guidance (SACLOS). This was to use semi-active homing, which would home onto an infrared-illuminated tank and would reach the target without further operator control. However Orange William was also specified with a 4,000 yards separation between the illuminator and the launcher – that was beyond available technology, and the project was soon cancelled. The contractor was Fairey Engineering, where Howard Surtees then worked on the air-to-air beam rider Blue Sky, that later became Fireflash. That was the project which required Brigadier Clemow to put things right, before he came to Vickers.

Fifty years before TRIGAT, Howard Surtees conceived a SACLOS missile solution with the 4,000 yards range of long-range TRIGAT and automatic guidance (requiring IR illumination of the target). His feasibility study still provides considerable detail.

The requirement was for this long-range missile to be operated from air-portable tracked fighting vehicles and from the Battle Series Chieftain tank, delivering a lethal hollow-charge warhead to penetrate the heaviest tank armour at ranges down to only 50 yards, as well at 4,000 yards. The weapon had to be as simple to operate as gun armament and have maximum reliability and probability of a first-shot kill. Quite a challenge… Surtees produced entirely original ideas for guidance, which had to be shown feasible.

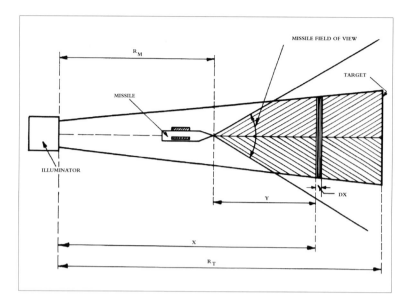

Fig.105. Missile beam-riding on back scatter from atmospheric molecules and particles ahead.[47]

Semi-active infrared guidance was chosen, requiring the projection of sufficient IR energy to be reflected from a dark protected tank of 3ft x 5ft size (hull down), in the presence of obstructions in the foreground and possible decoys near the target. Since targets could be moving at 15mph across the line of sight (30mph was assumed in the design, but then larger, at 7.5ft x 7.5ft), the flight time at maximum range had to be a short seven seconds, also enabling ripple-firing of several missiles. This required high launch acceleration of about 30g, to achieve a highly supersonic Mach 2.5 to Mach 3 maximum speed. The system had to be effective at night and in poor visibility conditions including haze and high moisture levels.

Lasers had not been invented in the late 1950s, so a searchlight of sufficient power in the far infrared (verging into the visible) spectrum was specified in considerable detail. Perhaps the main problem with this was the minimal IR energy that would be received back from the target at maximum range. This was insufficient for detection by a missile IR homing head and, in overcoming this problem, Howard Surtees came up with a bold solution requiring all of his brilliant mathematical ability and knowledge of physics and engineering.

His guidance studies centred on the use of a narrow pencil beam to illuminate the target and to use the back-scattered radiation from the molecules and particles in the beam as the guidance signal on which to control the missile, until it was close enough to the target, when it could home onto its IR reflection. This was something like following the beam normally visible from a searchlight, only employing the immediately surrounding reflections from the atmosphere for guidance.

Shown diagrammatically to show the basic elements of the mathematical analysis, the pencil beam appears to diverge and the scale of the searchlight and missile are not representative. However, it can be seen that, after calculating the energy scattered by atmospheric particles, their effect is considered by calculating the effect of thin slices ahead of the missile's guidance receiver. The energy from such slices over the length of beam ahead of the missile is progressively summed (added) by mathematical integration. This enabled the actual guidance signal received by the missile's IR detector cell to be calculated and the disposition of the signal over the area of the detector to be shown. The diagram below shows how the received IR energy is distributed on the area of the detector cell(s) and how it is affected by the missile's position relative to the beam.

When the missile is riding at the beam centre, the energy is symmetrically distributed. When the missile is displaced from the centre of the beam, the energy is concentrated away from the centre, providing a means of detecting the beam riding error and a measure of the correction required to bring the missile into the beam centre.

Other detection methods were considered, including rearward-facing detectors, that would receive the maximum amount of energy from the searchlight. The main advantage was the lower power of searchlight such a system would require, and lower susceptibility to jamming. However, this came with disadvantages related to the stability of missile trajectory since, as the missile turned to correct any error, its tail end would turn away from the searchlight and reduce the received signal. Following the chosen principle, as the missile approaches the target, the energy received from the target reflection would increase until it exceeds the back scatter energy from the beam and the total signal for guidance would increase.

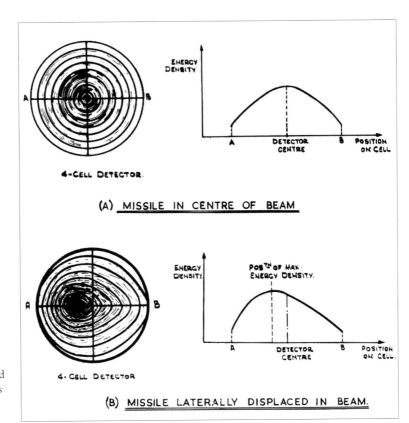

Fig.106. Distribution of IR energy on the detector and how it indicates missile position in the beam.[47]

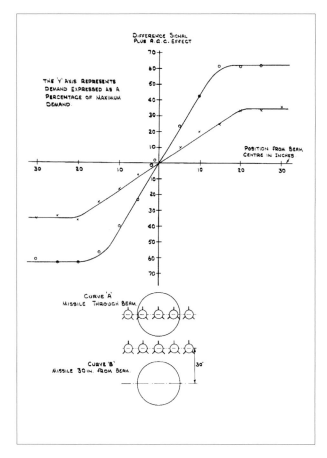

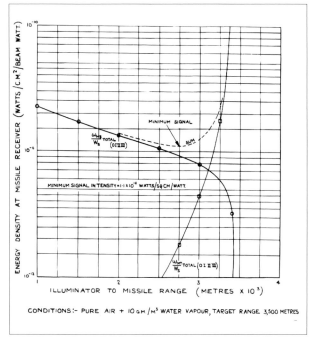

Left: Fig.107. Guidance signal as a function of missile position.[47]

Below: Fig.108. Sum of falling beam and rising target reflection signals in pure air and in haze to 3,000 yards.[47]

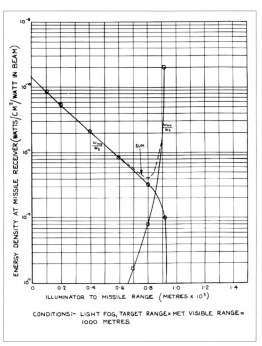

Assuming a 'static split' guidance system employing four germanium p-n junction detector segments, two measuring energy falling above and below the detector centre and two measuring energy falling to the left and right of the detector centre, it would be possible to obtain difference signals in the two planes of missile control, as corrections for feeding to an autopilot. The latter would then turn the missile in the required direction towards the beam's centre-line.

The difference signals can be plotted on a simple graph, to show how directional manoeuvre demands on the missile can be sensed, as well as the size of the demands, as the missile's position varies about the beam's centre-line.

The steeper graph (A) shows the condition when the missile is passing through the beam centre, while the shallower curve (B) shows the difference signal variation as the missile moves across the beam, 30in away from its centre. The closer to the centre, the more firmly the missile is held into it.

The note indicating 'Plus AGC' relates to the Automatic Gain Control in the electronic circuits discussed later.

Surtees also calculated this detected energy variation in the missile guidance head, for conditions ranging from pure air with 10gm/cubic m of water vapour out to a range of 3,500m, for haze with the same amount of water vapour and with limited visibility fog out to 1,000m.

The minimum value of these signals over a representative range of weather conditions was calculated to be sufficient for guidance, out to the maximum required range of 3,000 yards, as described. In the case of limited visibility fog, surveillance and target identification are, in any case, prevented at long ranges, and this affects both the tank's operations and those of the anti-tank weapon system. The total signal detected by the natural addition of the falling back-scatter energy and the rising target-reflected energy varies with distance from the searchlight and from the target, as shown in the graphs.

For light fog, the received energy is shown in Fig.109 out to 1,000 yards. As with the two graphs above, the back-scatter signal can be seen to be at its maximum near the launcher (on the left) and falling (even faster in fog) as the limit of visibility is approached. At the same time the rising energy reflected from the target equals the back-scatter energy at about 850 yards, after which the target reflection takes over and provides plenty of signal for the missile's guidance circuits.

Besides enabling the searchlight to be accurately specified, the data began to provide the basis for designing the missile itself. One important aspect of the 'heat seeker' IR guidance system following from this, and the later questions of missile stability and control, relates to how the seeker should be mounted in the missile nose. As a missile manoeuvres, its attitude constantly changes due both to the new headings it pursues in response to guidance demands, and to additional aerodynamic incidence angles relative to the airflow that are required to attain the manoeuvring accelerations. Since these attitude and direction changes would move the seeker's detector in relation to the incoming IR energy and distort the guidance demand, it was decided to mount the seeker on a gyroscopically stabilised axis. It would then see the same guidance signals and make the same demands, as if the missile were not manoeuvring – that is, only dependent on the missile's distance from the beam

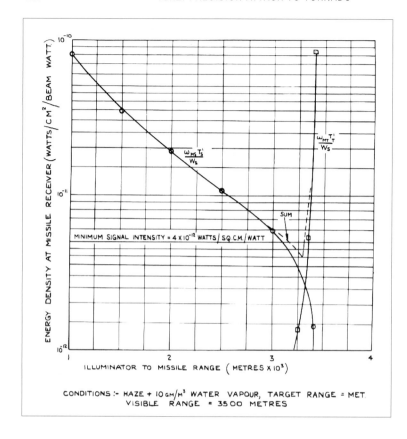

Fig.109. Energy at the missile as a function of range, in light fog out to 1,000 yards.[47]

centre-line. Thus, the basic missile design for delivering a lethal hollow–charge warhead containing 7lb. of high explosive within seven seconds at 4,000 yards range could be constructed in considerable detail.

The overall configuration was largely determined by the equipment, particularly the 3,000lb-thrust rocket motor (to provide the required launch acceleration to Mach 2.5), and by the need for sufficiently low aerodynamic drag, to permit full control-lability for guidance at maximum range, after coasting down from the end of the 2.4 second burn. The motor needed to be 'amidships' to maintain the missile's centre of gravity (CG) position near constant as the propellant was consumed. Behind the crush contact nose cone, the guidance head was located, with its plate-glass pyramidal IR window and its reflecting mirror focused onto the gyroscope-stabilised detector. The warhead was located behind the guidance head, with the autopilot's pitch and yaw accelerometers in between. The location of these instruments at a suitable position to avoid excessive sensitivity to angular accelerations of the missile axis was of some importance. The autopilot's roll, pitch, and yaw gyroscopes shared a space relatively close to the CG with the fuze, which would detonate the warhead on the crush contact closing a circuit on impact with the target.

For ease of stowage with other missile rounds in the confined space within a tracked vehicle, and also for engineering reasons, three folding low-aspect-ratio curved wings were chosen, to be equally spaced around the body circumference.

Initially wrapped around the body, the wings would then spring out into their flight condition by means of torsion coil springs, immediately following the missile leaving its 'zero length' launcher. The launcher located the missile safely until it had travelled a very short distance after rocket motor ignition, when the extended wings would slide back about 0.5in, and protruding feet at the wing roots would be securely locked into position by notches on the missile body.

Since the minimum target range was to be only 50 yards, the missile had to be under full control before it reached enough speed for aerodynamic control surfaces to be effective. The missile also had to overcome initial dispersion just after launch, which could occur due to any misalignment of motor thrust and of the wings to the body, besides dispersions due to any instability at near zero speed and in severe crosswinds. After considering aerodynamic controls which would have led to excessive storage and handling problems, the method of control was therefore chosen to be by jets near the tail of the missile, pulsing out laterally in three planes. The missile was to be roll-stabilised in flight, with the lower wing in the vertical 'plane' as seen in Fig.110. This arrangement would also permit control to be maintained at the end of the trajectory, when in adverse conditions speed may have dropped to 1,000ft/s. The control jets were powered by a cordite charge, in a similar manner to the gyroscopes in Vigilant, and electrical power was to be supplied by a thermal battery.

The searchlight design for creating a powerful pencil beam was critical to the feasibility of the anti-tank weapon system. The source had to radiate IR as efficiently as possible in the detector's far infrared spectrum, between wavelengths of 0.5 to 2.5 microns. Surtees found that the Xenon arc emitted powerfully at wavelengths between 0.3 and 1.5 microns and to a lesser extent in the shorter wavelengths of the visible spectrum. That would have some advantages, with minimal tactical disadvantage (the only disadvantage being that, over the short periods of acquisition and missile flight, this could provide information to an enemy).

The beam width, or divergence of the source and optics combination, needed to be less than 1 milliradian (0.057° or about $1/17$ of 1°). In order to minimise the effects of interfering background radiation entering the missile's IR detector, the beam would by modulated and the missile's detector would effectively filter out most incoming radiation that did not carry this modulation. For simplicity, mechanical rather than electronic modulation was favoured. For concentration of the IR source, the arc gap of only 1mm was available and the voltage required to create the arc was 13V – readily available in vehicles to carry the missile. Such a lamp differs from a gas discharge lamp in that the quartz envelope is largely spherical to withstand high pressures – operating at over 20 atmospheres. The cathode tip where most of the energy is concentrated runs at about 10,000°Kelvin and, by natural radiation cooling, the envelope temperature runs at an acceptable 1,000°K. An arc current of 100A would be required.

To keep the beam width to a minimum, some screening and filtering would be necessary, to limit the radiations emanating from beyond the cathode tip and from the lamp envelope. Electrical modulation would have the advantage of electrode or envelope radiation producing side lobes outside the desired pencil beam, but in view of its simplicity and particularly due to the 6kW of power needed to be available for

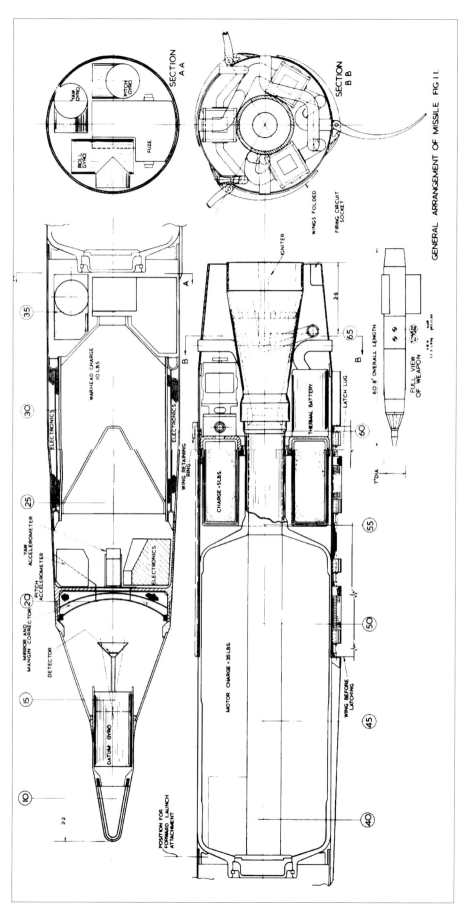

Fig.110. Proposed missile design, shown in two parts for clarity. Complete missile shown below, in miniature.[47]

Right: Fig.111. The Xenon arc lamp.[47]

Below: Fig.112. Typical brightness distribution for a Xenon arc lamp.[47]

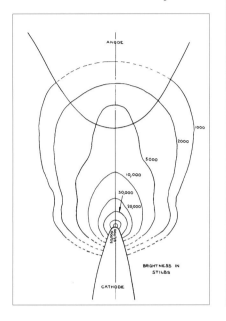

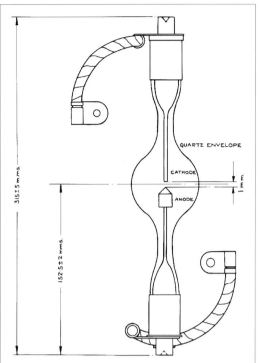

electrical modulation, it was decided to use screening and mechanical modulation at 100Hz. In order to minimise the system bandwidth beyond which radiations would be capable of interfering with guidance, sine wave modulation rather than a simple square wave shutter was chosen. Thus, a simple 'chopper' with sinusoidal teeth would run at 60,000rpm to create the 100Hz sine wave, and this would be driven by an air turbine of the type already developed for Vigilant.

The transmitter optics to throw the pencil beam required extremely precise shape, and the surface required a parabolic mirror of 1m diameter, eliminating the use of light aluminium alloy. The author was involved in investigating the alternative – a much heavier, glass astronomical–quality mirror. With a young engineer, Jim Cole, assisting, the author visited Grubb Parsons Ltd in Newcastle. There it was established that the accuracy specifications Howard Surtees had calculated would be met by their normal astronomical telescope mirrors. Slewing such a heavy mirror to follow tank targets would be more difficult, but sufficient power would exist for the requisite motors to drive the searchlight fast enough.

The transmitter optics design would therefore incorporate this 3m mirror, focusing the Xenon arc light source into a pencil beam with minimised dispersion around the edges.

Fig.113 shows the Xenon arc lamp, with a secondary spherical mirror behind it radiating through an aperture in the main parabolic mirror. The radiated energy is reflected back into the parabolic mirror by a plane secondary mirror in a 'folded' system that assists in shielding unwanted radiations.

The beam projecting is seen as a parallel beam in (A) opposite. Diagram (B) shows how the parabolic beam is formed and, in exaggerated form, shows the dispersion at the edges of the beam due to the effects of minor mirror flaws and due to the basic reflective design.

The circuit to switch on the arc applies a voltage of 5kV depending on the spark gap, via a capacitor. As soon as this voltage is reached and breaks down the spark gap, the capacitor is discharged into a step-up transformer applying a peak voltage pulse of about 20kV on the DC voltage already applied to the lamp. This starts the discharge and the arc then flows. The few seconds it takes for this to take place and the power reduction until it settles down are not sufficient to prevent reception by the missile's IR detector during its early gathering into the beam.

In the process of arriving at the missile configuration and detailed aerodynamic design, many factors were taken into consideration and alternatives investigated. Guidance considerations indicated that 6in missile diameter was required for the IR seeker mirror. This could be increased to 7in over most of the missile's length to accommodate the rocket motor and the warhead without unduly increasing drag. The overall missile length to accommodate all items worked out at just over 5ft (60.8in), employing a light alloy tube body cylinder and weighing 93lb overall. The stiffness required of such a tube was required more for handling, than for flight loads. Some consideration was also given to plastic and to magnesium alloy body tubes, offering low-cost manufacture in large quantities – but heavy investment in tooling.

Initially, a wingless configuration was considered. However relying only on body lift for manoeuvre would have required the missile to adopt higher incidence angles than would be tolerable for seeker performance, as well as large changes in the centre of pressure (CP), making for difficulties in stability and control. A low-aspect-ratio wing design using a magnesium alloy forging or possibly a scurfed magnesium casting was adopted – three wings of 5in length beyond the body cylinder and 12in chord. These were disposed at 120° around the body cylinder, with curvature enabling them to be snugly folded around the body before launch.

The 3,000lb 2.4-second-burn rocket motor with a conventional propellant specific impulse (SI) of 210 was selected, for a 'boost-coast' flight regime. This choice was made after considering a two stage 'boost-sustain' thrust regime and propellants of different SI values. Many such combinations and the resulting trajectory profiles, performance variations and weight effects were studied, before rejecting some lighter weight solutions in favour of the configuration described. This propulsion would enable the missile to accelerate off the launcher at about 30g and reach Mach 2.5, before decelerating to 1,000ft/s after covering 3,500m. Such a short flight regime was tactically important and also greatly reduced the effectiveness of possible enemy jamming or decoys.

Dispersion, as already mentioned, was investigated in Vickers' Pegasus digital computer, with assumptions of motor thrust being misaligned by up to 0.25 milliradian (0.014°), wing misalignment of up to ⅛° from the body axis and crosswinds of up to 30 knots.

The missile structure design allowed for excess lateral manoeuvre up to 10g in any plane and angular yawing accelerations of up to 100 radians per second^2, based on a missile 'weathercock' oscillation frequency of six cycles per second.

Warhead design was not required for this feasibility study, but based on knowledge already gleaned from development of Vigilant. The originally recommended 5in-diameter charge for the hollow charge was increased to 5.5in in order to ensure high lethality, allowing for difficulties of accurate manufacturing in large-scale production. The fuze design was based on the Vigilant fuze, modified for the much shorter minimum range and therefore the arming distance, under conditions of much higher accelerations off the launcher.

Assumed conditions and parameters relating to the missile's performance included a number of factors beyond those already described.

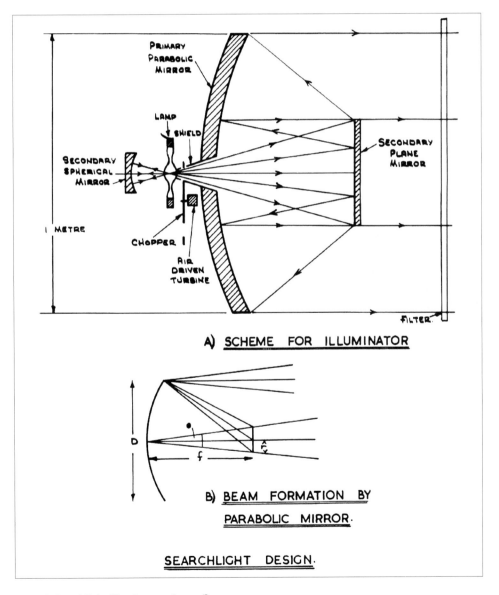

Fig.113. Searchlight illuminator scheme.[47]

With respect to guidance, everything was circumscribed by the amount of power that could be radiated into the pencil beam and the power received by the missile's seeker, compared with extraneous radiations that would confuse the system. Besides direct sunlight, energy due to the tropical sun shining on a 50 per cent-reflecting Earth would inject noise into the system's 20Hz limited bandwidth, roughly equalling the noise generated by the IR detector cell itself. The system would be designed to work on a signal-to-noise ratio of 4, and Surtees calculated that back-scatter signals coming from a relatively short distance ahead of the missile would provide enough energy density at the detector to overcome this noise effect.

Surtees estimated that 600W of the 3kW-rated Xenon arc would be radiated into the beam, producing 20W of energy in the spectrum of interest, between 0.8 and 3 microns. From experience, it was known that large dark objects are just visible against the horizon, when transmittance in the visible spectrum between them and an observer is about 3 per cent. Since the target must be in view before it is engaged and since it is small, camouflaged, and will often appear against dark backgrounds, it is considered that, under battle conditions, the target will not be spotted unless the transmittance in the visible (and therefore in the near IR) is at least 5 per cent between launcher and target. Under good conditions, the transmittance is much higher – per km typically between 79 per cent at 32°F and 40 per cent relative humidity, to 67 per cent at 68°F and 60 per cent relative humidity. However, most of the energy falling upon the tanks is absorbed, and special paints may keep the reflected energy down to 5 per cent, though in battle conditions this could rise to 20 per cent. In considering the terminal phase of semi-active homing, Surtees assumed a more conservative 10 per cent. For the back-scatter energy calculations already mentioned, the power available from the particles in the atmosphere was also based on the same effective radiation from the Xenon arc searchlight into the confines of the pencil beam.

The benefit of using a modulated beam, at the frequency on which the missile guidance system concentrates, could be undermined by other potential obstacles to accuracy. Direct sunlight shining into the guidance receiver has to impinge over very restricted angles (largely shielded by the seeker geometry), to have any likelihood of saturating the detector. The effect of smoke – laid by the enemy for countermeasure purposes – would affect successful acquisition of the target, but would also hamper the enemy and would therefore be of doubtful advantage. Smoke from the rocket exhaust in Vigilant had been minimised by the nature of the propellant and the nozzle and flare design. Such smoke from earlier fired rounds (say in a ripple salvo) was not expected to have significant effect as, at the limits of visibility, it would not really be possible to identify a tank anyway. A further effect studied was that due to background modulation due to boundary layer turbulence of the air around the missile's IR window. This did not appear to affect other supersonic IR-guided missiles, partly due to the thinness of the boundary layer at the nose. However, experiments and wind tunnel tests were proposed and, in the event that effects were found to be detrimental, the modulation frequency of the guidance system could be raised to a level where the turbulence no longer mattered.

Countermeasures were considered firstly by targets being painted so as to absorb 95 per cent of the incident IR energy. However, as already indicated, the missile would nevertheless receive sufficient energy during its terminal approach to the target and, in any case, this would have no effect during the main period of approach to the target using back-scatter beam riding. In order to defeat the missile during its terminal semi-active homing phase, a decoy source modulated at the operating frequency of the weapon would be required. The only effective position for such a source would be some 20ft above the target, depending on its power, and it would have to be mounted on the tank's turret, in order to avoid interfering with its weapons or guns. Furthermore, the source would have to be in permanent position since the missile's short flight time (only two seconds for the last 1,000 yards) is insufficient to allow the source to be positioned. This is hardly possible and would restrict a tank's movements and ability to take cover among trees. If the target can measure the beam's modulation frequency in the short time while it is running for a shot, a modulated jammer decoy would have to be operated on a continual basis. Otherwise, the modulation would have to run up in the very short time from detecting the searchlight beam just before launch and arrival of the missile within seven seconds. To run a high-power source up to the required modulation speed of 100Hz with sufficient energy in such a short time is unlikely to be achievable. Nevertheless, Howard Surtees explored several anti-countermeasures, such as employing phase measurements to modify the detection circuit in a manner that overcomes modulated incoming decoy signals.

Missile control system design was critical, together with the guidance system already discussed. The missile's accuracy would depend entirely on these interacting components of the system, and Surtees' mathematical analysis was meticulous. Pitch and yaw gyroscopes were placed to give stable heading references in those planes. Together with pitch and yaw accelerometers, these instruments would give inputs to the autopilot electronics, which would, in turn, respond to guidance signals.

During the beam riding phase, guidance signals would be very nearly proportional to the missile displacement from the centre of the pencil beam. Since the output sensitivity of the detector is a function of range, Automatic Gain Control (AGC) was employed to make the guidance loop independent of range. Atmospheric conditions affect the relationship with range, so it was important to maintain a suitably high signal-to-noise ratio. While full evaluation of the autopilot design detail was not possible within the funding of the study, the overall system kinematics received a great deal of attention.

The three main criteria for the autopilot design were: adequate speed of response to guidance demands and suitable damping of missile motions throughout the complete range of operating conditions of speed, angle of incidence, range and altitude (between sea level and 10,000ft); minimum complexity; low steady state errors throughout the flight envelope, for accurate guidance.

I have already mentioned the use of cordite gas jet controls near the tail end of the missile, which would have to operate for long enough to ensure control at the end of a long-range trajectory. Several methods of autopilot control were investigated, including various combinations of missile (gyroscope) heading, acceleration measurements (accelerometers) and a well-known electronic technique for stabilising otherwise oscillatory systems, known as 'phase advance'. As its name implies, phase advance involves anticipating the outputs of instrument measurements, in order to dampen movements otherwise prone to overshooting. Of five variants and combinations,

TARGET RANGE (ft)	DEMANDED ACCELERATION (g's)	ANGLE OF INCIDENCE	ERROR (ft)
500	3.86	9°	2.55
1000	2.75	2.2°	1.82
2000	1.8	1.4°	1.2
3000	1.42	<1°	0.94
5000	1.0	<1°	0.66
10000	0.48	<1°	0.32

Fig.114. Beam-riding errors due to target crossing velocity.[47]

TARGET RANGE (ft)	BEAM DIAMETER (ft)	ERROR DUE TO MOVING TARGET (ft)	OPERATOR PLUS TRACKING ERROR (ft)	ERROR DUE TO BACKGROUND NOISE (ft)	TOTAL ERROR (ft) R.M.S.
10000	5.82	0.32	2.45	1.16	2.74
5000	4.41	0.66	1.72	0.88	2.04
3000	3.85	0.94	1.43	0.77	1.88
2000	3.56	1.2	1.29	0.71	1.90
1000	3.28	1.82	1.14	0.66	2.24
500	3.14	2.55	1.07	0.63	2.84

Fig.115. Total beam-riding errors as the missile approaches the terminal homing phase.[47]

Surtees chose accelerometer control (which would demand lateral accelerations via controlled aerodynamic incidences) combined with feedback from rate gyroscopes, which would effectively give heading control when phase advanced.

I have already indicated how gyroscopes were to roll-stabilise the missile, which was necessary due to warhead considerations and to provide a 'gravity bias' that would give the missile a naturally horizontal trajectory in the absence of guidance demands. Roll control was thus specified to keep the missile within 20° of its orientation on the launcher. The estimated effects of misalignments of the wings, rocket motor and the rear-mounted control jets indicated that the resulting small roll rate could be held down by differential use of the jet controls in response to the roll rate gyroscope output, to keep the roll angle below 20° over an eight-second period – leaving one second to spare over the estimated longest flight time.

Control of the roll-stabilised missile in pitch and yaw, and its response to guidance signals determined the beam riding accuracy. Surtees' analyses covered a variety of mathematical relationships leading to suitable electronic control networks capable of dealing with the missile's low aerodynamic stability, variations in CG position, and the stability of both (the missile's) inner control loop and the overall kinematic loop, including the guidance element. The design had to utilise well-chosen operating ranges for the accelerometers and the rate gyroscopes and every mathematical control equation to which the electronics were designed. These required confirmation by simulator studies over all speed and aerodynamic incidence conditions that would occur over the launch, acceleration, coasting and terminal phases of flight. This was further taken to allow for movements in the searchlight's beam axis and the effect of crossing targets.

Beam-riding errors with the system were first evaluated due to crossing target velocity. The cross-country speed of a tank is usually taken as being 15mph but, allowing for the development of hydro-pneumatic suspension for future vehicles, the assumption was doubled to 30mph.

It will be seen that manoeuvre accelerations and incidence angles reduce as the missile exits the gathering phase soon after launch, and the beam-riding errors reduce from the missile being at the periphery of the pencil beam, then at long range, virtually in its centre.

Additional errors would be caused by 'background noise' (reflections from the ground and from sunlight). These were assessed, together with the effects of operator tracking errors with the beam, and then summed to give the total beam-riding errors as they vary with range *from the target*. Allowing also for the contribution of rocket motor thrust to lateral accelerations in the boost phase, the total beam-riding error is seen to reduce from 2.74ft at maximum range from the target, through less than 2ft around mid-range, to a little under 3ft at 500ft from the target. While beam riding, the missile must remain stable in the presence of possible sudden movements by the searchlight.

This puts the missile close to the target centre, before it enters the terminal phase, when the target signal gradually gets to exceed the back-scatter signals and enables the missile to home onto the tank with ever increasing accuracy.

Fig.115 summarises these highly acceptable beam-riding errors, which are quite small in comparison with the size of a hull-down tank.

Stability during the gathering and later beam-riding phases remains important, with the greatest importance being during gathering, since the minimum target range is only 50 yards.

Missile oscillations following launch, when the beam is offset by the assumed normal of 5ft, and up to 13.2ft from the launcher can be seen in Fig.116.

At 5ft separation, the missile is within the confines of beam width by 0.2 seconds and remains there. Even in the worst (an unlikely 13.2ft separation) case, the missile momentarily barely leaves the 3ft-diameter beam confines at 0.9 seconds and then remains close to beam centre. This should ensure hitting a close-range 5ft x 5ft target at 50 yards.

The missile's response to step displacements of the searchlight beam were also investigated in these simulations, over a missile speed range from Mach 1.5 to Mach 2.5. This would represent unlikely sudden movements that might conceivably occur under battle conditions. As Fig.117 shows, the missile would remain essentially within the beam within a very short time after the disturbance occurred.

Even when a 12ft displacement occurs, the simulations show rapid return to beam centre, after a minimal excursion to about 1in outside its periphery at 0.9 seconds during a less-than-one-second period.

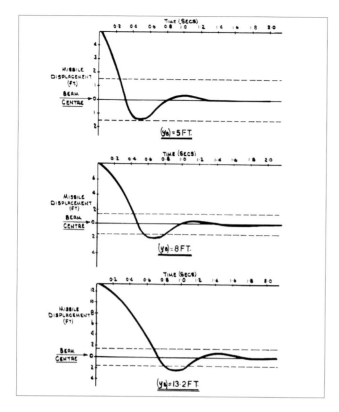

Fig.116. Gathering phase stability at Mach 0.5.[47]

The homing phase follows a gentle transition from guidance signals being predominantly from beam back-scatter, to the strongest signal coming direct from the target reflection. In pure air, this occurs at approximately 400m 'range to go'.

Any tendency for wild ('bang bang') swings in control would be eliminated by the gradual nature by which the beam-riding signals remain, to die away slowly as the ever strengthening tank reflection signal takes over.

As this occurs, the signal-to-noise ratio initially specified to be at least 4 now increases further as the target is approached. When the target image completely fills the field of view, no more proportional guidance commands will be possible but, by this time, the missile is within 40ft of striking the target, with only 40ms of time to go. The miss distance from the centre of (say) a 7ft diameter effective target was not expected to be significant.

It was hoped to obtain a spot of 1.9m diameter on a target at maximum range. It was shown that, if only 10 per cent of the searchlight's power falls within the pencil beam, then the effect of one-third of this power falling onto the ground is not significant. However, as earlier shown, calculations indicate 99 per cent of the power would fall within the pencil beam. Consequently, in the presence of the most adversely placed and shaped obstruction limiting the visible height of the target, the centroid of reflection would not be shifted outside the confines of a target, if its height above the target was 1.8m at maximum range. Under realistic conditions, the error in the apparent centre of a 3ft x 5ft target would be acceptably low.

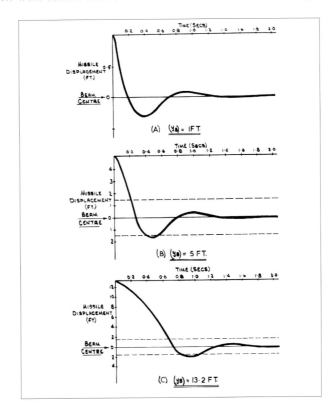

Fig.117. Response of the missile to sudden 'step' displacements of the searchlight beam.[47]

If, say, the narrowness of the beam proved optimistic and a decoy jammer were assumed to be at 20ft from the target, further protection may have been possible to provide the missile with an annular view. The size of the 'blind spot' could then be made to correspond to the likely distance of the decoy from the target. When the decoy or target spot came into the field of view, the hitherto falling guidance signal strength would start to rise, enabling the initiation of a final memory phase of no longer than a quarter of a second.

Achievement of this performance was dependent on a number of important missile components. Besides the already mentioned gyroscopes and the accelerometers of ±15g range and suitable natural frequency and damping, the Jet Control System is worthy of mention.

This was required to create maximum lateral control forces of 70lb in yaw, 50lb in pitch and 20–30lb in roll. These forces had to lag demands by not more than 0.04 seconds, and the system had to operate for seven seconds. Experience with Vigilant actuators led to the choice of a cordite cartridge, whose exhaust through the jet orifices would be metered by nominally 10ms pulses maintaining a constant gas flow from the propellant chamber. By applying pulse duration modulation of the gas effluxes, it was possible to create the forces required for control in each of the missile's axes, as demanded by the control and guidance systems. This led to a simple poppet valve system that switched gas to the appropriate nozzle. These valves were in turn to be controlled by an electromagnetic relay, to apply control torque to the poppets. This reduced the number and complexity of moving parts to a minimum and the feasibility study went into full detail, regarding the design of the charge, the pulse duration modulation (PDM) controls, the electromagnetic relay and the poppet valves. Transistorised electronics were fully detailed for the autopilot, signal amplifiers, summing and sign-reversing amplifiers, as well as the PDM modulator and driver.

The Air Portable Vehicle received equally careful attention, assuming the carriage of the weighty searchlight with its astronomical-quality glass parabolic mirror of 39in diameter and 43in length. This needed placing as high as possible for a free path to the target and was assumed to require splinter-proof armour, including an automatically opening front cover.

Two zero-length launchers were projected for missiles of 5ft length and 8in diameter, weighing 90lb each. It was envisaged that twenty missiles would be stowed and mechanically handled at a high rate for successive firings. An optical sighting aid rigidly fixed to the searchlight structure, as well as a periscopic viewfinder with x10 magnification, were required, and split-field and zoom lens types were considered. Traversing and elevating gear for the searchlight and launchers would be required, as well as 3kW of electrical power for the searchlight's Xenon arc lamp.

For rapid and accurate target tracking, all this equipment would be mounted on a single turret, providing common elevation and azimuth control. The accuracy of beam positioning would have to be within ±3 minutes of arc, to any desired point on the target. Additional fine beam positioning could be provided relative to the main mounting. Smooth power control of the lamp was specified at 5°/s in azimuth and 2°/s in elevation. For fast slewing, these rates needed to be 24°/s and 5°/s, with creep speed minimised, at no greater than 0.02°/s. Allowing a small preset datum angle with respect to the beam axis, the launchers would follow the lamp. In any case, the launcher datum needed to be maintained within ±6 minutes arc from the lamp datum. Azimuth coverage was required over ±30°, besides the coarse alignment possible using the vehicle's tracks. Elevation angles would range from +20° to -10° (downhill).

Missile handling would be designed for eight-second reload time for each launcher and provision would be made to discard any misfired missile without personnel leaving the vehicle. Once again, protection would be provided against small-arms fire and splinters in the launcher-loading areas. Lamp positioning had to be unaffected by rocket motor blast during launch. Similar requirements applied to launching from the Chieftain tank, with its 360° azimuth coverage and necessarily reduced stowage capacity of six missiles.

Although the feasibility study did not extend beyond these design analyses and simulations, Howard Surtees added proposals for a future programme of investigations that would increase the validity of the design prior to any full development programme. In the event, the Ministry of Aviation did not pursue the study any further, concentration remaining on Swingfire (to follow Vigilant – the surprisingly long-lasting 'interim weapon') – and, much later, TRIGAT developments (still in the making in 2004).

16.3 PRELIMINARY STUDY OF A 35-MILE ARTILLERY WEAPON SYSTEM

When the third Government Guided Weapon contract in a row (Red Dean) was cancelled in late 1956, Vickers made a strong attempt to secure work by proposing to develop a highly mobile artillery guided weapon for use with tactical nuclear and conventional high explosive warheads. It would have a maximum range of 35nm and a minimum range of only 6 miles, to be in service by 1965, implying that acceptance trials of a year's duration needing to commence in January 1962. That such a requirement was in the offing was known to Vickers in sufficient detail (from the Outline Military Characteristics) for them to embark on a serious private venture study – following which, the Army issued a formal requirement through ARDE. Since this came after the Vickers study was completed, the study report included a number of caveats before it was issued, indicating that some details may have to be revised, if aspects of the newly issued requirement had not been explicitly met.

The emphasis was on simplicity of operation (requiring the minimum of men and materials), as well as high mobility on roads and cross-country. This was to be achieved with a rapid-fire capability in the case of HE warheads, and highly accurate delivery, with 50 per cent of missiles hitting within 60 yards of target centre. A very important aspect of the Vickers design was to make the system immune to enemy jamming.

The entire weapon system had to accept the implications of nuclear warfare and had to be capable of being manoeuvred into, and operated from, restricted areas such as quarries. With HE warhead armament, reload time was not to exceed fifteen minutes. It had to be assumed that the enemy had full knowledge of any Radar elements used in the system. Ideally, the operating range should be wider – out to 45 miles and down to lower ranges than the 6 miles, if possible. The system would have to comply with the requirements of Phase II air transportation, implying the minimum number and sizes of vehicles. The warhead would have to remain safe and only be armed on approach to the target zone. There would have to be provision for the inhibiting of rogue missiles.

Guidance choices were the first critical factors to consider. Initial considerations were for Radar-based guidance, employing either a tracking Radar or two widely spaced ground-based transmitters. Besides the question of enemy jamming, the first hurdle was the Radar Horizon which, even in featureless flat terrain to 40 miles range, would be at 10,000ft. Any such system would require a form of additional terminal guidance after the missile passes below the Radar Horizon. Considering both possible choices, ground stations would have to be accurately located, and of a performance quality, in terms of accuracy and resolution, inconsistent with rapid mobility. The missile's low Radar echoing area and power required at the ground transmitter would require the complication of a transponder in the missile, while with systems where the ground station supplies (relatively weak) guidance commands, the missile would need a command link receiver whose antenna is always pointed towards the ground station. This is a serious complication involving much development. Consequently, Inertial Navigation guidance was investigated in

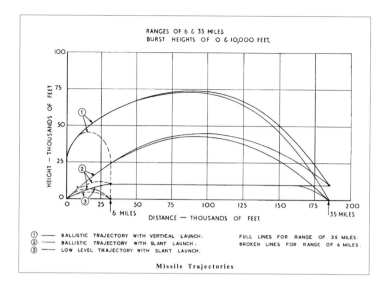

Fig.118. Comparison of possible missile trajectories.[52]

some detail. Totally self-contained within the missile, this would avoid all possibilities of jamming, since no transmissions of any kind are required.

Before embarking on missile design and its control and guidance in any detail, or on the design of the launching method and the vehicle, it was necessary to consider the kinds of trajectory that would best suit the operation. Ballistic trajectories with vertical and slant launch were possibilities, and a low-level trajectory with slant launch was also considered. While, at first sight, a vertically launched missile might appear to require a smaller site, it would also require a separate launch pad and be more easily detectable over perhaps quarter of an hour to half an hour as a missile site. In fact, the site size could well be determined by the need to move the vehicles into position. Furthermore, it could be relatively easily detected following launch by means of its heat signature and due to the longer time it would be at high altitude.

A high ballistic trajectory would require much more missile manoeuvre capability, whose body lift would be inadequate at stratospheric altitudes, leading to the need for wings and large control surfaces. This would, in turn, require a larger transporter and launcher. Furthermore, the large range of pitch angles from the upward vertical to a vertical descent would require a much greater degree of gimbal freedom in any stable platform used as a reference of for inertial guidance. This again would lead to greater dimensions, weight, cost, and lower accuracy. In the event of control failure, the directions and distances a rogue missile could cover would be very large indeed, with trajectories possibly leading far behind as well as towards the target and to each side. Thus, the safety trace for a vertically launched missile would be unacceptably large. From the mobility point of view, and in regard to speed into action, whereas in a slant launch the transporter vehicle could also be the launcher, a vertical launch would most likely require another vehicle to carry a launch pad.

Fig.118 shows how the three main trajectory alternatives compare. Note that No.3 follows a slant launch, but at the longer ranges (beyond 30,000ft), the missile cruises at 10,000ft until it reaches the vicinity of the target.

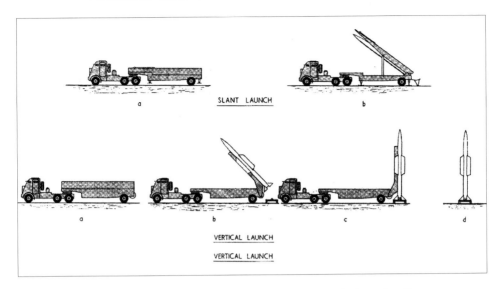

Fig.119.Vehicles and how they are affected by slant and vertical launch alternatives.[52]

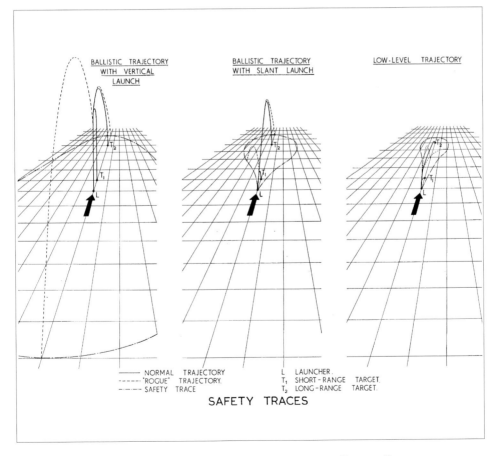

Fig.120. Possible dispersions of a rogue missile cover progressively smaller areas.[52]

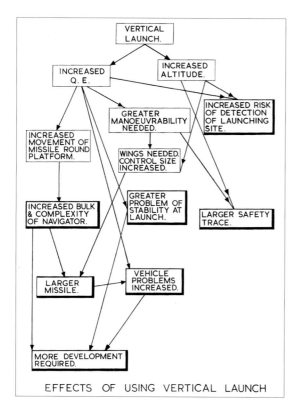

EFFECTS OF USING VERTICAL LAUNCH

Fig.121. Argument for slant launch shown as a logic block diagram.[52]

Compared with a slant launch transporter/launcher, the vertical launch vehicle is larger (taller) and heavier and carries a winged missile with large control surfaces. The launch pad is a separate item, shown on the right (Fig.119).

Ballistic trajectories were compared with low-level trajectories showing the short-range and the long-range extremes. It will be seen that the low-level trajectory results in a smaller safety trace for short and long ranges (Fig.120).

The result of these assessments was to choose a slant launch method, and design proceeded on this basis.

Detailed consideration of the vehicle system was now possible, with Vickers Elswick envisaged for detailed design and supply. After considering the American 'Corporal' weapon system's vehicle complement as well as the Army's new field defence anti-aircraft guided weapon system, both of these were found to be excessively complicated for the simple solutions envisaged for this artillery weapon. Two main schemes were considered: firstly, a lightly armoured independent column, whose task was to fire a limited number of nuclear-headed missiles, and, secondly, a missile battery system designed to cope with a considerable number of rounds, capable of rapid loading and firing. With advice from the Fighting Vehicles Research & Development Establishment of the Ministry of Supply, it was established that using specially designed prime mover vehicles should be avoided – leaving standard tugs or prime movers to draw trailer or semi-trailer type vehicles for special application – and that designs should be based on current in-service vehicles.

For the main Cold War requirement of tactical nuclear strikes, concentration on the vehicle complement and the logistics of handling the missile was as important as the design of the missile itself. The operating group comprised six vehicles, two of which were trailers (Fig.122).

The prime mover shown was a standard 10-ton tractor, modified to carry a 14mm-armoured cab. This would provide blast protection from missile launch and, remaining attached, it could realign rapidly in azimuth (Fig.123).

Note that the blast plate folded down from the rear, with stabilising legs bearing on the ground. Also see the hinged sides that drop down being moved by jacks for firing. The main stabilising feet are adjusted manually. The closed launcher/missile container is armoured, with heat insulation inside. When closed for movement, the launcher rail also forms the top of the launcher container. Loading the nuclear warhead from its separate transporter is achieved as shown in Fig.124.

With the missile/launcher container lowered and its front door lowered, the warhead is loaded and moved back to the missile, with the aid of a travelling gantry whose arms are swung forward from the top of the launcher. An electric winch was to be built into the forward end of the launcher rail, to draw a missile up for reloading from a transporter. The lower portion of the semi-trailer could be used for stowage of an electric power generating system.

The sequence of site operations commences with lining up the inertial navigator (described later). Power for this would be turned on about thirty minutes prior to a launch, allowing the gyroscopes to be run up to speed. On arrival at a suitable site, the launcher would be towed to an approximate bearing for the anticipated target. A 'bearing picket' is then established, with a reference direction and map coordinates. Meanwhile, the warhead loading can proceed as indicated above. Once the target coordinates have been established, the trailer can be swung round by the prime mover onto the approximate bearing, when the assembly is jacked up and levelled. After completing the functional checks and lining procedure, the quadrantal elevation (QE) is selected and the firing sequence initiated from the command car. Once the side doors and rear blast deflector plate are lowered, the launcher can be elevated to the required QE and the missile fired − estimated within twenty-five minutes of arrival on site.

A complete missile battery for delivery of numbers of conventional warhead missiles is depicted in Fig.125. Here the vehicles are thin skinned, and a special missile transporter is based on the same chassis as the launcher. Otherwise, the vehicle system is the same as for nuclear-headed missiles.

Here, a Battery Command Vehicle, with Reconnaissance and Survey Vehicles, leads four missile-launching vehicle groups, including Cargo Handling Vehicles and Warhead Transporters to carry 12,500lb HE warheads. The missiles would be transferred from RASC vehicles to the specialised unit semi-trailers for transport to the launcher site.

Arriving on site, the missile transporter is aligned some 30 yards behind the launcher. The ends of the three missile containers are removed and warheads are attached, using sheer legs for handling. To reload the launcher, the transporter is reversed up behind it, the missile container is slung from the two travelling

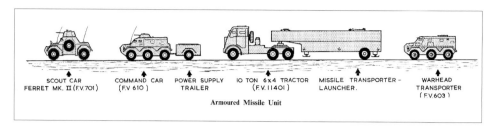

SCOUT CAR
FERRET MK. II (F.V.701) COMMAND CAR
(F.V 610) POWER SUPPLY
TRAILER IO TON 6x4 TRACTOR
(F.V.11401) MISSILE TRANSPORTER –
LAUNCHER. WARHEAD
TRANSPORTER
(F.V.603)

Armoured Missile Unit

Missile Elevated for Launching

Above: Fig.122. Existing vehicle types for the warhead, and towing specialised power supplies and the missile launcher itself.[52]

Left: Fig.123. Detached, the launcher container is opened and the missile elevated for launch.[52]

Below: Fig.124. Scheme for loading the warhead onto the missile, before elevation for firing.[52]

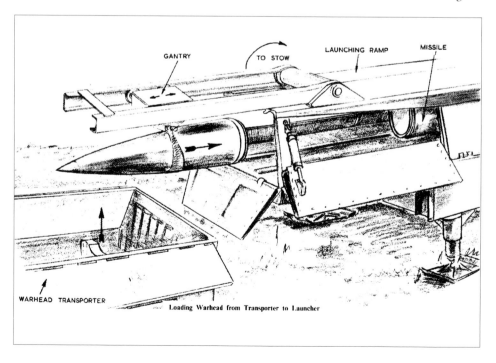

GANTRY   TO STOW   LAUNCHING RAMP   MISSILE

WARHEAD TRANSPORTER   **Loading Warhead from Transporter to Launcher**

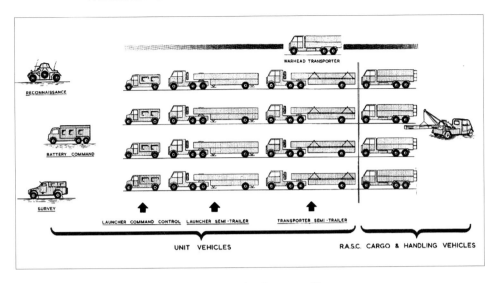

Fig.125. Missile Battery for conventional HE warhead weapons.[52]

gantries on the transporter, and its top flanges are engaged with the grooves in the launcher rail. After the winch cable is attached to the container lid, the winch can pull the container top, which forms the rail proper, from which the missile is already suspended. The remainder of the container (canister) is left on the transporter and the control surfaces are then attached. Once the launcher rail and the missile are fully engaged, the rail is clamped along its length to the main launcher using interconnected cams. The requisite electrical and temperature control connections to the missile can then be made. Once the transporter has been towed back about 30 yards and the missile navigator is aligned on target, the missile is ready for firing.

The battery commander would fire from each launcher in rotation, the whole battery achieving four firings every fifteen minutes, with a fifteen-minute cycle at each launcher.

This detailed design may have required fine-tuning during the development programme but, even in such a preliminary study, the Vickers team put a lot of thought into the solutions. For air transportable applications, the study offered the design of a Self-Propelled Launcher which could be driven inside large transport aircraft holds.

This sketch is self-explanatory and represented another prospective contribution from within the Vickers group of companies.

I have already alluded to some aspects of the missile design. As noted, this was based more on keeping the system as simple and mobile as possible, rather than achieving the very best technological result. Propulsion by the various kinds of air-breathing (jet) engines may have resulted in a lighter missile, but much greater complication. The same applied to liquid fuel rocket motors, which would have had the added complication of carrying corrosive and cooled fluids in the field as well as difficulties of fuelling the missiles on site. Consequently, Vickers chose solid rocket motor

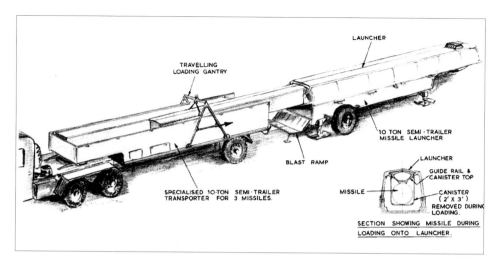

Fig.126. Missile transfer from specialised semi-trailer transporter to the launcher.[52]

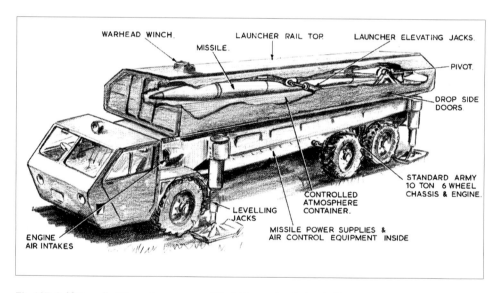

Fig.127. Self-Propelled Launcher on a modified 10-ton 6 x 6 chassis.[52]

propulsion and a wingless pencil-shaped missile body with rear control surfaces. To avoid separating boost rockets, the proposed rocket motor had boost phase and sustain phase charges in tandem, which burned in a cigarette-burning mode. This arrangement was chosen in preference to an optimised combination which would have required the boost thrust to be ten times the sustain thrust, resulting in the need for separate blast pipes and exhausts. By choosing a thrust ratio of only 8, it was possible to provide the required 5g acceleration off the launcher, followed by more than enough thrust to overcome drag during the cruise at 1,500ft/s at 10,000ft altitude. The missile would thus accelerate gently during the cruise, but could be allowed to coast during the last stages of a long-range shot, allowing a reduction in the burning time and of the associated propellant weight.

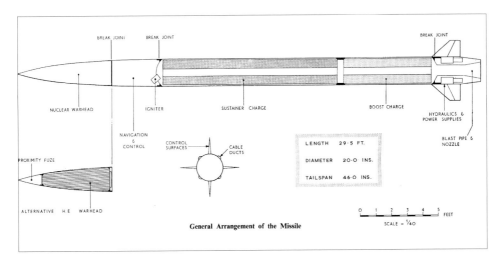

BREAK JOINT   BREAK JOINT   BREAK JOINT

NUCLEAR WARHEAD   IGNITER   SUSTAINER CHARGE   BOOST CHARGE
                                                                                                    HYDRAULICS &
                                                                                                    POWER SUPPLIES
        NAVIGATION
          &   CONTROL
        CONTROL   SURFACES   CABLE
                                            DUCTS   BLAST PIPE &
PROXIMITY FUZE   NOZZLE

                                                            LENGTH   29·5 FT.

                                                            DIAMETER 20·0 INS.

                                                            TAILSPAN 46·0 INS.

ALTERNATIVE H.E WARHEAD

                         General Arrangement of the Missile   0 1 2 3 4 5 FEET
                                                                                      SCALE = ¹⁄₄₀

Fig.128. General arrangement of missile, showing two-stage rocket motor and other components.[52]

The alternative nuclear and HE warheads are shown at the nose of the missile, followed by the navigation and control equipment ahead of the dual thrust rocket motor charges. Fairings interspersed around the body between the control surface locations carry electrical signals from the control system to the rear-mounted hydraulic actuators for the control surfaces, where local power supplies are also located. The missile body is virtually taken up with the rocket motor. Whereas the nuclear warhead detonation was expected to be essentially altitude-dependent requiring an accuracy of 200ft from the navigator, the HE warhead was to be (radio) proximity fuzed for near-ground detonation.

At 2,550lb, well over 50 per cent of the 4,700lb missile all-up weight was the rocket motor propellant. The missile 'all burnt' weight was 2,150lb, including the 500lb warhead, 1,070lb motor empty weight and 230lb for the structure. The total remaining equipment weight, including navigation, control and temperature controls, power supplies, control surface actuators, and cables and pipes, thus accounted for 850lb. This was all included inside a total missile length of 29.5ft and 20in body diameter, the tail span (when assembled before launch) reaching 46in.

The aerodynamic design included an ogival nose of 5.3 fineness ratio and, with its boat tail, the missile's drag at 1,500ft/s at 10,000ft cruising altitude totalled 1,885lb. Lift was provided mainly by the body, augmented by the presence of fairings that carried cables to the aft end control surface actuators. An aerodynamic incidence of 5° was estimated for level flight at the cruising altitude. After the eight-second phase of 23,500lb boost thrust, giving a 5g launch acceleration, the sustain phase rocket motor thrust of 2,950lb continued for a further ninety-two seconds, exceeding the average drag figure and allowing for some further acceleration before burn-out, after which the missile would coast.

The missile required power supplies to provide 3.75hp for its hydraulic load and 1kW of electrical load. The proposed system employed a closed hydraulic system driven by a hydraulic pump. The pump was, in turn, to be driven by a gas turbine, fed with the

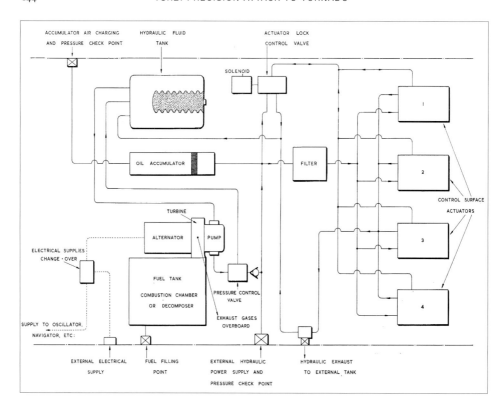

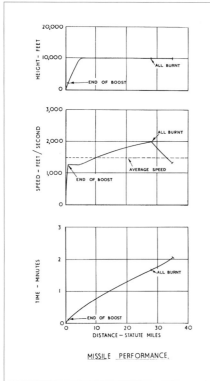

Above: Fig.129. Typical scheme for hydraulic and electrical power supplies.[52]

Left: Fig.130. Missile performance over maximum range showing cruise height regime, speed reaching a maximum of 2,000ft/s, and 35 miles range being reached in a time of two minutes after launch.[52]

Below: Fig. 131. A typical control surface hydraulic actuator working at 3,000psi.[52]

decomposition products of hydrogen peroxide (HTP) or isopropyl nitrate (IPN). The same turbine was expected to power the electrical alternator, possibly via the hydraulic motor. A crystal oscillator was projected for the highly regulated voltage required for the gyroscopes. Alternatives to be studied for the electrical loads included thermal batteries.

Retaining the principle of utilising equipment already proven and available where possible, a range of hydraulic components designed for aircraft and industrial applications working at 3,000psi was anticipated. This would keep the bulk and weight of the control fin actuators down and minimise sealing and other factors affecting reliability.

Note the external electrical supply, fuel filling, hydraulic power and exhaust connections, and also the external air charging, test and pressure check connections to the missile's external support equipment.

Navigation and control were the cardinal factors in the feasibility of such a missile being effective in its stated operational purpose.

As I have already indicated, after considering various Radar-based guidance systems and the missile's attendant vulnerability to enemy jamming, the study concentrated on Inertial Navigation (IN) as a means of achieving the required accuracy and field operation simplicity, with immunity from electronic countermeasures. In 1956, the art of inertial navigation was relatively young and, even in the USA, where missile technology was more widely applied to missiles and rockets, the performance of gyroscopes and accelerometers required by such systems was limiting. The principle of using a truly horizontal stable platform that was unaffected by aircraft or missile manoeuvre depended entirely on the establishment of a true vertical reference and the accuracy of platform-mounted instruments to measure the host missile's movements.

Using Great Circle navigation, in a similar manner to normal terrestrial navigation, for the most direct route to a target, a system was chosen using northerly and easterly Earth reference axes and the true vertical. Such a system requires the missile to compute its positions relative to a target corrected for the effect of a rotating Earth, aided by precessing the axes in sympathy with the Earth's rotation rate at the latitude of the missile. The azimuth channel being essentially 'null seeking' in guiding the missile towards the target, it can be separated from the remainder of the system for simplicity, and to minimise interference of cross-coupling effects in the computer (in those days, still analogue). This feature was considered to justify the additional pre-launch computation to convert target information into the Great Circle coordinates and the use of non-constant precession and correction terms.

Establishing and maintaining a true vertical in a moving body is mostly achieved by the Schuler Pendulum principle and, while this method was not mentioned in this study, it was used in American military aircraft that were in service in the early 1960s, and possibly before.

Dr Schuler's Pendulum depends on the assumption that if one could construct a pendulum of a length equal to the radius of the Earth and suspend it from a manoeuvring missile, it would always point directly towards the centre of the Earth – and therefore remain vertical. This vertical would remain correct, regardless of the missile's movements about the stable platform. Like any clock's pendulum, a pendulum of such a great length would have a natural period of oscillations and this period works out to be eighty-four minutes. Engineers building inertial platforms

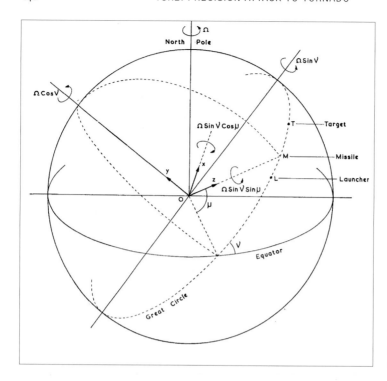

Fig.132. Great Circle
navigation and the
axes for navigation.[52]

found that they could synthesise the eighty-four-minute period without any actual
pendulum, by using servos to correct any errors in the horizontal and making the
natural oscillation period of the servomechanism equal to eighty-four minutes.

In this 'closed loop' levelling system, the key instruments are firstly accelerometers,
measuring any tilt away from the horizontal (and therefore the desired vertical
reference). Secondly, gyroscopes mounted on the platform can then be used to
maintain the platform's heading axis and its roll axis along desired spatial axes. The
same accelerometers mounted along these axes are then used to measure the missile's
accelerations in each axis, for integration into velocity and further integration into
distances travelled along the axes. If these measurements of distance travelled are
sufficiently accurate, the missile can be controlled to fly to the target.

This study also assumes the use of doubly integrated accelerometer outputs, to
give velocity and distance travelled along the three axes. However the proposed
platform appears to rely on the measurement of angular movements by rate-
integrating gyroscopes, to provide the correcting servo feedback for maintaining the
platform's vertical reference. Such an 'open loop' system may be more susceptible to
instrument errors such as gyro drift. However, the mathematical analyses appear to
show a sufficiently high accuracy of navigation to the target.

This gyro was a centrepiece of the proposed platform's stabilisation. Angular
movements of the missile caused the gyroscope gimbal to precess, and this was resisted
by the drag in a viscous fluid around the sealed gimbal assembly and by a torque
motor. The amount of movement against this resistance was a measure of the amount
of missile movement about the gyro's axis and was measured by an electrical pick-off.

On a stable inertial platform three such gyros are required, one for each navigation axis (while later gyroscopes were supported on air bearings or magnetically levitated bearings for minimising friction and the resulting drift, gyros of this time used high precision mechanical bearings with higher drift rates; later still, laser gyros avoided the use of mechanical elements altogether and achieved much lower drift rates).

Thus, the Stabilised Platform was designed with three HIG 6 gyros, with accelerometers accurately aligned to the three gyro axes, for their outputs to be correctly integrated to give velocity and physical missile travel along the navigation axes already described.

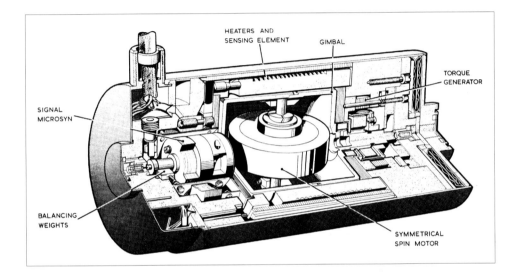

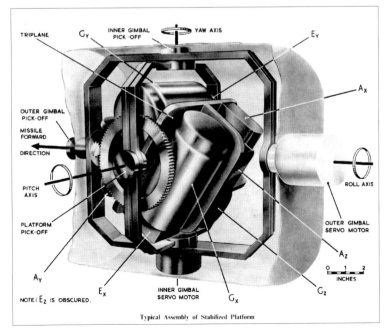

Above: Fig.133. Honeywell HIG 6 1°-of-freedom rate-integrating gyroscope.

Right: Fig.134. Assembly of a stabilised platform, showing main axes, gyroscopes and accelerometers.[52]

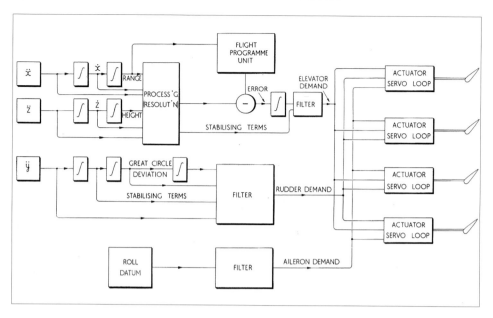

Fig.135. A typical navigation and control system block diagram.[52]

The illustration in Fig.134 of a mock-up designed for this project employs the three Honeywell gyroscopes described and three Sperry feedback-type accelerometers. The latter use electrical torque motors to keep a delicately spring-restrained moving mass centralised, the torque motor current to maintain this condition being proportional to the acceleration to be measured. The platform axes are mutually orthogonal and the gimbals and mountings form a triplane of aluminium alloy, with precisely machined surfaces for the alignment of gyroscope and the respective accelerometer axes. By choosing the slant launch and low trajectory indicated, the platform does not have to be 'fully aerobatic', the angular travels being limited to provide movement in pitch between +45° and -60°. In yaw (azimuth), the angular travel is only required to be ±25°, and in roll, ±20°.

The pitch axis was therefore chosen as the inner rotation, so that the swept volume of the assembly was minimised. The gimbal providing freedom in yaw was next and the outermost gimbal was pivoted to the missile to give freedom in roll. The whole assembly was for mounting between two lateral missile bulkheads. In contrast to today's highly miniaturised gyroscopes and accelerometers, this platform had to carry gyros of 5.9in length and weighing 4.6lb each. Their drift rates under laboratory conditions were 0.1° per hour. The Sperry accelerometers were also large by modern standards (3–4in long), weighing 19 grams including a preamplifier, and with a measurement threshold of 1/10,000g. This platform and gimbal system's overall weight was 56lb. Adding the navigator enclosure and temperature controller, computer and servo amplifiers, the flight programme unit, etc., the total weight of the navigation equipment amounted to 150lb.

The Control and Navigation System took its three axial inputs from the stabilised platform accelerometers, as seen in the block schematic diagram above (Fig.135).

Blocks for each of the three stabilised navigation axis channels are shown with successive integration blocks, producing velocities and then distances in the range, height, and Great Circle deviation (azimuth error) directions. The Processing Resolution Unit compares the missile range and height thus represented with inputs from a Flight Programme Unit to produce error signals. Similarly, in the azimuth axis, the computed Great Circle deviation (further integrated) combines with acceleration and velocity terms in a filter that adds to similarly filtered outputs from the other two axes to provide rudder and elevator control surface movement demands. The roll datum adds to these demands to give aileron-like differential demands to the rudders and elevators for maintaining roll stabilisation, assisted by a phase advance signal to provide damping of roll oscillations. Finally, the four demand outputs control actuators move the control surfaces for altering the missile's flight path.

Prior to launch, the navigation system, including the stabilised platform, has to be aligned with the target and, while further study of alternative methods remained to be made, the study illustrated one possible procedure. This required suitably adequate maps or the conduct of a survey before bringing the missile to the launch site. The process consisted of establishing the vertical datum and the bearing and range of the target, with the stable platform being aligned to the requisite launching attitude (QE). Details of the trajectory to be flown were then to be entered into the Flight Programme Unit.

A bearing picket, consisting of two men with optical instruments, would next be established within sight of, but some distance away from, the launcher, in such a position that a view of suitable prominent objects could be obtained, for triangulation purposes. Knowing the coordinates of the prominent objects, a reference direction (e.g. grid north) would be established. The bearing picket would then determine the coordinates of the missile by triangulating on two widely spaced marks on the launcher, thus establishing the launcher starting position for navigation. Since the angles are measured in a horizontal plane, the bearing picket did not need to be at the same height as the launcher, which could be down inside a quarry, for example, or similarly hidden from reconnaissance viewing. This process does not require great accuracy in the position measurement, compared with the required accuracy at the target. The most favourable system of axes for alignment was determined to have one vertical and others horizontal, along, and at right angles to, the line from launcher to target. The platform would then be aligned to the true vertical and rotated about this axis, so that the longitudinal axis was parallel to the instrument at the bearing picket. The platform would be continually levelled during the final phase of the lining up, to adjust for any subsidence of the launcher. At this point, the study recognises the possibility of using the accelerometers to sense any error from the true vertical and anticipates the possibility of servos driving the platform back to the level, by zeroing out the accelerometer outputs – approaching the Schuler Pendulum principle.

The complexity of the above procedure is illustrated overleaf.

Shortly before missile launch, the stable platform would be decaged allowing it freedom to move relative to the missile structure and function as the heart of the Navigation System. It was estimated that the time taken from arrival at the launching site to firing was twenty minutes, possibly adding five minutes for any

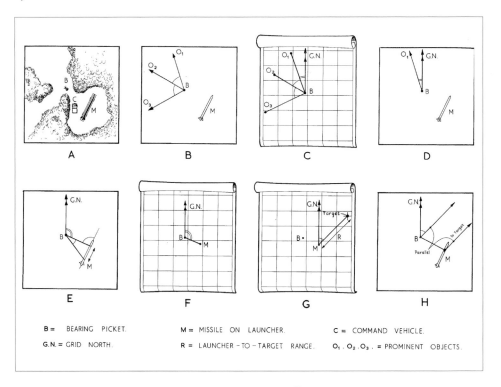

B = BEARING PICKET.   M = MISSILE ON LAUNCHER.   C = COMMAND VEHICLE.

G.N. = GRID NORTH.   R = LAUNCHER – TO – TARGET RANGE.   O₁ . O₂ .O₃ . = PROMINENT OBJECTS.

Fig.136. Diagrammatic sequence of the lining-up procedure.[52]

physical realignment of the launcher heading if target coordinates were greatly off this direction. The time between decaging and firing would be kept down to about twenty seconds, to maintain weapon accuracy.

Oh, for GPS! Had Global Positioning been available at the time, much of this complexity would have been eliminated, and timesaving possible.

Accuracy estimates allowed for errors in range due to map errors, initial platform tilt, gyroscope drift, accelerometer errors, integration errors and other navigation errors. Similar errors were considered in the azimuth direction. Height errors were also considered (with the possibility of reducing this with the aid of a barometric altimeter in the missile).

For the maximum range of 35 miles, the table in Fig.138 separately shows the root mean square (RMS) errors in range, line, and height (ft), for each main error source.

Combined into overall errors at the target, these result in Critical Error Probabilities at the 35 miles-range target shown in Fig.137.

Thus, the final assessment from this feasibility study indicates total errors to be within 180ft at 35 miles target range. At shorter ranges, such as 20 miles, the total error with 50 per cent probability reduces to about 75ft. Clearly, for nuclear delivery, these errors would be devastatingly accurate, and even for conventional HE delivery with 500lb warheads it would not take many missile launches to destroy a military target. However, no evidence of the Army's response comes to hand in the Public Record. A good try for the times!

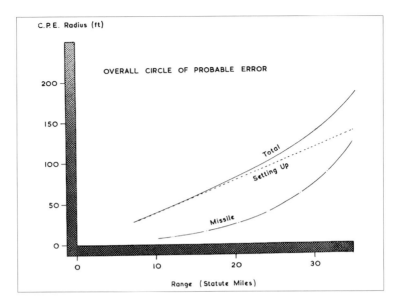

Fig.137. Total probable errors varying with target range.[52]

Source of Error	Error		Range	Line	Height
Setting Up Error External to Missile	Map Error		185	185	
	Bearing Error			81	
Missile Error	**Instrument Errors**	Bearing Error		27	
		Initial Tilt	19	19	14
		Gyro Drift	121	121	
		Accelerometer	19	19	19
	Computation Errors	Integration	12	1·5	10
		Gravity			188
		Precession		5	
		Accelerometer Correction		5	

Fig.138. Table of errors due to main causes.[52]

16.4 AIR-TO-AIR WEAPON AGAINST MACH 3 BOMBER AT 80,000FT

Well-known for his design of the Mixed Power Rocket Interceptor aircraft and the Black Knight ballistic rocket at Saunders-Roe, Maurice Brennan had moved to Weybridge for Vickers Special Aircraft Projects. Ironically, this was soon after my earlier boss, Paul Leyton, fell out with him and unnecessarily left Saunders-Roe, whence he had moved from Vickers! Brennan worked alongside Alan Clifton, who had moved from his chief designer role at Supermarine. Also a legendary figure in the aircraft industry, and now in his sixties, Alan had a significant part in designing the Spitfire under R.J. Mitchell, as well as the latest Supermarine jets. In 1959–60, these two designers were engaged on an advanced project to meet the Joint Naval/Air Staff Target OR 346, for a variable geometry, supersonic, aircraft-carrier-based fighter. Another engineer of great experience working with them, 'Spud' Boorer, had worked with George Edwards in his earlier designer years at Vickers, and then for years as chief designer for Barnes Wallis.

Combat Air Patrol (CAP) at 36,000ft at Mach 0.7 for endurance was the preferred readiness and attack profile. Alternatively, aircraft could intercept by using an 'off the deck' launch trajectory.

Brennan met with Howard Surtees one day and asked 'How large should we make this airplane's weapons bay?', to which Howard replied cryptically: 'That depends on what you want to put in it.' Maurice shot back 'Well, you're the weapons designer, you tell me!'

That was when Howard called me into his office to offer an extremely challenging work proposition. He wanted me to start from 'square one' (the threat to be met by the proposed fighter) and to work from this through to a weapon system design that would give the fighter a high kill probability – one that would also fit within a weapons bay that suited the fighter's design specification. Apart from obtaining advice and help from colleagues like Dab in the next office, the various Government research establishments, and Howard himself, I was to work virtually on my own.

I had made the metamorphosis from horny-handed and high-jet-flying trials engineer (with Blue Boar and Red Dean) to group leader for Development Testing and Environmental Testing (mainly of Vigilant), and finally to project engineer. In 1960, my Aeronautical Engineering degree was ten years past and, although not totally forgotten, despite designing the trials model Red Dean ground-launch booster rocket early on, and lots of aerodynamics trials analysis, my mathematics and aerodynamics were definitely somewhat rusty. Yet, this would be a project I could fairly claim to be largely my own.

Spud Boorer sat down with me first and explained 'The Threat' against which the new fighter and my weapon system were to operate. The Soviet Air Force was highly competitive with the best of American and British aircraft and also, in view of already well advanced ground-to-air missiles, the Royal Navy and the RAF perceived the danger of a Russian bomber attacking a British Naval Task Force with a long-range 'stand-off' weapon. Furthermore, the bomber was assumed to be flying at Mach 3 and at a great height – 80,000ft. The stand-off weapon launched by this bomber was

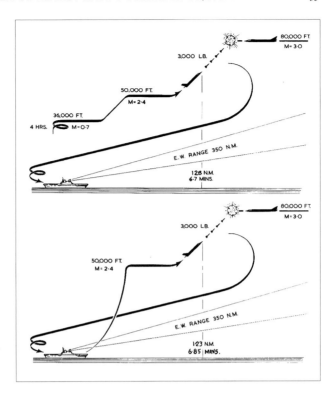

Fig.139. High-altitude and low-altitude interceptor roles for the Vickers variable geometry fighter to meet Naval/Air Staff target OR 346.[48]

expected to have a greater range than the range of ship-to-air guided missiles – up to 150nm. It would therefore be capable of destroying the aircraft carriers of a Naval Task Force without approaching closer than this distance, after flying 600nm of its 1,500nm radius of action at the prodigious speed of Mach 3, at 80,000ft. It was expected to be capable of up to 2g evasive manoeuvres at this altitude and also of zooming up to 105,000ft to evade air-to-air attack.[48]

A tall order, particularly since the fighter being designed to meet this threat after launching from the deck of an aircraft carrier would be speed-limited to Mach 2.5 and to the much lower altitude of 60,000ft. The fighter would also have low-level strike roles, so its variable geometry wings design and performance resulted in a number of compromises to accommodate these roles, including short-distance take-off and landing.

In designing a guided weapon system that overcame the considerable performance advantage of bomber over fighter, everything would firstly depend on how far out the bomber might be detected, as it approached the fleet. This would depend on the performance of ship-borne Radars that might be in service ten to fifteen years ahead. Howard Surtees started me off by accompanying me on a visit to the Admiralty Surface Weapons Establishment (ASWE) near Portsmouth. In great secrecy, ASWE was developing large Radars for future carriers, with power for long-range detection and with accurate height-finding capability. These Radar projects' antennae resembled large cylindrical rooms big enough to climb inside and employed the latest ideas for concentrating power into the narrowest possible pencil

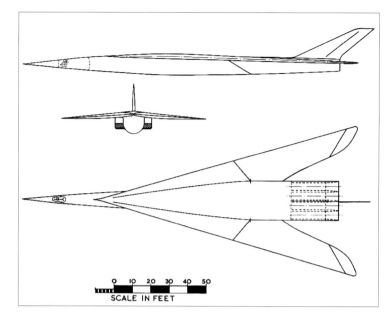

Left: Fig.140. The assumed Soviet Mach 3 (at 80,000ft), stand-off-weapon-carrying bomber threat.[48]

Below: Fig.141. Artist's impression of the Vickers carrier-based variable geometry fighter with Mach 2.5 capability at 60,000ft.[48]

and fan-shaped beams. With the target's Radar-echoing area assumed to be 5–10sq. m, in the absence of jamming, these search Radars would be expected to detect our target at a range of 350nm.

The further the detection range, the more time the fighter would have to intercept. However, even at 80,000ft, the Radar Horizon would limit detection to a range of just over 340nm. If the bomber approached at a lower altitude, the Radar Horizon would prevent detection until it was closer to the fleet, although, at these lower altitudes, the bomber's speed would also be lower. Detection had to occur before the bomber could launch its stand-off weapon – which was assumed to use inertial guidance and would therefore not need to radiate detectable transmissions.

If the stand-off weapon had a range of 150nm, the Radar Horizon would prevent detection before the weapon was launched (assuming there was no additional Radar cover from high-flying reconnaissance aircraft). The assumption of stand-off weapon range nearer to 100nm meant that detection and interception out beyond this range might be possible, preventing the launching of a stand-off weapon.

The bomber was also assumed to have a low-level attack capability, its sea-level speed being Mach 1 at most, where it would have a manoeuvre capability of 6g. The graphs of my calculations in Fig.142 shows that a 100nm stand-off weapon launch could only be prevented if detected at over 10,000ft.

This began to set the initial conditions for considering how the fighter should be deployed and the necessary performance of the air-to-air missile. One thing was abundantly clear: I would have to come up with a missile design capable of jumping up to 80,000ft from the fighter's cruise ceiling of 60,000ft, and one sufficiently manoeuvrable at this height for accurate guidance. In the event of the Soviet target zooming even higher, our missile would need to manoeuvre in the rarefied stratosphere of up to 105,000ft. Yes, quite literally a tall order!

Assuming sufficiently early detection, I had to ask what would be the most effective and cost-efficient flight regime off the aircraft carrier to ensure reaching a target soon enough for a successful interception. To answer this question, I embarked on a series of flight pattern and trajectory calculations considering interception by leaping off the carrier on detection of a target, to flying fighters on Continuous Air Patrol (CAP) at various radial distances around the fleet.

'Off the deck' interception would appear to require the least number of fighters, if interception could be achieved in time. However, even with the carrier sailing into wind, besides the time to arrive at altitude, a take-off delay of at least three minutes would be incurred. This compares with one minute to get onto an interception course from CAP. Assuming a 100nm stand-off range as a likely threat, this would be the very minimum range at which a kill would be required.

The next possibility, requiring a further raft of calculations, was a fighter patrolling overhead the fleet. We would assume Airborne Interception Radar (AI) detection range of 100nm and a missile launch distance of 20nm from the target, evading either by turning horizontally at 2g or by a zoom climb.

The fighter is directed by ship's Radar towards the approaching target as soon as it is detected. Possible interception points are shown for the target turning through 30°, 45°, or with a zoom climb after turning 59°. If the target turns through more than 65°, there is no interception course possible, unless the fighter turns back in an S-turn, as shown in Fig.143, and the target also turns back to attack the fleet. In each case, interception occurs when the stand-off bomb is beyond 100nm. However, the maximum kill range from the fleet at 80,000ft would be between 140nm and 150nm.

Considering a single attack from any direction, alternative CAP regimes were studied, to compare the effectiveness of patrolling with four aircraft at a radius from the fleet of 200nm, and three fighters patrolling at a radius of 100nm and 200nm. These regimes appeared to have the advantage of starting the interception from further out towards the stand-off weapon's own maximum range. By the placing

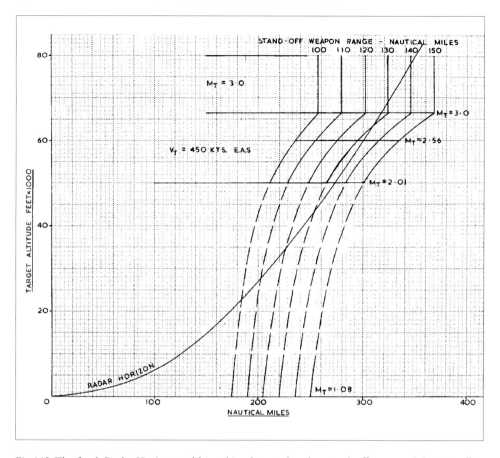

Fig.142. The fleet's Radar Horizon and how this relates to bomber stand-off range and detection.[48]

of, say, four fighters around the CAP circle, with the possibility of being up to 45° ahead of the target's flight path toward the fleet, the nearest interception would still be at 150nm.

Assuming a target capable of 2g evasive manoeuvre at 80,000ft, applying the same aerodynamic lift it could zoom with an initial 1.24g in the vertical plane and, climbing on a quasi-ballistic trajectory, it could reach its probable ceiling of 105,000ft in ninety-seven seconds. It would still be flying at Mach 2.79 before it would start its descent (engine and stability considerations were assumed to prevent it from zooming any higher). Such a zoom manoeuvre would cover a distance of over 80 miles, before arriving back at 80,000ft. The target would have been at over 90,000ft for ninety-two seconds, covering 52 miles over this altitude. Although it would have to execute this manoeuvre flying in a straight line towards the fleet, the effect of its high altitude would be to increase the missile's wing area requirement by a factor of 3.9, for a given missile weight and manoeuvre capability.

Now, the 'no collision course' target manoeuvre is after turning through only 18°, and the zoom climb is assumed to commence at 20°, just after turning through this angle.

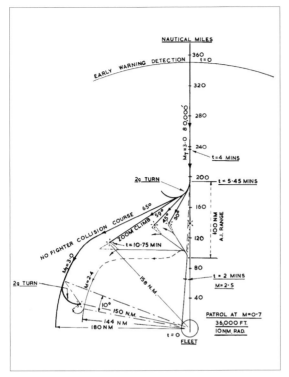

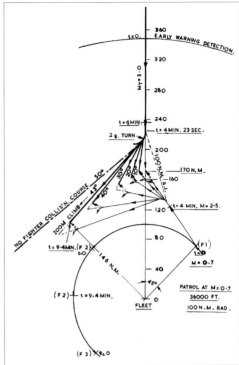

Above left: Fig.143. Interception pattern, single fighter patrolling very closely over the fleet.[48]

Above right: Fig.144. Interception pattern with four fighters patrolling around a CAP radius of 100nm from the fleet.[48] Here, the 'no collision course' target manoeuvre is after turning through 50°.

Right: Fig.145. Interception pattern with four fighters patrolling around a CAP radius of 200nm from the fleet.[48]

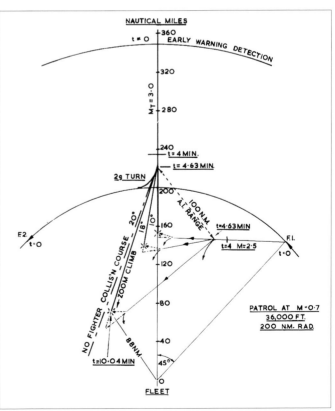

Clearly, tactics could be varied, depending on the number of fighters available to place on CAP. The diagrams show how the interception process and the resulting range depends on when the target starts its horizontal or zoom manoeuvre in relation to the fighter's initial position on the CAP circle and its own interception manoeuvre towards the evading target. The assumed 100nm range of AI detection and the assumed 20nm missile range affect the picture fundamentally. I assumed that the target would start its evasive action as soon as it detects that it has been illuminated by the fighter's AI Radar.

In the case of the 200nm radius CAP, with the target turning through 20° to avoid an interception course, unless the target zoom-climbs and the fighter then turns towards it, a hit at 88nm may be possible, assuming the missile is designed to operate successfully at these excessive altitudes. Depending on the stand-off weapon's ability to also operate at such a great height, this could be too late to prevent it from being launched. However, notwithstanding interception ranges varying between 170nm and, in the zoom-climb case, 146nm from a 100nm CAP, a closer-radius-over-the-fleet CAP indicated greater flexibility against varying target evasive actions. This close-to-the-fleet CAP may therefore be considered nearer to an optimum, still offering interceptions beyond the stand-off weapon's assumed 100nm range, at between 140nm and 150nm.

In working towards the criteria for designing the missile, an interception technique became the next thing to define. As I just indicated, we established an initial preference for 'directly overhead the fleet' CAP, flying at 36,000ft and Mach 0.7. Following early warning, identification, and the decision to intercept a particular target, the fighter would have to dive to accelerate, and then climb in an optimum manoeuvre until limiting speed Mach 2.5 was reached at 60,000ft. This manoeuvre would take four minutes, covering a distance of 65nm. The aircraft would continue in the direction of the expected interception under ship's radar control at Mach 2.5 at 60,000ft until AI contact was made, when the interception course computer commenced to direct the pilot (or autopilot) on to a collision course.

For targets at altitudes above 60,000ft, the fighter will remain at 60,000ft during most of the interception course, so as to make use of the increased turning capability at this relatively lower altitude. Where excessive manoeuvre was required, it may have become necessary to reduce height to 50,000ft, with a 4 per cent speed reduction penalty. The turn rates in the previous figures have radii of 8.1nm, corresponding to 3.65g. However, the missile would then be required to 'jump up' some 30,000–40,000ft, requiring the fighter to execute a computed manoeuvre in the vertical plane just before launching its missile(s), in order to reduce the vertical angle through which the missile would have to turn. Such a climb would best be commenced from 50,000ft, where more lift is available. We estimated that a climb angle of 20° could be achieved over a distance of 11.5nm, resulting in a launch at 65,000ft. This would leave the missile to climb some 40,000ft if it were to climb against a zooming target. While this need would result in an increased missile weight, missile launching errors could be considerably eased by commencing the trajectory at the lower altitude.

When intercepting low altitude targets, it would be necessary for the fighter to dive (while reducing speed) after AI lock-on. This would be at the maximum descent rate, as late as possible in the interception phase in order to make the best use of the higher speed possible at 60,000ft.

Enemy Radar jamming was not investigated in great detail. However, it was evident that the range at which target range information could be obtained could be greatly reduced by the expected carcinatron jamming from the target. Even with the future ship-borne Radars anticipated in 1970, detection range was expected to be reduced by 40 per cent, reducing the 350nm range to 140nm. Nevertheless, here the Radar Horizon was also in the fighter's favour. If a jammer appeared, it could not be less than 350nm away (unless it was flying at a height greater than 80,000ft). Then, by triangulation of azimuth Radar information from the Radars of two ships on an adequate baseline, target information could be obtained with sufficient accuracy for the direction of an interceptor to within AI range.

The main effect of enemy ECM on the AI Radar was to deny range information, which is necessary for determining the missile launch instant. This was expected to necessitate the computation of launch range from the initial conditions and from the subsequently obtained relative target motion. This motion could be defined from the angular information obtained from the Radar, during the fighter's proportional navigation interception. The accuracy of this would very much depend on the accuracy with which the ship-borne Radar could obtain the initial conditions of target track and speed, and on how up-to-date this information was when fed into the interception course computer. Ideally, therefore, the missile launch range should preferably not be a critical quantity, but should have as wide a tolerance as possible. In addition, a less jamming-susceptible Q-Band Radar, acting with the AI Radar in the fighter, was considered a worthwhile development for obtaining target range. Furthermore, that would add the complication of another band of operations required of the ECM jammer. It should enable accurate range information to be obtained at around the launching range.

The tactical situation could be summarised by saying that, for this project's ten-year timescale, projected ship-borne Radars, and additional airborne early warning Radars to cover the low-flying targets, would provide sufficiently early warning to enable interceptions at target ranges in excess of 100nm and at altitudes between sea level and over 100,000ft. Fighters should be on CAP at a small radius from the fleet, or be ready for launching 'off the deck' as the tactical situation demanded. The foregoing studies over several months required enough aircraft interception and missile trajectory calculations to keep my slide rule thoroughly warm.

Missile design requirements were now beginning to emerge. The above interception diagrams already showed that the missile would have to engage targets at up to 105,000ft and that the direction of attack would vary from directly head-on through beam-on, to some 30° behind the target beam. To achieve the requisite manoeuvres at such high altitudes, the missile would need a large wing area and its weight would have to be severely limited. To accommodate large wings inside the fighter's weapons bay, classical missile 'Cartesian' wings in the pitch and yaw planes would take up much too much space, and folding wings were undesirable due to their complication and difficulties of maintaining sufficient stiffness.

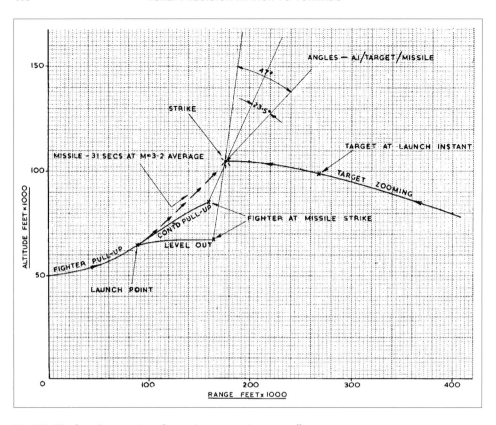

Fig.146. Head-on interception plan against a zooming target.[48]

Consequently, a 'twist and steer' operation similar to conventional aircraft would be preferred and I took a trip to Filton, where Bristol Aircraft's chief engineer, David Farrar, had developed the successful Bloodhound ground-to-air missile, employing 'twist and steer' control, for the RAF. David looked at our study as far as it had gone and, considering the arguments and the limitations, he agreed with my proposition. We went for 'twist and steer'.

The number of stowed missiles with vertically parallel wings in a weapons bay and missile body depth, were roughly interchangeable. The weapons bay width suggested the possibility of four missiles of 8in depth. While stowed for carriage before firing, this still required any control fins to be foldable parallel to the wings. These considerations led to limiting the missile weight to 600–700lb, to ensure that it could achieve its required manoeuvre up to 5g or 6g at 105,000ft. Handling and storage aboard ship could be feasible, for missiles up to a weight of 1,500lb.

Now I had to consider the type of guidance the missile should employ. Attenuation difficulties with infrared in cloud tended to rule that out, so our proposal was for Radar guidance. The fighter's AI Radar could be utilised as a lamp set for a semi-active homing system and calculations showed that, with a 6in-diameter Radar antenna dish in the missile, with current techniques it could achieve a lock-on range of 30nm against a 10sq.m echoing area target. The maximum possible protection against enemy noise jamming would be required, with optimised reduction of missile response to target noise. We also considered the possibility of a terminal homing phase employing infrared at the high altitudes where cloud would not be a factor.

The missile's flight plan now called for a range of 30nm with a flight duration of about thirty seconds against head-on targets, with a missile speed increment over the fighter of Mach 0.5. This led to a boost sustain propulsion rocket thrust programme giving a propulsion range of 15nm with allowance for the missile to climb from the fighter's height limit to the target's maximum altitude. Since most of the missile's drag at extreme altitudes would be due to the resolved part of lift at the high incidence required to achieve manoeuvre, at intermediate altitudes requiring lower aerodynamic incidences, a greater propulsion range would be achieved. At these altitudes, a greater useful missile range could be achieved, by ensuring that missile power supplies lasted long enough to make use of a coasting phase after rocket motor 'all burnt'. This property would also allow for the increased missile ranges required for beam and near-tail attack that would result from heavy target manoeuvre at and below 80,000ft. At low altitude the drag, even at the lower cruising speed, would be much more significant and, in order to avoid excessive deceleration at sea level, the sustainer thrust would need to be higher than for extreme altitude. This would require a balanced choice of rocket thrust regime, to allow for the differing extreme conditions.

This interception plan illustrates how the missile would have to overcome the fighter's inferior performance compared with that of the target, by means of its 'jump up' capability. The nominal Mach 0.5 speed increment would ensure that the fighter could evade target wreckage – or a target that had not been destroyed – and that the Radar reflection angle from fighter-target-missile would not exceed 60° during an evading target manoeuvre.

The highest target altitude expected for purely horizontal interception was 50,000ft, where the target speed would be Mach 2 and its minimum turn radius 8nm. Here, the fighter speed would be Mach 2.4 with a similar minimum turn radius. For head-on attack under these conditions, the launching range would have to decrease, since the target can turn through 70° in thirty seconds, thereby greatly reducing its approach towards the missile. Even more study and slide rule 'bashing' would be required to confirm the optimum propulsion range and flight time over the whole altitude range to be covered. However, it appeared that any reduction of the proposed propulsion range would result in a need for much higher speed. That was considered undesirable, due to the greater heating effects and the reduced ability to cope with launching errors, which may become larger in the more severe tactical situations. A long flight time was also expected to allow for better optimisation of miss distance.

Warhead and miss distance relationships were based on the use of continuous rod warheads, such as I had learned about on my GW course at Shrivenham in 1953. These warheads were considered to be more lethal than blast warheads or fragmentation warheads, when used against the kind of high-strength structures from which supersonic high-altitude aircraft were constructed. When detonated, a

R.M.S MISS	WEAPONS	% TARGET SURVIVAL	MISSILE RELIABILITY
40 ft.	2 x 1,400 lb.	46%	80%
	2 x 700lb	56%	
	3 x 700lb	42.5%	
	4 x 700lb	32.2%	
20 ft	2 x 1,400lb	24.5%	80%
	2 x 700lb	32.3%	
	3 x 700lb	18.4%	
	4 x 700lb	10.5%	

Fig.147. Survivability of target, against 80 per cent reliable missiles with 20ft and 40ft miss distances.[48]

continuous rod warhead creates exactly that – a continuous circular ring of steel rod that expands in diameter until it eventually breaks. If the missile can be guided to a miss distance that is smaller than the radius of the ring, this high-energy ring of steel cuts through the target's thick-skinned structure, severing major components. Additional effects of blast and fragments add to its lethality, somewhat depending on the altitude. Clearly, the smaller the miss distance, the greater the lethality.

The power and lethality of the warhead also depends on the weight of the explosive charge and the rod-producing steel casing. It would therefore appear that the bigger and heavier the warhead, the greater the missile's lethality. However, the weightier the warhead, the larger and heavier a missile would be needed to carry it – and the more difficult it would be to achieve a small miss distance. More compromises had to be considered and, in terms of the fighter's assumed total weapon load of 2,800lb, comparisons were made between the carrying of two large (1,400lb) missiles with correspondingly large warheads, and carrying four smaller missiles weighing 700lb each, with commensurately smaller warheads. Assuming a warhead weight equal to 11 per cent of missile weight and factoring in an 80 per cent missile reliability assumption, information about continuous warhead lethalities from ARDE showed that 46 per cent of targets will survive two 1,400lb missiles, whereas only 32 per cent would survive four 700lb missiles. These lethalities applied to a root mean square (RMS) miss distance of 40ft. If the RMS miss distance could be reduced to 20ft, the survivabilities reduce, respectively, to 24.5 per cent with two 1,400lb missiles, and to 10.5 per cent with four 700lb missiles. With three of the smaller missiles, the survival rate is still only 18.4 per cent.

Even allowing for only 80 per cent missile reliability, two 700lb missiles achieving 40ft RMS miss distance fired in ripple would reduce a target's chances of success from, say, 50 per cent (allowing for stand-off weapon lethality and reliability) to 28 per cent. With an improved miss distance of 20ft RMS, the bomber's *mission* survivability reduces to 16 per cent with two missiles and only 5 per cent with a ripple of four missiles.

Doubling the interceptor's weapon load would, of course, pay considerable dividends, leading to target survival chances against eight 700lb missiles of 80 per cent reliability with 40ft RMS miss distance being 10 per cent and only 1.1 per cent if the miss distance were 20ft RMS. However, the choice of whether to double the fighter's size or to double their number would be a logistical choice involving the possibility of a totally different aircraft. The principal figures are tabulated in Fig.147.

This is also illustrated by the graphs below, showing the effect of improved reliability.

These curves show the effects on lethality with continuous rod warheads, of missile total weight, the number of missiles in a ripple firing, and reliability. The vertical scale of 'Probability of Target Avoiding a Kill' is the inverse of 'Lethality'.

Though obviously enough an important benefit, the importance of minimising miss distance is made very clear by the big improvements in lethality between 40ft RMS and 20ft RMS miss distance. The effect of firing ripples of missiles is also clearly evident. The above arguments are based on somewhat over-simplified assumptions, but clearly show the trends.

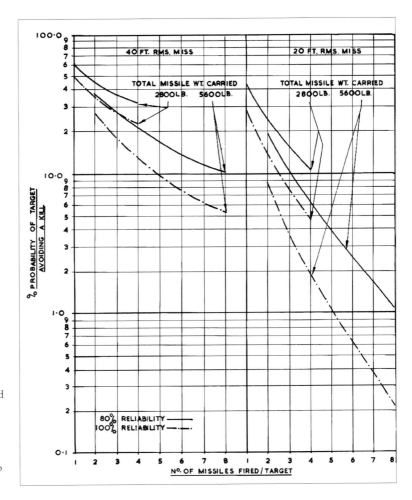

Fig.148. Target survivability and how it reduces with improved miss distance, for total missile loads of 2,800lb and 5,600lb.[48]

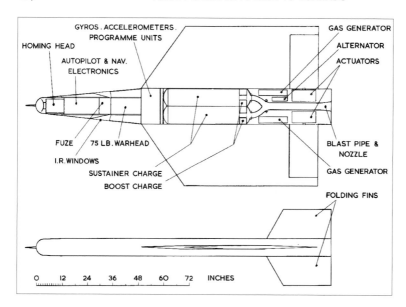

Fig.149. Configuration and component layout for the air-to-air missile for OR346.[48]

The missile configuration and design details could now be sketched out with sufficient confidence to advise Maurice Brennan as to a suitable size for his aircraft's weapons bay – his original question posed to Howard Surtees. Subject to many more confirmatory studies, I was able to draw a missile configuration that would correspond with the main criteria I had established.

This conventional aeroplane-like configuration had the large cropped delta wing area and elevator controls required to pull the 'g' manoeuvres at up to 105,000ft, together with two all-moving vertical control fins above and below the missile rear body. These fins would also move differentially, to act as ailerons for roll control. The fins folded parallel to the wings for stowage in the weapons bay. The body cross-section is non-circular, being 8in deep and 16in across in the spanwise direction, to accommodate the twin rocket motor bodies and their common blast pipe. Ahead of the wings, the body tapered down to a circular cross-section at the hemispherical radome. For low-altitude sorties, a spike was to be fitted on the radome for drag reduction and to provide rain protection. The elevators had a mid-chord hinge line, to reduce hinge moments and inertia. Alternative configurations using a movable rocket exhaust remained to be studied, with a view to reducing the rather large wing area. The possibility of using variable geometry wings in view of the missile's large Mach No. and centre-of-pressure range were also considered worthy of study.

This missile configuration was not exactly my preference for elegance and beauty – but it was a practical and seemingly effective solution for meeting the Mach 3, 80,000ft–105,000ft specification required to overcome the fighter's relative performance inferiority. Overall length including the spike was 12ft, wing area was 28.2sq.ft, and the 13in fin heights provided a total area of 4.45sq.ft. Wing thickness was kept low for supersonic conditions, at only 2 per cent of the wing chord, and consisted of parallel slabs representing 70 per cent of wing chord, with equal leading and trailing edge wedge sections.

The resulting total weight was estimated at 685lb, including a 75lb warhead and initiator, with possible growth to 700lb. Within this, the total structure weight was 174lb and propulsion accounted for 292lb, carrying about 220lb of propellant. The all-important equipment for electrical power and gas generation, control, guidance and fusing accounted for 218lb. The resulting centre of gravity (CG), at 2.3ft behind the wing root, corresponded well with the propellant CG, so that there was only 1in shift in the overall CG position as the propellant was consumed during flight.

The choices and estimates for the guidance head, autopilot, navigation, and fuze entirely depended on the best forecasts I could obtain concerning the micro-miniaturisation of electronic equipment that might occur in the ten years ahead. Transistors were still relatively new and the forward thinking regarding integrated circuits was largely dependent on experimental work in the USA and in the UK. The RAE at Farnborough, TRE at Malvern and industrial collaborators at the GEC, Smiths and EMI, with whom we had worked on Red Dean, were able to shed some light on the future. However, it was more a matter of estimating volume, weight, and power consumption of equipments to be designed using these emerging techniques, than firm projection of equipment designs against our well-defined criteria. Had I been able to see into the future, I would have known the immense progress that would be made with integrated circuits and could have felt more confident about the choices and the assumptions we were making. In hindsight, these choices were not too far off the mark.

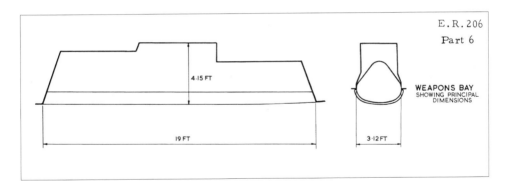

Fig.150. Outline dimensions of the fighter's weapons bay.[48]

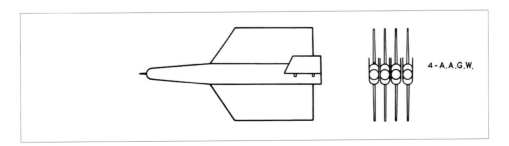

Fig.151. Stowage of four missiles in the weapons bay, with folded vertical fins.[48]

In the absence of wind tunnel tests at that stage, aerodynamic estimates indicated the drag forces to be overcome and how these could be reduced by about 12.5 per cent at Mach 1.4 with the addition of the radome spike for low-altitude interceptions. Aerodynamic pitching moment estimates enabled me to choose elevator travel of ±30° to produce an incidence of 20° at Mach 3.0 and higher. This elevator power would be higher than required at low altitude and stability would have to be augmented by acceleration feedback in the autopilot. We expected the balanced elevators to have reduced effectiveness at low angles, due to a thick boundary layer near the wing trailing edge. Without allowing for this effect, the elevator power was estimated to produce 12.4g of manoeuvre per degree of its deflection at Mach 1.3 near the 'all burnt' motor condition and beyond, during coasting, when the missile weight would be down to 500lb.

This 'carpet' plot (Fig.152) shows that, at the higher speeds up to Mach 4.0 at the top-end altitudes, the missile could 'pull' nearly 7g, while at a 'modest' 65,000ft, the missile could pull up to the structure limit designed at 15g. At 80,000ft, the limits occurring soon after the end of the boost phase would be structural rather than aerodynamic. Under these conditions, there would be a lag in the generation of incidence angle, with a time constant of approximately 2.5 seconds. This would increase to eight seconds at 105,000ft. At this same weight and the corresponding estimated moments of inertia, the missile's natural aerodynamic frequency of oscillation would be one cycle per second, which could be increased without difficulty to a higher value by using acceleration feedback. Rate gyroscope feedback would probably also be required, to increase the damping of any oscillations.

In the yaw plane, all-moving control fins were proposed and, to overcome insufficient damping at 105,000ft, rate gyroscope feedback would again be used to control the two-cycles-per-second natural oscillations. The splitting of fin area above and below the body would reduce any cross-coupling effects and enable control to be effective while the wings were at pitch incidences in either direction. The greater power of the fins at low altitude could require only one of the two to be used for control, so long as this did not produce excessive rolling moments.

Roll control at the highest altitudes and speeds would be obtained by differential movement of the fins, since the elevators would need to use their full operating range of angles to achieve the 20° of incidence for the required manoeuvres. Rolling rate would be important for setting the plane of turning in an interception, as for a conventional aircraft. We estimated that, at 105,000ft, 20° of aileron-wise deflection of the fins would produce a 90° roll datum change in 0.6 seconds. At 80,000ft, this could be achieved in 0.33 seconds. We estimated that this order of control would be well within the power available with ±30° of fin travel. At sea level and speeds of Mach 1.3 and higher, however, it was expected that, instead of the fins, use of elevator controls within their lower effectiveness within the boundary layer could be worth selecting.

Thus, it appeared that the missile's flight could be adequately controlled over the very wide range of conditions existing over the altitude and speed ranges described. With the elevator effectiveness under the most adverse conditions producing around 12 'g's per degree of deflection using actuators of average performance, the

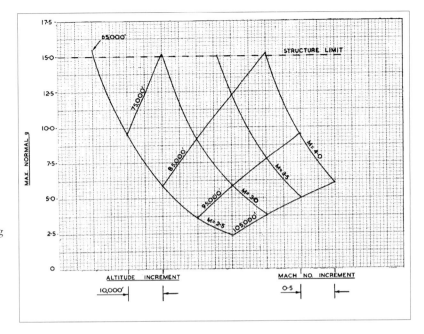

Fig.152.
Manoeuvring
capability of
the missile
at the higher
altitudes and
speeds up to
Mach 4.0.[48]

missile should not be in danger of exceeding its structural limits. The next step in confirming the aerodynamics of the missile would have to be wind tunnel testing.

By the time we had reached this point, my slide rule was running seriously hot!

Peter Mobsby made up for what I lacked in structural design experience, and produced the necessary detailed designs and weight estimates. Due to the missile's high speed, the complete structure up to the rear of the nose portion carrying the equipment packages would be constructed from steel. He designed a steel sandwich construction for the wings and control surfaces, based on a maximum temperature of 350°C. Forward of the wings, the body was to comprise a light alloy tubular inner structure carrying the various components, with bulkheads between each section (see Fig.149). These bulkheads would form the external body shape and support the external structure made of light steel sheet, with spot-welded longitudinal reinforcing corrugations. The 'shell' would fit over the internal structure and maintain its shape by virtue of the engagement with the bulkheads.

The centre body section of steel shell construction would have channel frames at about 6in spacing, to provide attachment for the wing roots and to diffuse the loads into the body shell. The main frame at the end of the body section would take the rocket motor thrust and the main shear and bearing loads from the front wing spars. A similar but lighter frame would carry the spar loads and the rear ends of the rocket motors.

The wings and control surface leading and trailing edge wedge sections were to be of solid steel, between two steel spars. The space between these main members would contain 0.002in stainless steel honeycomb, while the outer skin facings would be of 0.01in stainless steel. Such complete assemblies would be brazed together, probably using an oven technique with boron trifluoride as the gas flux. The main spars of the vertical elevator fins would also form the actuator shaft.

Propulsion with 6,000lb of thrust for two seconds and a sustainer level of 1,500lb for a further twenty-nine seconds has already been mentioned. Solid propellants were considered from Bristol Aerojets Ltd, employing polyurethane, and alternatively from ICI, using their high-energy propellant. Both of these had similar 'specific impulse' energy values (SI) of 250 seconds. While the ICI propellant would not have been suitable for the extended high temperatures occurring during external carrying under a fighter, the internal stowage in a weapons bay avoided this potential problem. Such performance was readily available from the 7.5in-diameter charges that would suit our 8in-diameter body.

The Bristol Aerojets Ltd propellant was still the more likely choice, in view of its lower sensitivity to temperature changes. Its slower burning rate pointed to a case bonded charge that could be burned from both ends, with a central blast pipe to take the gases out rearwards. However, complications with the need for a nozzle area change between boost and sustain phases led back to the ICI propellant, whose temperature sensitivity could be tolerated in the absence of external carrying. Two fibreglass rocket motor bodies were assumed and, in order to avoid passing two blast pipes and nozzles through the missile's rear compartment, a manifold joining the two motor end closures was proposed, with a single subsonic blast pipe and expansion cone assembly.

In contemplating the critical factors of Radar Guidance for homing, we had to take advantage of RAE's highly esoteric and advanced mathematical analyses that related various forms of Radar noise, the missile's stability and manoeuvre performance, to the miss distance that could be achieved. I tried my best to apply my rusty mathematics to understanding the RAE's computations with confluent hypergeometric functions. While I could not claim to be totally successful in this, with the help of Howard Surtees I was able to gain some confidence in the resulting miss distance estimates.

Target sightline information as the prime data was to be obtained using a semi-acting X-Band Radar receiver, probably operating on Continuous Wave (CW). We could carry a 7in-diameter paraboloidal dish, which would be fitted with a 'static split' angle tracking system. This would be less susceptible to jamming than the Red Dean-style pulsed Radar with conical scanning. We calculated the effective lock-on range in conjunction with the AI Radar lamp, set to be 30nm on a 10sq.m target. Since the missile would be shielded from the target during the pre-launch sequence, lock-on would have to be after launch. We assumed this could be achieved with the space-stabilised antenna dish that would be locked to follow the AI Radar's sightline until after launch. The 12° Radar beam angle produced by our 7in-diameter dish would be able to 'see' the target and lock on independently soon after launch. The natural frequency and damping ratio of the dish system would have to be optimised between the response to noise and target-following requirements. A total dish system angular coverage of 60° would allow for attacks from the beam and possibly 30° behind the beam, as indicated by the interception patterns (see Fig.144).

A high-temperature-tolerant pyro-ceramic radome was expected to suffer near-zero aberration, and the addition of the aerodynamic spike for low-altitude interceptions was not expected to create more than a small aberration effect. Target noise considerations were the main factors to affect miss distance, and the static split angular detection system was largely expected to eliminate the effects of angular noise. In the project's timescale, the effects of glint noise were also expected to be largely eliminated. These expectations were based on work in progress at ministry establishments, to correlate phase front variations with signal fading, and the possibility of using intermittent sightline information. Isolation of the sightline source-of-error signal was also considered to be a likely means of error correction, for reduction of miss distance.

Subject to simulator studies to be pursued for more accurate assessment of the guidance requirements, the consensus was that, in the ten-year timescale of the project, the proposed design would achieve reduced miss distances from 40ft RMS without full optimisation, to nearer 20ft RMS. The possibility of using a terminal infrared phase to reduce miss distance at the maximum altitude was considered with the existing dish system and angle-tracking circuits of the Radar receiver. A small active IR source of about 20–30W would be adequate for short terminal ranges in the absence of atmospheric attenuation. Alternatively, passive target radiation could be used.

With its 'twist and steer' regime, this missile's command roll stabilisation system would be required to operate on information from the guidance system. For the rapid roll rates already given above, a bi-stable roll system would ideally be used, if stability problems could be overcome. Once the missile has rolled into the selected plane of manoeuvre, navigation towards the target would be by homing, according to the measured rate at which the missile-to-target sightline rotates. The missile would then be commanded to turn at a rate proportional to that rate. The proportion factor 'k' would depend on the direction of attack. The setting of this value would be controlled from the interception course computer in the fighter, and locked at launch. For a head-on attack, requiring the tightest turning speed, the factor would be at the maximum of six times sightline rate. The sightline rate signal would be passed through an optimisation filter, whose character will allow a compromise between the conflicting needs of minimising response to target noise and following rapid target manoeuvres.

The required flight path pitch rate would be converted to a pitch acceleration demand proportional to missile speed. Dependent on launching speed, this 'k' term would probably be accurate enough if taken at an average value over the range of missile speeds during the interception trajectory, and it would be set into the Navigation computer by the aircraft. To match the structural limitation, it was proposed to limit this acceleration to 15g. The autopilot would compare this demand with 'g' measured by an accelerometer, and the resulting error signal would be the prime means of control. The error signal, together with rate gyroscope stabilising signals, would operate on servo amplifiers, whose outputs control the elevator angle in a closed loop actuator system. The placing of the accelerometer ahead of the missile CG provides a form of phase advance, and consequent damping effect. Without autopilot modification, the missile natural frequency in pitch at 105,000ft was estimated at only 0.85 cycles per second. By appropriate choice of loop gain, the frequency can be modified to two or three cycles per second and rate feedback could be arranged to produce the desired critical damped response.

In the yaw plane, the autopilot's function would be to reduce to zero any accelerations outside the manoeuvre plain. Here again, a well-damped response to any disturbances would be required, particularly since aerodynamic damping in yaw would be virtually absent.

In all axes, aerodynamic gain variations would necessitate autopilot gain variations dependent on altitude and speed. In view of the large altitude range covered to maximum height – such as from 60,000ft to 105,000ft – the autopilot gains may require variation throughout the missile's flight, starting from a datum set in at launch. This would preferably be done on a time basis, in order to avoid the need to measure actual aerodynamic (pitot) pressure. Consideration was to be given to further sophistication, by the use of the 'sympathetic servo' method of control, where the gain is always held to the effective maximum within the stability limit. It was also proposed to employ cross-coupling cancellation by the measurement of angular accelerations and feeding these back, in addition to the individual pitch or yaw loop response signals. Rate gyroscopes for this would need to be run up very quickly before launch, requiring cordite cartridges or springs for run up, when wheel speeds would be sustained electrically.

Warhead design has been mentioned earlier. With advice from ARDE, its 7.5in diameter, within the available missile diameter, and 14in length allowed for a double layer of 0.25in x 0.25in square rod sections forming an unbroken hoop radius of 26ft after detonation. This hoop of steel would expand at a rate estimated to be between 3,250 and 3,500ft/s, propelled by detonation of the RDX/TNT filling. Against an aircraft like the Soviet 'Badger', the lethality (fed into the earlier calculations and graphs) was estimated to be 31 per cent at 40ft RMS miss distance and 54 per cent at 20ft RMS. Lethality against aircraft of sandwich or honeycomb construction was expected to be greater, while the effect of steel in the target's construction was not considered to be of great significance. The initiator would fit within the warhead dimensions and it was considered that, in view of the limited flight duration in an interception, adequate heat insulation would be obtained from the air gap between the missile skin and the rods.

The proposed infrared fuze design was predicated on the 7,000ft/second maximum relative velocity of approach to the target in head-on attack at high altitude. Since geometry mandated that passive I.R. detection of radiation from the target's jet plumes would only operate from within 9° of the missile's longitudinal axis, an active I.R. fuze was proposed. This would use a 10 to 20 watt Infrared source, radiating in the 2–3 micron region. Such an arrangement would operate at a target range of 30ft to 40ft in adverse cloud conditions and it would have a considerable range margin over the required miss distance in the more favourable atmosphere at high altitude.

A conical sheet polar diagram of I.R. radiation at 45° from the missile axis would allow for a rod impact 40ft behind the target nose under the worst case of maximum target approach speed conditions, corresponding well with a maximum of 40ft miss distance. Considering an approach from 30° behind the target beam at high altitude, the relative velocity is very nearly equal to the 3,500ft/sec. rod velocity, resulting in a near 45° rod vector which coincides with the fuze polar diagram. Thus, the maximum I.R. detection range required at high altitude will be between 60ft and

80ft. At low altitude, the missile approach relative velocities are much smaller, varying between 1,500ft/sec. and 3,000ft/sec. Since the rod velocity is little changed, a time delay would be required, which would have to be varied with altitude (effectively with relative speed). This again would be set into the missile before launch. Further study was anticipated to determine whether fuze timing needed adjustment with attack angle. This could be most effectively computed form the available sightline angle in the terminal homing phase. However with wide enough tolerance, it may suffice to set the delay based on launch conditions.

A further detailed study was considered desirable, to determine the best form of discrimination against sun, cloud and sea returns. In the event of excessive miss distance, a self-destruction signal was to be used. Fuze arming was to occur after launch, dependent on distance covered ahead of the fighter and would be based on acceleration measurements.

Control actuators were specified to powered by cordite or similar gas generating solid, and the working fluid could be the gas itself or possibly oil, pressurised from a gas driven oil motor. The total running time was required to exceed the rocket motor life by three seconds before launch and twelve seconds after 'all burnt' to allow coasting for increased missile range. Feedback of control movements to the autopilot servo amplifiers would provide a closed loop control with a natural frequency of about 20Hz, this being well outside the missile aerodynamic response range. A maximum control velocity of 500°/second was envisaged. Control torques applied to the elevators could be 200lb/ft, while those to the fins would only be required at half that value. The total weight of actuator and its motive power was estimated at 70lb. To protect the missile structure from the effects of any actuator 'run away' soon after low altitude launch, altitude variable physical stops would be essential. In addition, zero angle control locks would be required to prevent any unfolding or fouling within the weapons bay prior to launch. These locks would be removed at rocket motor ignition.

Electrical power supplies were specified to be generated with an alternator driven by gas generators through a turbine. Alternatively, they could be coupled to the hydraulic motor described above. About 100 watts of single and three phase power would be required for all services except for the fuze, which required a separate supply from a high voltage thermal battery.

Throughout the study and the design process I have described, there was continuous consultation with the aircraft design team, principally Spud Boorer and also with (occasionally) Maurice Brennan, but more often Alan Clifton. This gentle and supportive top designer from Supermarine would come into my little office and sit down to discuss the missile installation and particularly the $64,000 question of lethality. His whole aircraft project depended on delivering the kill, before the fleet could be decimated by the Soviet stand-off weapon. An important design aspect within the weapons bay was the automatic ejection of a missile with sufficient impulse, to throw it fast enough and far enough below the aircraft for the safe ignition of the rocket motor.

Having thus completed fairly detailed design and specification of the missile using the 'steam power' of my slide rule, it was necessary to compute missile performance over a much more comprehensive range of conditions. With only slide rules, this would

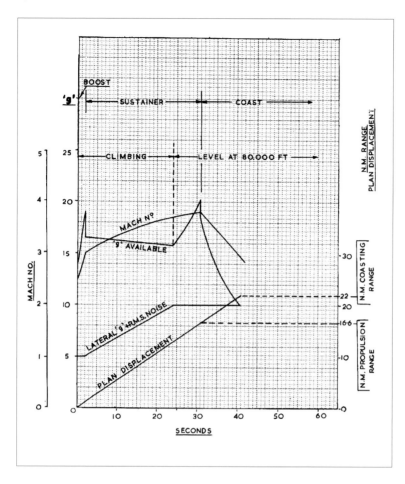

Fig.153.
Performance
against
manoeuvring
target at
80,000ft.[48]

be impossible to complete in a reasonable time and now after establishing the range
of conditions, I decided to have the necessary several hundred trajectories computed
by Vickers' Mathematical Services Department, employing the recently operational
Pegasus Digital Computer under the leadership of Harry Hitch. Occupying a large
room behind the main Drawing Office, Pegasus probably had about the power of
my 2001 vintage laptop PC. However, it performed all kinds of complex operations
including wing flutter simulations and it should make short work of my needs. My
trajectory equations worked simply and smoothly with the slide rule, assuming
approximately constant conditions during half-second iteration periods.

Full of confidence for a quick turnaround with which to finish the Study, I
delivered the equations and the many interception conditions for which we needed
to verify the missile's performance in terms of manoeuvre capability, Mach Numbers
during its flight period and distance to target. However, Harry Hitch's programmers
just could not get the equations to work on Pegasus. Drumming my fingers, I sat
and waited for an eternal five weeks, when Pegasus finally began to cough up with
trajectories. Once it learned how to do the job, the results cascaded out and provided
all I needed within a day or two.

The results are shown as graphs (Fig.153 and Fig.154), covering the basic performance cases against a manoeuvring target at 80,000ft, a zooming target at 105,000ft and a low altitude target (Fig.155). Without covering the homing trajectories in plan, the computations allow for the effects of Radar noise and the aerodynamic factors associated with manoeuvre, confirming that the missile as designed should in fact reach the target area. Verification of missile homing accuracy and actual miss distances would require further work involving detailed simulations, such as those used to produce the RAE's miss distance criteria and calculations to which I referred, under the discussion on guidance and miss distance.

The graphs show the rocket motor boost, sustainer period followed by coasting after 'all burnt', while the missile is making its 'jump up' from the fighter's attack altitude, to the target's altitudes. Missile speed rises to Mach 3.8 against the 80,000ft manoeuvring target and it reaches beyond Mach 4 against the zooming target at 105,000ft in the face of the most conservatively assumed drag. Missile manoeuvring 'g' available only falls to a still adequate 10g for successful homing guidance, (requiring up to just that amount including noise effects), at the 80,000ft manoeuvring target altitude. Similarly, at the non-manoeuvring zooming target's 105,000ft altitude, the 'g' available during the missile's approach to the target is sufficient at 7g, for good homing guidance. The distances travelled are compatible with the Interception diagrams shown earlier.

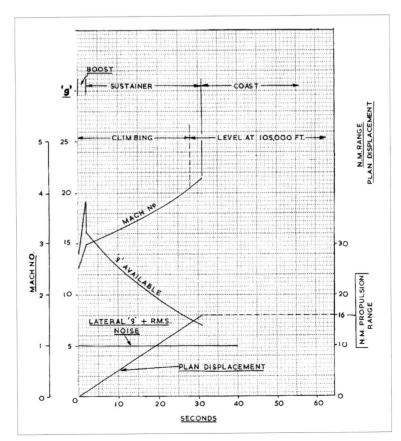

Fig.154.
Performance
against zooming
target to
105,000ft.[48]

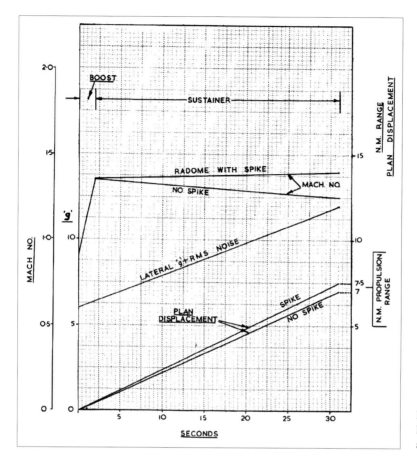

Fig.155.
Performance
at sea level.[48]

The drag effect of the Radome spike on Mach number and on distance travelled is seen not be enough to affect performance. The lateral 'g' after adding the effect of Radar noise is high enough for homing manoeuvres and remains below the 15g structure limit.

Launching errors were allowed for in all of the above interceptions. Calculations showed that at a missile speed of Mach 3, even a 90° launching error could be corrected within fifteen seconds by a 10g turn. This corresponds to a total interception flight time of thirty-one seconds, leaving a further sixteen seconds plus coasting time for collision-course homing.

Mean miss distance was further considered in the light of an oscillating missile's response time lag denoted by the parameter 'ξ' (number of time lag periods to strike) and the parameter 'α'. In the case for a head-on attack, with the homing Navigation Constant 'k' set to 6, 'α' (= k x missile speed/range rate to target) will be at optimum value of 3 or 4, assuming zero launch error. Allowing for a 0.5 second missile time lag, the maximum value of 'ξ' for a thirty seconds flight time would be about sixty, but allowing for even fifteen seconds launch error corrections, the value of 'ξ' is still greater than 30.

With these values of 'α' and 'ξ', the mean miss distance against a steadily manoeuvring target would be zero, so long as the missile was subject to no 'g' limit.

With the most adverse value of 'ξ', the miss distance is only 2½ft. This value of 'ξ' corresponds to three seconds of flight, or about one half of a six seconds period – thought to be near the target's optimum for evasive manoeuvre in the pitch plane. Incidentally, this is also the worst case for causing crew airsickness. Now considering the realistic missile 10g limit and a low value of 'ξ' (= 6), the mean miss distance works out as 10ft. During the climbing approach to a target at 80,000ft, the missile limit will be much more favourable at 15g for the whole propulsion range making this estimate quite conservative.

During (only) the final stage of missile pursuit to 105,000ft, the missile manoeuvre is limited to 6g. However, at this top of its ballistic trajectory, the target is incapable of manoeuvre other than its predictable free fall. In the absence of other information, we could assume that the mean miss distance at this height would be similar to that at 80,000ft.

Glint noise on the Radar return has the effect of creating scatter of the guidance commands. The extent of this depends on the power spectral density of the noise created by the Glint. With the values of 'α' and 'ξ' taken above, this power spectral density (according to the experts measured as $15ft^2$/radian/sec.) results in a scatter of 20.6ft RMS. The consensus at the time was that in the ten-year time scale, this effect would be substantially reduced by the measures already described. Scatter due to angular noise was assessed by the RAE in its Report GW No.18 and found not to apply with Static Split Radars such as we proposed. Furthermore, the noise power spectral density assumptions on which the above figures were based had already improved in the missile's favour by a factor of 70. We therefore concluded that the effect of scatter at 80,000ft was likely to be less than 5ft and would be similar at 105,000ft.

With the effects of Radome aberration already discussed and concluded to be acceptable and allowing for the anticipated improvements, the estimated total RMS miss distance was 23.5ft. This placed the 20ft to 40ft range used for the lethality figures into a conservative bracket. We appeared to have a viable missile design for Alan Clifton's fighter proposal, with a substantial lethality in ripple firings – approaching 95 per cent with the four missile load to be carried.

Some practical considerations concluded the weapon system study. The number of interconnections between the missiles and the aircraft would be kept to a minimum and the missile was therefore designed for rapid warm up on its own gas generated alternator power supplies, avoiding complicated electrical matching and change-overs from aircraft supplies. Connections would be required for firing up the missile cartridge and the thermal battery, for harmonisation of the guidance antenna dish to the AI sight line, the setting of autopilot gain, control mode and the navigation parameters and for the fuzing delays. In addition, mechanical means of altering the actuator stop positions were likely to be required. Launching would be by downward ejection, applying the main load near the missile CG at the wing root leading edge. Ripple firing would have to be with sufficient spacing in time, to ensure against a fuze being triggered by a leading missile. This spacing was expected to be between 0.1 second and half a second, depending on aircraft speed at the point of launch.

The launching sequence would start at −1min. 15 seconds before missile ejection, when the aircraft's AI Radar was locked onto the target. After setting the fin stops at − 1 minute, the autopilot gains would be set at −30 seconds, followed at −20 seconds by the navigation constant and fuze delays, when the conditions of the interception could be confidently set for the average conditions pertaining to the particular interception trajectory. Power supply would be fired up at −3 seconds and the guidance dish harmonised with the AI Radar direction a second later. Zero of the count down was the moment of missile ejection, the rocket motor firing being delayed to ¼ second later when the missile was safely clear. Radar lock on to the target was anticipated by +¾ second and ¼ second after this, the controls locks would be removed at +1 second. Fuze arming would be at the end of the rocket motor boost phase at +2 seconds, with the missile safely far ahead of the fighter.

This largely one-man study occupied my waking hours for a total of six months and in March 1960, it found its way into the Vickers Publication SPEC./206/3 as Appendix 3. After ten years of more practical duties since qualifying, it went some way towards restoring my facility with technical matters to a more worthwhile level – and taught me much besides. My experience of working with Spud Boorer and Alan Clifton left me with a long lasting respect and regard for both of these high flyers in British aviation – and incidentally earned me a salary raise of £100 p.a.! Perhaps this was when I finally crossed the magic 'secret salary rule' of £1,500 p.a. and qualified for that otherwise unattainable privilege of travelling by First Class.

Fig.156. The author of the Air-to-Air Weapon System Study in a different 'busy mode', at almost exactly the same time as the study was published.[103]

EPILOGUE

The details I have recorded from Public Records Office archives show how attitudes were set in the concrete of Government's desire to bring about amalgamations in the Aircraft Industry. As I have recorded, the 1 January 1959 TSR2 contract was effectively the midwife to the birth of BAC.

The TSR2 Navigation & Attack system developments and work described in the chapter 'Missiles Projects for the Future' were proceeding throughout the accompanying corporate turmoil, also associated with the 1962 ending of GW activity in Weybridge. Though we knew about the overall plan, engineers below the top management level, such as I, saw little day-to-day evidence of the turmoil. Nevertheless, even the acknowledged leading expert Brigadier John Clemow, who had been specifically recruited from the Ministry of Supply by Sir George Edwards in 1957 to head Guided Weapons and then the TSR2 'Nav/Attack' System, was evidently not privy to the Ministry correspondence and shenanigans relating to the private venture Vigilant Anti-Tank Missile development. These seemed to be going on behind John Clemow's back and when the final decision was being made to move the Weybridge GW work to Stevenage, John first heard about it by a chance comment, while he was attending the 1961 Paris Air Show. Back in Weybridge, he tackled Sir George, who confirmed the intention and asked John to move with the team to head up the Stevenage operation.

In the early summer of 1961, Sir George called a meeting of all the more senior GW team members, to promulgate the Stevenage move policy and undoubtedly, also to gauge reaction and extent to which we were willing to make the move. Sir Geoffrey Tuttle, lately an RAF Air Marshal, and other Vickers Board members attended this large gathering and in anticipation, I got together with some of my contemporaries. A few levels down the organisation, we were senior enough to be invited and I wanted to prepare our best shot at a defence of GW at Weybridge. We were also conscious that since the end of the Red Rapier ground-to-ground radar-guided missile, Sir George Edwards had taken little interest in the GW work. John Lattey, Arthur Carter and I sat down to discuss tactics, around a summary of the main points I had listed - the anticipated reasons for making the 'split' − with our possible counter arguments.[108]

To streamlining the organisation, I argued that a separate operation at Stevenage effectively duplicating Weybridge would not amount to streamlining. Against quantity production having to be at Stevenage, I countered that liaison with a

Weybridge technical team would be equally feasible as was already occurring with Supermarine at Hurn. Against arguments for projects requiring the employment of large facilities and staff numbers at Stevenage, we would counter that moving extra staff to Stevenage would increase problems and require extra housing – and that Weybridge facilities were largely adequate. Numbers would need to be reduced at some time anyway. To any suggestions that the Weybridge buildings would be required for other purposes, we would cite the multiplying buildings and floor space over the past ten years – and the small amount of area GW would now need. Regarding Government policy directives, our answer was the benefit of utilising available GW talent at decentralised facilities – and contended that BAC was sufficiently powerful to decide for itself, how to arrange its facilities around the UK, without bowing to Ministry influence.

After we heard the Directors' statements, I started our responses by pointing out the success of Vigilant, the work on (Howard Surtees') Long Range Project and other extended studies resulting in all the anti-tank work now going to BAC. I contended that the team which achieved this must be kept together. John Lattey followed by pointing out that the factor of the Navigation & Attack System part of TSR2 being handled by the GW Department was as significant, as the design of the aircraft itself. For this reason, the prospect of obtaining a military aircraft contract such as Swallow (originated by Barnes Wallis) would be greatly increased, if a team with GW's exceptional leadership remained in being. The same argument if properly pressed at high Government levels would also apply to a Supersonic Airliner (Concorde).

I continued – the team had had its back to the wall for five years and in the face of severe setbacks and redundancies remained loyal and enthusiastic. John Lattey continued – the team lived in Surrey and was not inspired by the prospect of moving to Stevenage. Weybridge was much closer to ARDE, the RAE, Larkhill and the London ministries. I resumed, indicating our fear that we would all lose two or three years of seniority vis-à-vis our opposite numbers at Stevenage until we could be accepted, then John Lattey chimed in to say that the numbers at Stevenage would have to be reduced in the next year or so; adding to numbers there would only make this more difficult – and anyway, who would be the first to be laid off in any redundancy?

Sir George took the view that we should be glad to 'get into the main stream'. However, John Lattey eruditely quoted in his best Latin – '*Maximum in udam ite, et immergiti*' – and for everybody's benefit translated it to, 'Get into the main stream and drown!' To which Sir George's sardonic response was, 'You don't only stick the pin in, you twist it round!'

Arthur Carter continued the attack, contending that the weapon systems concept of military aircraft such as TSR2 represents a major part of any (Weybridge) aircraft contract. Its efficient execution depended largely on coordination of the whole by one company and the prospect of gaining further contracts of this type would be greatly enhanced by the presently constituted Weybridge facility. John Lattey continued, arguing that the techniques available in a GW team are those, which apply to aircraft navigation, scheduled automatic landing, airborne communications and the air traffic control of modern subsonic and supersonic transports. The future of BAC Civil Aircraft may well depend on those skills. I continued the arguments further, contending that besides aircraft systems, the weapons to be carried must have their effect on the design of a military aircraft. In the project stage, these effects can only be properly allowed for by close cooperation between the Military Projects Office and a well informed and up to date Guided Weapons team – as was the case with TSR2 and with the projected supersonic fighters on which I was working. Arthur then continued by referring to Lord Caldecote's recent discussion paper to the Institution of Electrical Engineers citing the advantages of close integration between GW facilities and an aircraft design organisation.

Arthur and John had further questions affecting any engineers who were asked to remain at Weybridge to work on TSR2. How reliable career opportunities would Electronic Engineers, Control Engineers and Physicists have in the Weybridge aircraft organisation? And – how would the TSR2 Navigation and Attack system team be used after TSR2 was completed – or if it were cancelled? I concluded with questions concerning any of us who might elect to stay in Weybridge, to be absorbed into the aircraft team – would all including the more senior members be able to find sufficiently interesting work offering an adequate degree of responsibility and status, with continuing prospects? To what extent would GW team members be accepted on equal terms with aircraft staff at management and other levels?

Perhaps unsurprisingly, we did not receive too many direct answers to this raft of questions and assertions. George Edwards concluded by saying 'Well, I am going home' and we dispersed without much expectation of any reprieve. On 31 July, I sent a memorandum to John Clemow on behalf of the Guided Weapons Department, with copies to my two colleagues asking for answers to the many questions that would influence our decisions as to moving to Stevenage. What compensation might we expect for the many and varied costs associated with moving house and children's schools? What would happen to our Vickers Pension Fund? Would the company agree to a three years contract for those uprooting to Stevenage? Under what working conditions would we live and what kind of organisation and work prospects could we expect within the English Electric part of BAC?

No copy of the reply survives in my archives, but in the end, very few of the team were willing to make the move to Stevenage – I only remember Sam Hastings. John Clemow quite openly told us that had he been, say sixty years old, he might have thought of his continuity in employment – but he was only fifty and would therefore look to newer pastures. It was 9 October, before we received a memorandum from top management, setting out the responsibilities relating to the TSR2 Navigation and Attack System. This quoted a press report of the Guided Weapons work at Weybridge having now been transferred to the English Electric Guided Weapons Division – and that 'further to this, Mr. J. Clemow has left the Company'.

Chief Designer (Weapons) Howard Surtees started the new Elliott Automation Space and Missile Systems company ('EASAMS'), joined by Dab and Frank Bond – with an offer for me also to join.

To ensure continuity for TSR2, the aircraft division's chief of electrical design Harry Zeffert was appointed Chief Systems Engineer/E at Weybridge, responsible 'for the co-ordination and progress of the TSR2 Navigation/Attack System and its associated equipment'. Mike Still was appointed Deputy Chief Systems Engineer/E – effectively running the day-to-day TSR2 Nav/Attack work. John Lambie would continue his existing responsibilities as Chief Project Officer on TSR2 weapon systems and in this continuing Weybridge team, they were joined by Arthur Carter, John Lattey, Dennis Harris, John Goodwin, Jim Cole, John Doyle, Les Vine, Bob Taylor, Bob Elen, Pete Inglis, John Stroud, Charles Reeves, Colin New, Teddy Pearce, Sid Horwood, Don Streatfield, Tony Parsons, Peter Mobsby, John Teague, John Garrett, and a number of others.

Some of these, notably Dab, Frank Bond, Dennis Harris, John Goodwin, John Doyle and Jim Cole later followed Howard Surtees into EASAMS, for Navigation and Attack System work on projects including the Nimrod 1 anti-submarine avionics system and particularly relevant to TSR2, the Multi Role Combat Aircraft (MRCA). As International Test and Integrations Manager at EASAMS, John Goodwin continued the TSR2 systems approach to development, with which he was associated (initially under John Clemow's leadership as already described). This employed Staged Development of the systems and the software, where Stages 1, 2, 3 and 4 perfected integration, employing rigs and simulators such as already earlier described with TSR2 where equipment manufacturers lacked flying and ground test systems capability. The equipment manufacturers cooperated with this and provided staff to work with the Vickers TSR2 and later the EASAMS team. Thus, the integration philosophy applied in developing the TSR2's Navigation and Attack System was continued by the same team at EASAMS and over some nine years, it was successfully applied to Nimrod 1, whose timely and within budget conclusion earned EASAMS' Managing Director, Howard Surtees, the honour of an OBE. The same philosophy was successfully applied to some Buccaneer programmes and particularly, the internationally developed MRCA – which became the Tornado GR4 attack version, still in service in the twenty-first century. The heritage of the cancelled TSR2 survives!

As the year unfolded, I was already considering my future career. I had spent ten years in engineering, caught a whiff of the business side with the private venture Vigilant – and especially now, could not see a clear path towards management at BAC. From my starting in early 1952 as a novice under Barry MacGowan's earnest and friendly tutelage when I was launched into serious trials in Canberra jets, through the "Hen Coop's" late 1954 visit of to our home – each bearing a knitted garment for our imminently due firstborn, the sympathy and friendship shown by my colleagues after my mother died in a motor accident in 1956, Paul Leyton's rumbustious leadership and Frank Bond's humorous if sharp edged leadership till I was promoted to head the Test Group in 1957, the innovative period with Vigilant in that group where I had my first taste of managing three laboratories full of engineers – all the way through my latest two or three years Project Engineer period under a brilliant Howard Surtees, I could hardly have had a happier work experience. John Clemow had already reinforced his style of leadership, when he gave me free reign to take whatever reasonable time off I may need, while my wife Mary was unwell during the later stages of her fifth pregnancy. Only later elsewhere, in a company that suffered that corrosive problem was I to realise bliss of working at Vickers in a team without serious 'company politics' to overshadow the worthwhile challenges. Now I was hankering toward getting into Marketing and to experiencing the world of business.

Judiciously attending interviews, by the time of the October memo, I had obtained job offers from Peter Hearne at the highly divisionalised and entrepreneurial Elliott Automation to market avionics, from Dick Haines at Decca Radar to market ground Radar data handling systems – and from Howard Surtees, who was about to start up EASAMS. They all offered promising careers and starting salaries around the still desirable level of £2,000 per annum – a modest if not insignificant improvement on my current £1,650 p.a. With our family well on the way to producing a fifth child, any good career prospect was worth pursuing and every penny would count.

Then suddenly, I was asked to accompany Dab and Les Vine for a two-week stint with Honeywell in Minneapolis, to help them with their proposal for the tube-launched TOW anti-tank missile. Ever since the Vigilant team had been travelling to America while I remained in my Weybridge labs, I had felt some envy for those able to sample the America one otherwise only saw through Hollywood and the media. And here was an opportunity I could hardly miss. But now my conscience pricked, since the new baby was due towards the end of the American project – should I leave Mary at such a time? On unburdening myself, Mary was emphatic. 'I have had four babies and I know exactly what to do, so you don't have to worry. In any case, you may never have the chance to go to America again.' Not only did I have her permission, I had marching orders!

Dab and I flew out together, with a stop in New York just too short to get further into Manhattan than a few minutes walk from the East Side Terminal. We finally arrived in Minneapolis around 1 a.m. London time, to be met by an ebullient crowd from Honeywell – who promptly took us to a smart night club. For several hours, bemused in such unfamiliar surroundings, we sat in low armchairs drinking large whiskies on the rocks served by long-legged, short-skirted waitresses. After this unexpected introduction to American hospitality, we got to bed in our overheated hotel at around 6 a.m. London time, with a few hours to go before we were picked up and taken to meet Clyde Parton, vice president in charge of Honeywell's Ordnance Division. Before long, we were on chummy terms with Clyde and his group of engineers, who took nightly turns after work, to drive us in one of their pair of enormous cars to even more enormous homes, fitted throughout with unfamiliarly deep pile white carpets. At each place we were treated as family – 'home from home', to our great surprise among people who not only failed to ram America down our throats as I had expected – but who actually asked how we did things in England. They had super kids, responsible teenagers who worked to earn their own money while at school and college. At work, it was a matter of getting down to it and getting an urgent job done. Even on Thanksgiving Day, we worked till lunch time, when all three of us were invited to the house of a senior engineer, who could not say exactly how may rooms they had. We were seated among about twenty relatives for the traditional turkey and pumpkin pie dinner and then the older of his six children showed us around their vast house. Perhaps the Hollywood version of America was not entirely correct.

Thinking of my recently completed NATI/VSTOL project study for which I selected a Litton Inertial Navigation System, before leaving Weybridge I suggested making a side trip to Woodland Hills in California, where I could view the Litton platform, its test programme and results - and the total operation. We would all feel more comfortable with my choice, if a first-hand inspection confirmed the credibility of Litton's claims. Henry Gardner agreed to this and after a week in Minneapolis, I took the Sunday evening flight to Los Angeles. Litton was to arrange a Hertz Rent-a-Car for my journey to Woodland Hills and for my use until I returned to Minneapolis on Tuesday. I had never driven an American car, nor any car with automatic transmission, and the 17ft 'small Chevy' kangaroo hopped out of the parking lot, until I got used to keeping my left foot away from the pedals. Then it was only a matter of following some pencilled directions on a scrap of paper and the LA road map through the unfamiliar dazzling array of traffic lights and signs along roads with strange names like Sepulvada Boulevard then through the Santa Monica Mountains before getting back on the I-405 Ventura Freeway going West. All totally unreal, especially in the dark. Somehow, I navigated the 25-mile maze without getting lost or hitting anybody, reaping admiring exclamations by the Litton folk waiting at my motel. As in Minneapolis, straight out – this time for dinner at The Smokehouse and after a large steak, to bed and another exploration to find 'The Plant' next morning.

In a couple of days of whirlwind laboratory and clean room tours, presentations around their hardware and in response to my intensive questioning, explanation of their flight test and operational results with the systems in the F104 Starfighter, I had also seen a working LN-9 platform such as I had proposed for the Vickers NATO/VSTOL project – and was thoroughly impressed. Before leaving for the LA International Airport on Tuesday afternoon, I telexed my confirmation of the Litton platform choice back to Weybridge and was being shown back towards my Hertz car. Bob Marcille was my guide and before making my goodbyes, I told him that if the project moves ahead, somebody else would be handling the project because I was shortly expecting to leave Vickers.

A hand descended on my shoulder and another took my elbow, as I was propelled into the General Manager's office. Somewhat resembling Orson Wells, Bill Jacobi took a couple of minutes to offer me a job. I could choose between three options – come to California and join the team there (on an American-sized salary), go to Litton's company in Hamburg at Plath GmBH – or set up a new London Office, to market Litton navigation systems to the British Government and establish relationships with British Industry. If I took a job in Europe, I would report to Litton's Director of Marketing (Europe) – one Bob Kirk (years later to be a Director of BAe) located in Zurich. I would be able to make my office at Bush House in London, where another Litton company was established. Despite the attractions of sunny California, the challenge of setting up one-man operation to represent this great company in the UK looked by far the best, particularly in view of our recently acquired first own mortgage on a semi-detached in Surbiton – and with that fifth baby about to arrive.

We finished the proposal on time in Minneapolis, where I was able to track down a first cousin in Chicago whom I had never met. She promptly invited me to bring Les

Vine for a weekend – and to meet her family of seven children. Mary still showed no sign of going into labour and becoming both confident and ambitious to see something of Washington and New York I made plans to delay my return by a few more days. That is, until I made (for those days) a rare telephone call to her from Pittsburgh. The precious three minutes was mostly taken up with her tearful description of keeping her legs crossed – since pains had begun. In a great panic, I took the first available plane back to London and as I walked into the house, she was waiting – 'take me to the hospital NOW'. Fourteen hours later, another daughter had arrived.

Although Howard Surtees, Dab, Frank Bond, Dennis Harris, John Goodwin, Jim Cole and others were going to start up EASAMS and the temptation to join these long established colleagues, I decided to take the job with Litton. However, while higher than my other three, Bob Kirk's offer did not reflect my expectations from an American company. It was unfortunately clear, that in Europe, Litton would not pay an American salary (except to American 'expats'), so I turned down £2,150 p.a. Nothing like this had evidently ever happened to the burgeoning Litton and after some delay, Bob increased the offer to £2,250 p.a., a good £600 or 35 per cent more than my salary at Vickers. Before I left the company, I went to see Henry Gardner, who had first recruited me into Guided Weapons nearly ten years earlier. He shook me warmly by the hand and said that I would always be welcome to a job if I wanted to come back. The TSR2 work carried on (without me) until its 1965 cancellation. However, as I heard later, Gardner had suggested that I engineered the Litton Specification and the visit to them, in order to get a job there! Such a false accusation was my least expectation and had to be sorely resented.

When I told Bob Kirk I had arrived home fourteen hours before our baby's birth, his immediate repost was 'Well – you had time for at least three more meetings.' I started my new life and flew to Zurich in the New Year, followed by many visits to the US – and much later to live there for over twenty years. So much for 'perhaps you may never get the chance to go to America again'.

Twenty-six years later in 1988, the Vickers operation at what had (between 1907 and 1939) been the famous Brooklands Motor Racing Track closed down altogether and most of the vast factory and office buildings complex was demolished. On one of the regular trips home from our current life in Atlanta, sagging structures with wires and conduit forming drooping spaghetti-like vines viewed through my taxi window en-route from Gatwick Airport was surely one of my saddest experiences. Fortunately, Spud Boorer and others saved the barely budding Brooklands Museum buildings – particularly the Brooklands Club House, which had for years served as Barnes Wallis's 'R&D Department' headquarters and the W103 Hangar – now known as The Wellington Hangar, where my Test Group Leader office was located, while I controlled Development and Environmental testing. Much of the banked racing track remained, but most of the large site was redeveloped, to house business parks, 'superstores' and some residential housing. With much lobbying and hard work, Spud and the others saved the Club House and enough of the original hangars and motor racing sheds from the developers' wrecking ball. With hard-won funding from sponsors – and later the National Lottery – an enthusiastic team assisted by many volunteers developed the existing fine Brooklands Museum.

When I retired back to Weybridge from Atlanta in 2002, Spud had already given me a conducted tour of the many aircraft, aero engines, racing cars and other exhibits. I went along to see if I could do anything useful as one of the many museum volunteers, when it suddenly struck me that there was not a single sign of the guided weapons and TSR2 avionics work that had occupied so many of us between 1950 and 1962. On asking about this, I was met with a blank stare – clearly, nobody realised what had taken place. My dismay at this was quickly met with a simple invitation – 'can you create a guided weapons exhibit'. This became much of my life thereafter, although at first, there appeared to be nothing remaining to exhibit. Neither missiles, nor any mention of TSR2 Navigation Attack Systems – zilch! It took many visits to other museums around the country, searches in the National Archives, Vickers Archives and unearthing many thankfully saved archives within Brooklands, before I could locate technical information and examples of each of our missiles – hopefully for transfer into a GW and TSR2 exhibit at Brooklands. I also 'unearthed' many TSR2 Nav/Attack system files and manuals and helpful ex-colleagues who remained on this Earth. Writing up the history became my next obsession and this book is the result.

REFERENCES

1. Brooklands TSR2 archived files and photographs.
2. TSR2 Navigation & Attack System Supplementary Brochure, Section 2.3.3, Brooklands Museum Archives.
3. EMI Electronics Ltd, Report No.DP950, September 1961, Brooklands Museum Archives.
4. MOS Meeting Report, Equipment Procurement TSR2, 27 January 1959, Brooklands Museum Archives.
5. TSR2 Navigation & Attack System Supplementary Brochure, Section 3.1.1, Brooklands Museum Archives.
6. TSR2 Navigation & Attack Systems Supplementary Brochure, Appendix B, Brooklands Museum Archives.
7. BAC TSR2 brochure No.6, November 1961, Brooklands Museum Archives.
8. TSR2 Navigation & Attack System Supplementary Brochure, Section 2.1.9, Brooklands Museum Archives.
9. *War Monthly* magazine, 1978, article by Graham Wilmer.
10. TSR2 Navigation & Attack System Supplementary Brochure, Section 2.2.1, Brooklands Museum Archives.
11. TSR2 Navigation & Attack System Supplementary Brochure, Section 2.1.3, Brooklands Museum Archives.
12. BAC Systems Division/E SD-E/F/25/955, 'TSR2 Central Computing System: The Computer Capacity Problem', D.J. Harris/J.I. Lattey, 25 September 1964, Brooklands Museum Archives.
13. TSR2 Navigation & Attack System Supplementary Brochure, Section 2.3.2, Brooklands Museum Archives.
14. TSR2 Navigation & Attack System Supplementary Brochure, Section 2.3.6, Brooklands Museum Archives.
15. TSR2 Navigation & Attack System Supplementary Brochure, Section 2.2.3, Brooklands Museum Archives.
16. Vickers Research Ltd, Report No.19, 'Investigation of Navigator's Task', Brooklands Museum Archives.
17. NACA Research Memorandum RM A56I10 by Barnett and others, Brooklands Museum Archives.
18. RAE Technical Note No.IAP1101, J.M. Naish, Brooklands Museum Archives.
19. TSR2 Navigation & Attack System Supplementary Brochure, Appendix 1, Brooklands Museum Archives.
20. Elliott Automation Handbook TSR/HB/PROV, May 1963, Brooklands Museum Archives.
21. Vickers-Armstrongs (Aircraft) Ltd, Report AERO/S & C/047, Sept. 1960, Brooklands Museum Archives.
22. AERO/S&C.040 'Progress Report on Digital Simulation of the "Ski-Toe" System', R.W. Penney and M. Salisbury, 12 January 1960, Brooklands Museum Archives.
23. 'Vickers Aerodynamics Dept Interim Report MWS/RWP/MW257 on Simulation of Automatic Terrain Following, in Turning Flight at CAL' (Nov. 1960), reported on 12 December 1960.
24. AERO S&C 054 'Design of a Terrain Following System', 9 March 1961, A. Roberts and M. Salisbury, Brooklands Museum Archives.
25. Vickers Systems Div/E Report SD-E/H/26/9, 'Aircraft survival at low terrain clearance heights', 19 April 1963, J.I. Lattey.
26. TSR2 Navigation & Attack System Supplementary Brochure, Section 3.1.3, Brooklands Museum Archives.
27. TSR2 Navigation & Attack System Supplementary Brochure, Section 3.1.4, Brooklands Museum Archives.
28. TSR2 Navigation & Attack System Supplementary Brochure, Section 3.3, Brooklands Museum Archives.
29. Vickers GW Dept GW2/N/85/164, 'The General Purpose Section of the Verdan Computer. Its

Operation and Programming', D.J. Harris/A.H. Carter, 4 April 1960, Brooklands Museum Archives.

30. Vickers GW Dept GW/N/85/6, 'Scaling the Digital Differential Analyser (DDA) in Verdan', G.A. Wimbush/D.J. Harris/A.H. Carter, 27 October 1960, Brooklands Museum Archives.

31. RAE Tech Note No.IEE 21, 'The Central Computing System for the TSR2 Aircraft: Coordinating Document for the Carry Trials', D.J. Faddy and T.R.H. Sizer, December 1963, Brooklands Museum Archives.

32. Vickers-Armstrongs (Aircraft) Ltd and English Electric Aviation Ltd, 'Design Specification V.E.S. 1002, Issue 2; Digital Computer for Type 571 Aircraft', D.J. Harris/J.B. Lambie, approved by H. Surtees, 23 September 1960, Brooklands Museum Archives.

33. Elliott Bros (London) Ltd and BAC correspondence 1963–1965, Brooklands Museum Archives.

34. TSR2 Navigation & Attack System Supplementary Brochure, Section 2.4.1, Brooklands Museum Archives.

35. TSR2 Navigation & Attack System Supplementary Brochure, Section 2.4.3, Brooklands Museum Archives.

36. Ferranti report IFC/123, 'Vol.II – Application to Weapon Aiming', 6 April 1960, Brooklands Museum Archives.

37. BAC TSR2 brochure No.6, November 1962, Brooklands Museum Archives.

38. TSR2 Navigation & Attack System Supplementary Brochure, Section 2.1.4, Brooklands Museum Archives.

39. Vickers SD-D4/F/22/122, 3 July 1962, Brooklands Museum Archives.

40. Vickers SD-D4/Z/33/110, 26 July 1963, Brooklands Museum Archives.

41. Vickers SD-D6/A/OO/128, 25 February 1964, Brooklands Museum Archives.

42. Vickers SD-D6/F/23/929, 1 January 1965, Brooklands Museum Archives.

43. English Electric September and October 1961 publications K2/94 & K2/95, Mobile Automatic Checkout Equipment (MACE), Brooklands Museum Archives.

44. Seminar looking back at 'TSR2 with Hindsight', book published by The Royal Air Force History Society.

45. *Aeroplane Monthly*, September 1973, 'TSR2 – what went wrong?', by Bill Gunston.

46. Public Records Office archives for TSR2.

47. LRP Anti-Tank Guided Weapon Feasibility Study VGW Report No.46, H. Surtees, Brooklands Museum archives.

48. Vickers-Armstrongs (Aircraft) Ltd, Publication SPEC/206/3, Brooklands Archives.

49. Author's scans of aerial view photograph representing CRT resolutions.

50. Brooklands Museum drawings archives.

51. *Illustrated Encyclopaedia of the World's Rockets and Missiles*, by Bill Gunston, Salamander Books Ltd.

52. Report No.VGW/P3, Brooklands Archives.

53. Brooklands Museum, Photo Archives.

54. MOA draft memorandum sent to CGWL, DG(GW) and US/LGW in mid-1959; Public Records Office archives.

55. Author's photo archives.

Copyrights: Document and photograph references to Brooklands Museum Archives, BAC and related companies are included with permissions, under the Copyrights of BAE SYSTEMS.

MINISTRY PERSONALITIES

History of GW at Vickers – Personalised at govt ministries, from PRO documents

Harold Watkinson,
Minister of Defence

John Profumo,
Minister for War

Christopher Soames,
Sec. State for War

Geoffrey Rippon
Parliamentary Sec.
Minister of Aviation

T. J. Bligh
10 Downing St.

Benjamin
A.P.S. to Minister of Aviation

George Brown
Sec. of State, Economic Affairs

Denis Healy
Sec. of State, Defence

Roy Jenkins, Sec. of State, Aviation
Harold Wilson, Prime Minister

LIST OF FIGURES